For Tyler,
So you can
come and visit!
Happy Birthday
Vrindevani

a5 LOS ANGELES

Architecture, Interiors, Lifestyle

Casey C.M. Mathewson, Editor   Frances Anderton, Introduction

CONTENTS

004 INTRODUCTION

016 ABRAMSON TEIGER ARCHITECTS
018 Lima Residence
026 Kelly Residence
030 Davis Residence
032 Lehrer Residence

034 BARTON MYERS ASSOCIATES, INC
036 Residence in West Los Angeles
044 Bekins Residence
048 Tempe Center for the Arts

052 BELZBERG ARCHITECTS
054 Conga Room
062 Brentwood Residence
066 Skyline Residence

070 CLIVE WILKINSON ARCHITECTS
072 VCU Adcenter
078 FIDM San Diego
082 JWT Headquarters
086 Maguire Associates

088 DESIGNARC
090 Bel-Air Residence
098 Mussel Shoals Residence

104 EHRLICH ARCHITECTS
106 700 Palms Residence
114 Zeidler Residence
118 Asu Walter Cronkite School Of
    Journalism & Mass Communication

**120 FREDERICK FISHER
AND PARTNERS ARCHITECTS**
122 Santa Ynez Residence
130 Oceanside Museum of Art
134 The Annenberg Community Beach House
    at Santa Monica State Beach
136 The Walter and Leonore Annenberg Center
    for Information Science and Technology
138 The Contemporary Museum of Honolulu

140 GRIFFIN ENRIGHT ARCHITECTS
142 Keep Off the Grass SCI-Arc Exhibition
146 [WIDE]BAND – Nomadic Café
150 Point Dume Residence
154 Schindler's Paradox Box

**156 JOHN FRIEDMAN
ALICE KIMM ARCHITECTS**
158 Graduate Aerospace Laboratories,
    California Institute Of Technology (Galcit)
166 King Residence
170 Green Dot Charter High Schools
172 FIL Guadalajara
174 Fitness And Athletic Center,
    Claremont Mckenna College

176 JOHNSTONMARKLEE ARCHITECTS
178 View House
184 Helios House
188 Vault House
190 Poggio Golo Winery
192 House House

194   KANNER ARCHITECTS
196   United Oil Gasoline Station
202   Oakland House
206   26th Street Low-Income Housing

212   RAY KAPPE ARCHITECT
214   Santa Monica Prefab Residence
222   Rochedale Prefab Residence
226   Sunset Plaza Residence

230   LEAN ARCH
232   Kuhlhaus 02
238   Wild Oak Residence
242   Kuhlhaus 01

246   LEHRER ARCHITECTS
248   Museum of Water and Life
256   Lehrer Architects Office
258   Santa Monica Canyon Residence

260   MARMOL RADZINER
262   Palms Residence
268   Vienna Way Residence
272   The Accelerated School (TAS)
276   Desert House

278   MINARC
280   Rainbow House
286   MINARC House
290   Library Hafnarfjardar

292   PATRICK TIGHE ARCHITECTURE
294   Moving Picture Company
302   Tigertail Residence
306   Morocco Residence

310   Sierra Bonita Affordable Housing

312   RANDALL STOUT ARCHITECTS INC.
314   Taubman Museum of Art
322   Hunter Museum of American Art
328   Art Gallery of Alberta

330   SHUBIN + DONALDSON ARCHITECTS
332   Biscuit Filmworks
338   Nathan Residence
344   Saatchi & Saatchi

348   STUDIO PALI FEKETE ARCHITECTS SPF:A
350   Oberfield Residence
356   SPF:a Headquarters
360   Somis Hay Barn
362   Caverhill Residence
364   Wallis Annenberg Center for the
         Performing Arts

366   wHY ARCHITECTURE
368   Grand Rapids Art Museum
376   Royal/T
380   The Tyler Museum Of Art
382   Mulholland Residence
384   Great Wall Of Los Angeles Interpretive
         Green Bridge

386   XTEN ARCHITECTS
388   Sapphire Gallery Extension
394   Openhouse
398   Dubai ZPO Tower
400   DiamondHouse
402   Silverspur Office Building

404   APPENDIX

This generation of architects does not fetishize the detail. We are interested in spatial relationships, structure, technology. Nothing is pure.

Austin Kelly, XTEN Architecture

For the inventive and gutsy young architect, Los Angeles has long been a magnet, with its promise of adventurous clients, affordable virgin land, its vacation climate and dramatic topography, as well as a lack of history and bureaucracy to impose constraints. As a result the region has yielded 100 years worth of highly experimental, if mostly residential, architecture.

But with success comes a price. LA has been a magnet not just for architects, and the influx of millions of people has made Los Angeles, for good and bad, less of a frontier town. LA's signature contribution to lifestyle -- the automobile-dependent, single-family home -- has become increasingly untenable. The "city of the perpetual future," says Austin Kelly of Xten Architecture, is now more concerned with remaking itself in the mold of older cities: with "greater density and urbanism, more public space, more housing, more public transportation, more walkable and mixed-use neighborhoods…"

Meanwhile, the distinctive Angeleno attitude has gone global. The onetime Venice-based iconoclast, Frank Gehry, has become an international brand; the formal experimentation that defined Los Angeles architecture in the 70s and 80s can be found from London to Beijing to Dubai, as can the technical innovation that had defined our region's pre-and-post war Modernist architects, now being applied worldwide in new materials and systems to mitigate the energy crisis and global warming.

Having said all that, the work that comes out of here still astonishes with its chutzpah and invention. A drive through the hills of Malibu, Brentwood and Hollywood for example, takes you past just some of the newly built, large private homes shown in the following pages. They stand confidently on precarious sites, demonstrating a brazen scale and boldness. Theirs is an architecture of formal abstraction and material experimentation that thumbs its nose at pallid gestures, and has found clients and exceptional builders willing to go along for the ride, with the same gung-ho, only-in-LA spirit that pulled investors into

James Cameron's dream of a world of blue-skinned people on Pandora. "LA is still," says Casey Mathewson, author and producer of this book, "the creative center in the United States." This book is a snapshot of contemporary architecture in this creative center.

Mathewson is an architect based in Berlin, who believes his own work is nourished by continuous reflection on what his peers are doing. "A5: Los Angeles," is his latest -- a valentine from an architect working in chilly, if artistically bracing, Berlin to his fellow travelers in Southern California. It was realized in collaboration with the San Francisco-based publisher, Gordon Goff of ORO *editions*, and Ann Videriksen, an architectural advocate in Los Angeles who brings to the table a rare qualification: past acquaintance with Richard Neutra and other leading lights of the mid-century modern period. Together they have assembled a line-up of architects that are both established and emerging, younger practices often co-helmed by a husband and wife team. Most of the architects featured are working both in LA and overseas, and are producing residential as well as public buildings.

Furthermore, and very importantly to Mathewson, they are architects for whom construction matters. Where LA architecture had gained a reputation in the last two decades for formally exciting buildings whose details were either shoddy or overly tortuous, "crude detailing is typically a thing of the past in LA," says John Friedman of John Friedman Alice Kimm Architects "Architects here care deeply about how all the pieces of a project come together - from an exterior material change to a stair guardrail. These details may not be the central feature of a project... but if the details don't support the large idea, or are executed poorly, the impact of the project is not as high." In his own essay, Mathewson talks in more depth about construction details, and many of the projects in this book are supported with working drawings.

Another goal of the book was to show architects' public work. As Austin Kelly pointed out, "density and urbanism, more public space, more housing, and more walkable and mixed-use neighborhoods" are high on the agenda in LA at present. In the following pages you will see some examples of civic buildings and multi-family housing, low-cost

apartments, for example, by Stephen Kanner, the Annenberg public Beach House by Frederick Fisher and a Museum of Water and Life by Michael Lehrer. You will also see contemporary spins on a quintessential LA building type: the gas station.But in the end, houses still dominate, and mostly, very large houses (the size of private homes has grown, paradoxically, in tandem with the need for space and affordable housing). Even though, as John Friedman points out, "the innovation that occurred primarily in LA's private residences in the past has finally been welcomed into the city's public spaces and structures – Disney Hall, Caltrans, the Cathedral, and the Performing Arts school being the most prominent examples," it is still in the private, personal realm that younger architects tend to express themselves. This is partly because, without a public competition system as in some countries, it is hard for young LA architects to break into public building, and because LA is still home to people who are able to invest in building an experimental, new or substantially remodeled home.

The book also assembles architects with some common values; and to the extent the buildings in these pages share a language it is that, in Mathewson's view, they build upon the legacy of Southern California's Modernists -- Schindler, Neutra, Lautner, Charles and Ray Eames, Pierre Koenig and other Case Study House architects – in their abstract form, their inside-outside relationship, and their concern with beauty in construction and materials. To reinforce their bona fides in this regard, the book features the work of Ray Kappe – a third generation Socal Modernist, held in high esteem for his magnificent 1960s and 70s houses of interlocking vertical and horizontal planes in wood, concrete and glass, who is now enjoying a second career designing prefab houses for the developer LivingHomes (pp00). But in terms of sources for today's LA architects, one could equally turn to a contemporary of Kappe's – one who is Dionysus to Kappe's Apollo: Frank Gehry. For as much as today's architects are informed by the mid-century Modernists, they are also influenced by the formal expressiveness unleashed by the architect of Bilbao and the Walt Disney Concert Hall.

Gehry was considered radical when he modeled his buildings on experiments by his Venice artist friends or earlier painters like Malevich, but it is now completely commonplace for architects to draw from the work of artists, not to mention their private clients will oftentimes be artists or art collectors. Michael Lehrer (pp00) speaks for many in this book when he states that his thinking about building design is informed not just by the high priests of architecture but also by the "Serialists and Minimalists (Judd, Le Witt, Andre, Richard Long, Kelly, Frank Stella, Serra, Flavin), the Cubists (Leger, Braque, Picasso, Gris, Ozenfant/Le Corbusier); the Constructivists (Malevich, El Lissitzky) the phenomenalists (Turrell, Irwin, Bell), and many more."

While work by Marmol Radziner or the Bekins Residence by Barton Myers might bring to mind, respectively, Kappe and Pierre Koenig, you will generally find that buildings in this book are as much experiments in pure phenomena -- space and light and form and color -- as they are pure rational thinking. See Clive Wilkinson's washes of vivid color in his designs for FIDM, for example, Johnston Marklee's earthen, sculptural View house, or Patrick Tighe's leaping forms. And while the focus of this book is not the parametric design experiments so dominant in recent years, you will find examples of buildings that explicitly express the aesthetic and formal language of the digital design age.

Austin Kelly of XTEN Architecture neatly sums up the general design approach by the architects in A5, in words about his own firm that could apply to many others: "From Neutra we learned how to separate a glass wall from a structural element, so that they read independently and slip past one another. . . From Schindler we learned about interlocking spaces and the plasticity of surfaces. . . From Ray and Charles Eames we learned about a collaborative and open-ended design process... (but) we do not think that the buildings really look or behave like Case Study or California Modern buildings. . . .the structures are more complex, the spaces are more irregular and the buildings are more precisely shaped by and tuned to their specific surroundings than by any a priori ideas about architecture."

The buildings in this book were largely built in the oughts (or noughties), an era of easy borrowing and rising land values that came to a screeching halt at the decade's end. Now many of the architects featured in A5 are feeling the freeze or focusing on building elsewhere. So unwittingly, this book, conceived two years ago, stands as testimony to a moment in LA time – a moment when high consumption met panic about declining resources and global warming, and when a revival of interest in midcentury Modernism met phenomenalism and digital design. The architects whose work is shown in this book channeled these impulses and these buildings are the fascinating result.

—FRANCES ANDERTON

Photographer Benny Chan has worked diligently over the past few years to photograph overhead views of Los Angeles freeways during the height of rush hour. Using a camera designed and manufactured exclusively for this project, Chan has taken pictures from high in the sky from a helicopter and has rendered monumental sized prints. With his almost omniscient perspective, Chan explores and sheds light on the conundrum of traffic as a symptom of a society being unable to keep pace with its own expansion, while at the same time rendering a serene beauty from the chaotic scene.

CROSS SECTIONING LOS ANGELES

Los Angeles - long damned or praised as the hotbed center of artificiality, but now evidenced by the quality of the body of new work presented here - is hovering on the verge of a more inclusive future.

As a California-born architect now living and working in Berlin, I have always been fascinated by, and wary of, Los Angeles architecture. Its perpetual fast-lane redefinition of itself, combined with its laid-back surf culture has always made me envious. But a lack of concern for deeper issues, such as the realities of construction detailing faced by those of us who work in less gentle climates, made it seem as if Southern California architects were somehow exempt from dealing with some of the basic issues central to the profession of architecture. Now, after spending two years dedicated to compiling this book, I see this widespread preconception as unfounded.

After the heyday of Californian modernism in the 1960's, one sensed that a smog-like architectural haze had settled across the topography of Los Angeles. Charles Moore, one of my heroes of early environmentally-conscious West Coast architecture, seemed to stray in building Baroque-like explorations such as his Beverly Hills Civic Center (1988-90). From today's perspective, this frolicking experiment seems at best humorous. But back then such projects were taken dead seriously, and considerably influenced international architectural thought – all the way to my expatriate office in Berlin. But by 1989, when I analyzed Frank Gehry's Edgemar Project in Santa Monica and Morphosis' Cedar Sinai Cancer Center for Berlin-based Bauwelt magazine, the architectural smog in Los Angeles had begun to lift.

One personal moment of awakening occurred for me when I was visiting my parent's native city of Pasadena in 1995. I headed up the hills behind the Rose Bowl to drive up under the soaring bridge of the Craig Ellwood's Pasadena Art Center College of Design (1976). Treasuring Mies van der Rohe's hallmark Nationalgalerie in Berlin (1969) as I do, I sensed that Ellwood and his chief designer Jim Tyler had taken the language even further, creating an austere temple in this quiet arroyo that exerts an understated, yet powerful attraction – the essence of a successful architectural venture - and much closer to timelessness than the more hectic film-set type architecture that sprawls out across Los Angeles. This is a timelessness that results from the reduction of forms, and the precise detailing of these forms.

When it came to selecting the projects to include in this volume of *a5*, I looked for the same high level of attention to detail and have therefore included many construction details that illustrate how the buildings are actually made. So while this book explores the architects' formal relationship to earlier Southern California modernism – through interviews conducted by Frances Anderton – a primary focus has been put on these details that are presented in combination with precise architectural photography by a host of gifted photographers to create a final result very different from typical coffee-table books.

Over the past 10 years a myriad of building physics, codes, sustainability, structural, and liability issues have redefined some of the central challenges facing architects and led to an increased concern for construction detailing. Fred Fisher explains, "Today's energy codes and a growing consciousness of sustainability, as well as a narrower range of comfort demand more attention in construction and systems to maintain the sense of openness and lightness." [1] As a result, the nonchalant "stick and stucco" style that has characterized much LA architecture has now been overtaken by a new generation of designers that lavish careful attention to detailing.

Even the most quintessential trait of Los Angeles architecture – the easy intertwining of indoor and outdoor space facilitated by the gentle climate and, perhaps most poetically, spatially translated by the frameless glass corners and "spider legs" of Richard Neutra's '50s residences – continues to experience evolution in the work presented in this book. New building technologies, as well as refining existing materials, have facilitated this. Fleetwood Windows and Doors, one of the leading manufacturers sliding glass elements, addresses today's increased demands by minimizing the details to the essentials and utilizing state-of-the-art precision components with sleek, yet strong aluminum extrusions. At Michael Lehrer's Santa Monica Canyon House, entire double-height walls of folding glass elements open up to dramatically interconnect the living spaces to the landscape. Canadian-born Angeleno Barton Myers integrates multiple roll-up garage doors into his recent steel residences; perhaps in reverence to another essential component of the local cityscape – the neighborhood auto repair shop.

Environmental Responsiveness

This Californian dream of seamless indoor-outdoor living is not without its downside. Wildfires, droughts and earthquakes occur often and recall the harshness of Los Angeles' original arid landscape, characterized by early settlers as a desert sliding into the sea. Today's architects are addressing these threatening issues with innovative structural engineering systems, use of inflammable exterior materials in wildfire-prone locations, and thoughtful responses to sustainability issues that earlier generations of Southern Californians notoriously didn't consider. Minarc's recently completed Rainbow House (Fig. 1), a conversion of an existing apartment building into a residence, continues their series of sustainable residences with a non-compromising stance. In addition to the strict elimination of carpet, tiles, and paint, reclaimed wood from the existing building was reused. Finishing in the kitchen and bathroom sinks is made of recycled rubber, and the internal courtyard eliminates the necessity for air conditioning.

A common thread shared by the diverse architects featured in *a5* is that the response to environmental concerns is seen an integral element to each design that needn't be flaunted, but rather seamlessly integrated.

Renaissance of Prefab Technologies

The implementation of prefabrication construction technologies in residential architecture was a formative tenet in L.A.'s post-war era explored by Berlin émigré Konrad Wachsmann at USC, Raphael Soriano's own all-aluminum Soria Structures Company, and others. But despite the success of prefabrication technology in many California Modern houses that employed steel frame construction, the prefabrication of residential modules did not to gain widespread acceptance. Only in recent years has the industry seen a resurgence of interest, and the results by Ray Kappe and Marmol Radziner featured here suggest promise for the future development of this inherently green technology (Fig. 2).

However, while the green benefits - minimizing waste due to precise cutting, reusing and recycling excess materials, reducing noise, dust, and damage to the existing building site, centralizing trades, reducing vehicular emissions from travel to construction sites, and shortening construction times - are convincing arguments, the remaining challenge

1

2

3

4

to be met by prefab advocates is cost reduction. Due to challenging topography and high property costs, the recent modern prefab homes they have failed to break into a medium-low price bracket.

New Materials

One of the dominant features of the buildings included in this book is the wealth of new materials that have evolved over the past few years and are being creatively interpreted by the architects featured in *a5*.

Eco-Resin Organics composite panels by 3form offer the opportunity to collage wild grasses or other plant materials into in translucent panels. These can be hung as back-lit lighting installations, or modeled sculpturally and imprinted with graphic patterns to form intriguing elements (Fig. 3). The material is made of rapidly renewable and sustainably harvested materials, and is free of plasticizers, stabilizers, and PVC.
Trex composite siding slats are made of wood and plastic fibers from reclaimed or recycled resources, including sawdust and used pallets from woodworking operations, and recycled plastic grocery bags. The composite formula unifies the best qualities of wood and plastic to create a superior alternative to both (Fig. 4). The plastic components shield the wood from moisture and the wood components protect the plastic from UV damage while providing a natural, attractive look.

UltraTouch natural fiber insulation is made from 85% post-industrial cotton fiber, "denim-jean" scraps recycled as a by-product of the textile industry. The insulation is treated with a natural fire retardant, and is 100% recyclable, VOC and formaldehyde-free.
CeasarStone is a stain-, scratch-, and heat-resistant material pioneered in Italy in 1987 by harnessing the physical properties of quartz, one of nature's strongest minerals (Fig 5). The product spectrum includes a recycled range of quartz slabs that incorporate 17-42% first quality reclaimed quartz from the fabrication process (post-production recycled) and post-consumer recycled glass and mirrors.

Trespa Meteon architectural panels are flat panels that comprised of thermosetting resins that have been homogeneously reinforced with wood based fibers (Fig. 6). The durable panels with an integrated decorative surface available in a large range of colors, patterns and textures can

be used for exterior applications such as facade cladding, as well as for interior use. In several *a5* projects, exterior panel surfaces have been extended inside the spaces to interconnect the outdoor/indoor living spaces.

Swisspearl or Eter-Color, cladding panels made of fiber cement and available in a wide color range, allow expressively modeling exterior surfaces. For XTEN's DiamondHouse, a facade pattern was created from natural elements taken from the canyon site – and then abstracted, scaled and arrayed across the building as CNC-perforated 3/8" thick Swisspearl fiber cement panels (Fig. 7).

CNC routing technology was also used to perforate the metal panels of Patrick Tighe's Moving Picture Company project. Here, patterns derived from animated studies created by the client - are emblazoned onto the laser cut walls that circumscribe the interior spaces.

A New Social Awareness?

Clive Wilkinson says of the eminent social disparities within which Los Angeles architects operate that "Los Angeles is a place where the incongruity between public poverty and private wealth became visibly zoned into the landscape. Disparities are celebrated as diversity..." [2]
As a result of these disparities and the non-presence of governmental guidance in many architecture-related sectors – at least in comparison to international models still practiced widely in Europe - Angelenos have learned to rely on newly developed societal models. These new networks, often based in self-determination, have achieved some of the most exemplary architectural results presented in *a5*.

In response to increasing property values and a population increase of 3.8% since 2000, the single-family suburban residence as the prevalent form for housing in Los Angeles has been challenged. High property prices prohibit much of the population from buying a single-family suburban home and have led to the emergence of multi-family housing urban infill projects. This building typology has emerged as a platform for some of the most creative solutions being explored today.

For example, Stephen Kanner teamed with the non-profit Community Corporation of Santa Monica for his low-income 26th Street Affordable Housing project, completed in 2007, located, in departure from the traditional separation of commerce and residential uses in Los Angeles, on a commercial strip. Executive director Joan Ling says CCSM "prefers sites with proximity to mass transit and jobs, because they introduce a level of sustainability...that helps reduce traffic congestion and air pollution."

Patrick Tighe was commissioned by the West Hollywood Community Housing Corporation to design the Sierra Bonita Mixed Use Affordable Housing Project (Fig. 8). With an aim to be "for the community, from the community", it addresses an affordable housing shortage for tenants living with disabilities and also serves as the pilot project for a new municipal green ordinance.

Finding an acceptable school for their children – especially for the Latino and African American populations that respectively make up 44.6% and 9.8% of Los Angeles County's population - has remained a pressing problem. Just as the newest developments in housing suggest, the solution here can also lie in increased community involvement and private philanthropy, to counter the inefficiency of encrusted institutions and create new hope. By reactivating the California law that allows a public school to become a privately operated, publicly funded charter school if more than 50 percent of the tenured teachers vote in favor of the switch, new charter schools are spreading fast throughout Southern California to replace poor-performing large pubic schools with smaller, better managed neighborhood schools.

The largest charter school operator in Los Angeles, Green Dot, hired John Friedman Alice Kimm Architects to create two neighboring new 500-pupil schools in South Los Angeles, historically underprivileged region whose school population made up 91% Hispanic and 9% African American students. Each school has its own separate administration, as well as its own architectural identity.

The charter schools vividly illustrate the phenomenon that has most profoundly and increasingly shaped recent Los Angeles architecture – the role of philanthropy in design. The Eli and Edythe Broad Foundation supports many cultural institutions, including the $30 million, 2009 MOCA (Museum of Contemporary Art) bailout, $10 million for the Broad Stage at the Santa Monica College Madison Campus (2008, Architect Renzo Zecchetto), and $60 million for the Broad Contemporary Art Museum wing at LACMA (Los Angeles County Museum of Art, 2008, Architect Renzo Piano).

The Annenberg Foundation is another Los Angeles-based philanthropic organization that has provided many local architects the rare opportunity to explore non-residential, public building commissions. Founded in 1989 with the goal of advancing public well being through improved communication, the foundation encourages the development of more effective ways to share ideas and knowledge. Some recent examples included in a5 are the Wallis Annenberg High School at the Accelerated School, the Caltech IST Building, the open-to-the-public Annenberg Community Beach House on Santa Monica Beach, and the Wallis Annenberg Center for the Performing Arts planned in Beverly Hills to preserve and adapt a landmark post office with a new building.

John Friedman states that although there is "vibrant public debate about the success of new public spaces and public buildings, no one suggests that the City should not expand its progressive sensibility into the public realm."[4] In spite of Friedman's hopeful tone, the projects documented in a5 illustrate that much recent public architecture has often only been possible through the initiative of community groups and the financial support of philanthropic organizations. As Ray Kappe put it in 2003: "Government has abdicated its importance in our cities. As tax-payers we deserve more from our investment. Public places and public spaces must provide the most creative and desirable attributes, not the least."[5]

Looking Toward the Future

Sammy Hoi, President of Otis College, who tracks LA's 'creative economy', believes "an unbridled creative potential – empowered by the hybridization of the many cultures that meet and come to fruition in Los Angeles – is

5   6   7   8

still internationally recognized here" [6]. Some, however, believe that Los Angeles is losing steam. The architect Zoltan Pali says Los Angeles, appears in a sense, to be "falling behind. That is not to say that Los Angeles architects themselves are falling behind and in some ways some of our big boys are still producing compelling work - in other places." [7] This, too, is one of the messages of a5 - almost all of the firms portrayed have turned outside Los Angeles proper to realize some of their best projects.

The findings of the 2009 Otis College "Report on the Creative Economy of the Los Angeles Region" [8] confirm LA's creative potential and the importance of the creative industries for the local economy (the demand for architectural services could even increase by up to 6% by 2013 - if the current economic doldrums recede). According to Sammy Hoi, "Los Angeles is the most futuristic of all cities. But the region can only retain its position as a premier creative center in the face of growing global competition from newly rising cities if economic leaders and governmental bodies unite for common action more coherently then has been the case in recent times." [9]

The Otis Report also provides a list of "Some Things 'Born' in L.A." that have undeniably changed world culture and include; the T-shirt, Barbie, the Plastic Frisbee, as first commercially viable passenger plane (the DC-3), the Space Shuttle, the skateboard, the electric guitar, the first drive-through restaurant, and the Internet. With the exception of Ray and Charles Eames' furniture and Disneyland, no architects or buildings made the "Some Things 'Born' in L.A." list. A reoccurring theme surfaces when one looks back on the decades of architecture in LA. Architectural developments that originated elsewhere have customarily been co-opted to the local climate, lifestyles and technologies, but only seldom have new solutions originated here.

Upon further consideration, Richard Neutra's psychoanalytically-based design method developed while designing residences in the 50s [10] could perhaps be a candidate for the "Some Things 'Born' in L.A." list. By extending the scope of his consideration beyond mere formal or stylistic concerns to explore the deeper needs of his clients and translate these

into built form, Neutra achieved holistic results that made the residences more than aesthetically pleasing architectural statements. This increased sense of identification with a healing focus can be seen as an architectural approach "born" in Los Angeles

After the uncontrolled cycle of property overvaluation and the resultant economic consequences that now confront not only Los Angeles, many architects are now taking the time to assess their role and purpose. In the work presented in a5, a new sensitivity reminiscent of Neutra's approach can be witnessed. Trevor Abramson speaks of this as "architecture that can raise your soul to a higher spiritual level. As the world around us grows to be more fast-paced, coming home after a busy day has taken on a deeper meaning." [11] Seen in this light, Los Angeles – long damned and/ or praised as the hotbed center of artificiality, but now evidenced by the quality of the body of new work presented here – is hovering on the verge of a more inclusive future.

This book has been made possible by the tireless efforts of architectural advocate Ann Videriksen in Los Angeles. Frances Anderton brought all the pieces together at the end. Publisher Gordon Goff and his team at ORO editions have had the courage to believe in the project. My thanks go out to all of them, to the architects, and as to the sponsors from the building industries who have generously provided financial support for this project.

—CASEY C.M. MATHEWSON
Berlin   March 2010

1. In answer to a question posed by Frances Anderton for the Q&A section of this book
2. ibid
3. Sarah Amelar, "26th Street Housing, Santa, Monica", *Architectural Record*, October 2008
4. In answer to a question posed by Frances Anderton for the Q&A section of this book
5. Ray Kappe, *Ray Kappe_A Retrospective* (A+D Museum, 2003), 99.
6. Radio interview on KCRW Santa Monica by Frances Anderton, December 22, 2009
7. In answer to a question posed by Frances Anderton for the Q&A section of this book
8. Otis College of Art and Design, "Report on the Creative Economy of the Los Angeles Region", November 2009
9. Radio interview on KCRW Santa Monica by Frances Anderton, December 22, 2009
10. Sylvia Lavin, *Form follows libido : architecture and Richard Neutra in a psychoanalytic culture* (MIT Press, 2004)
11. In answer to a question posed by Frances Anderton for the Q&A section of this book

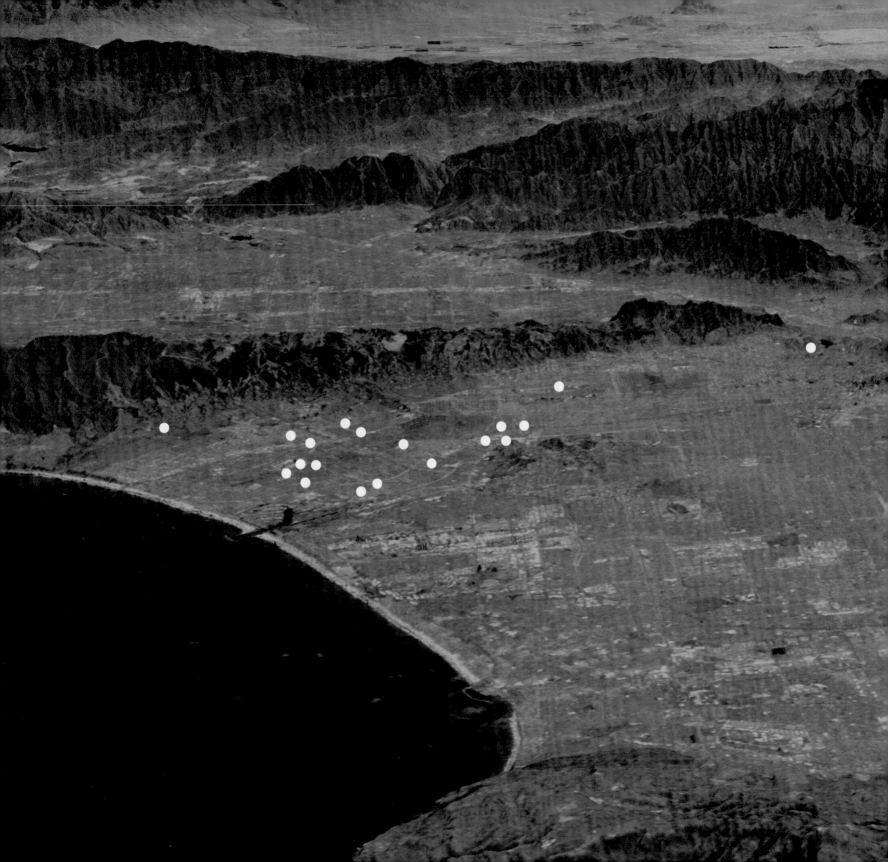

a5 LOS ANGELES

Architecture, Interiors, Lifestyle

ABRAMSON TEIGER ARCHITECTS

**Douglas Teiger, AIA
and Trevor Abramson, FAIA**

www.abramsonteiger.com

In the heart of downtown Culver City, CA, a team of award winning, dynamic Architects-Thinkers-Designers are making many prestigious clients very happy in their quest for inspired modern living in architectural homes. Abramson Teiger Architects is led by Trevor Abramson, AIA, and Douglas Teiger, AIA, who strive for a constant balance of practical needs and dramatic artistic expression. The principals treat every project as an exercise in collaboration, with the client's design, scheduling and financial goals at the center of all consideration, while unearthing the provocative symbiosis between architectural integrity and home tranquility.

The touchstone of the firm's design philosophy lies within the exploration of modernism and how it can inspire the people who dwell and work in architectural homes. Their architecture does not simply rest on clean exact lines resonating order and starkness, but integrates light and air within structured spaces of material and form. The result is space that flows, merging function and form without prejudice to indoors vs. outdoors.

Rooted in the Bauhaus, and evolved into Modern Southern Californian Lifestyle, the firm's design concepts use subtle and stripped down forms and shapes, allowing the simplicity of mass and its material to govern. Light is used to modulate surfaces, and when possible, the designs diminish walls and expand glass. Across all functions and applications, the result is visually dynamic architecture, which opens dramatically to expansive views and vistas, evokes a sense of peace, sanctuary, productivity and celebrates the "Home as the Ultimate Retreat".

Abramson Teiger Architects received the highest design award given by The American Institute of Architects, The National Honor Award as well as three AIA design excellence awards for its design of the First Presbyterian Church of Encino. In addition, for its design excellence, the firm has been recognized with numerous other awards, has been featured on Home Tours and has been published in more than 145 magazines and books.

LIMA RESIDENCE

YEAR OF COMPLETION 2008
LOCATION Calabasas, California
SIZE 5,000 square feet
PHOTOGRAPHY Jim Bartsch

Situated on the edge of a natural preserve this house takes full advantage of the uninterrupted natural landscape that it faces. The compound consists of the main house building and the garage, guest room building which are separated by a courtyard. The house form is a rectangle, in plan, with the long side composed of large glass doors and windows that face the view. The plan is essentially open with living-dining room and family room separated by a free-standing cabinet. The living-dining space is voluminous with its 14 foot high ceilings and clear story windows. It opens to the kitchen which runs perpendicular to the main space. The dining sequence transverses the living space in a series of spaces that each open up to the other and to the exterior in a dramatic manner. The kitchen has a series of sliding doors that disappear into a wall resulting in the exterior eating patio and the kitchen to be unified as one eating cooking environment. Likewise the kitchen and formal dining area are open to each other and are on the same axis. They face the view and connect to the exterior with another set of sliding doors that open up completely.

The form of the house is conceived as a series of folding roof planes clad in factory painted charcoal gray metal. At some points the metal roof is either folded up or down to become wall planes. These walls frame openings that are focused on the view to the hills beyond. At points the folded walls lift up revealing poured in place concrete walls that are part of the first floor enclosure. A wood grained phenoelic resin clad "box" protrudes from the house. The "box" which is a storeroom, has a greater purpose

of truncating the visual axis on approach to the glass front door, and is an integral part of the enclosure that makes up the exterior eating patio. The wood grained resin panel box thrusts into the house, containing the kitchen, and introducing a warm hue to compliment the palette of natural materials. Behind the kitchen is a raised landing area that leads to the steel staircase. This landing separated from the family room by a built in bar, is an in informal study and home office. The staircase is a steel butterfly frame with apparently floating wood treads that lead to the second floor master bedroom suite. The stair is free of the perimeter walls.

The swimming pool runs parallel to the house and is a blue dash of water that compliments the view to the natural preserve. Between the pool and the house is a strip of low maintenance artificial turf. The pool forms one edge to the courtyard between the two buildings. A fire pit is the focus of this outdoor living space. There is a strong indoor outdoor connection reinforced by large sliding doors and glass walls that visually unite the interiors with the exterior.

far left entrance view left various exterior impressions

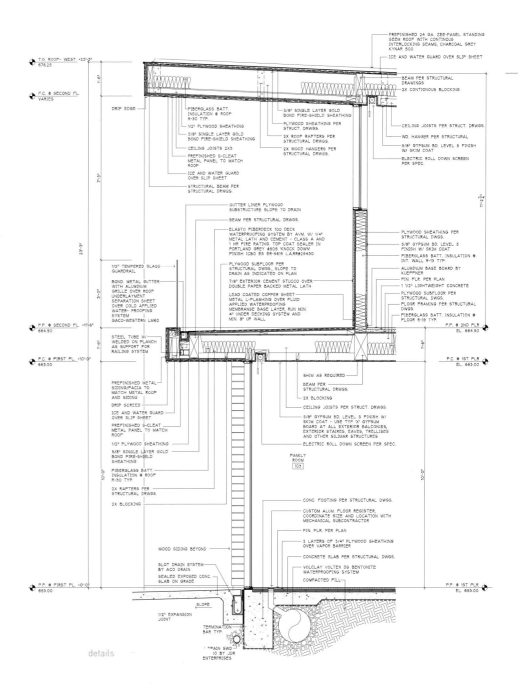

PREFINISHED 24 GA. ZEE-PANEL STANDING SEEM ROOF WITH CONTINOUS INTERLOCKING SEAMS, CHARCOAL GREY KYNAR 500

ICE AND WATER GUARD OVER SLIP SHEET

BEAM PER STRUCTURAL DRAWINGS

2X CONTIONOUS BLOCKING

CEILING JOISTS PER STRUCT. DRWGS.

WD. HANGER PER STRUCTURAL

5/8" GYPSUM BD. LEVEL 5 FINISH W/ SKIM COAT

ELECTRIC ROLL DOWN SCREEN PER SPEC.

T.O. ROOF- WEST +23'-3"
676.25

F.C. @ SECOND FL.
VARIES

DRIP EDGE

FIBERGLASS BATT. INSULATION @ ROOF R-30 TYP.

1/2" PLYWOOD SHEATHING

5/8" SINGLE LAYER GOLD BOND FIRE-SHIELD SHEATHING

CEILING JOISTS 2X3

PREFINISHED S-CLEAT METAL PANEL TO MATCH ROOF

ICE AND WATER GUARD OVER SLIP SHEET

STRUCTURAL BEAM PER STRUCTURAL DRWGS.

5/8" SINGLE LAYER GOLD BOND FIRE-SHIELD SHEATHING

PLYWOOD SHEATHING PER STRUCT. DRWGS.

2X ROOF RAFTERS PER STRUCTURAL DRWGS.

2X WOOD HANGERS PER STRUCTURAL DRWGS.

GUTTER LINER PLYWOOD SUBSTRUCTURE SLOPE TO DRAIN

BEAM PER STRUCTURAL DRWGS.

ELASTO FIBERDECK 100 DECK WATERPROOFING SYSTEM BY AVM. W/ 1/4" METAL LATH AND CEMENT - CLASS A AND 1 HR FIRE RATING. TOP COAT SEALER IN PORTLAND GREY #605 'KNOCK DOWN' FINISH ICBO ES ER-5615 L.ARR#25450

PLYWOOD SUBFLOOR PER STRUCTURAL DWGS., SLOPE TO DRAIN AS INDICATED ON PLAN

7/8" EXTERIOR CEMENT STUCCO OVER DOUBLE PAPER BACKED METAL LATH

LEAD COATED COPPER SHEET METAL L-FLASHING OVER FLUID APPLIED WATERPROOFING MEMBRANSE BASE LAYER, RUN MIN. 4" UNDER DECKING SYSTEM AND MIN. 8" UP WALL

PLYWOOD SHEATHING PER STRUCTURAL DWGS.

5/8" GYPSUM BD. LEVEL 5 FINISH W/ SKIM COAT

FIBERGLASS BATT. INSULATION @ INT. WALL R-13

ALUMINUM BASE BOARD BY KUEFFNER

FIN. FLR. PER PLAN

1 1/2" LIGHTWEIGHT CONCRETE

PLYWOOD SUBFLOOR PER STRUCTURAL DWGS.

FLOOR FRAMING PER STRUCTURAL DWGS.

FIBERGLASS BATT. INSULATION @ FLOOR R-19 TYP.

1/2" TEMPERED GLASS GUARDRAIL

BOND. METAL GUTTER WITH ALUMINUM GRILLE OVER ROOF UNDERLAYMENT SEPARATION SHEET OVER COLD APPLIED WATER- PROOFING SYSTEM GACO-WESTERN LM60

STEEL TUBE W/ WELDED ON FLANCH AS SUPPORT FOR RAILING SYSTEM

F.F. @ SECOND FL. +11'-6"
664.50

F.C. @ FIRST FL. +10'-0"
663.00

F.F. @ 2ND FLR
EL. 664.50

SHIM AS REQUIRED

BEAM PER STRUCTURAL DRWGS.

2X BLOCKING

CEILING JOISTS PER STRUCT. DRWGS.

5/8" GYPSUM BD. LEVEL 5 FINISH W/ SKIM COAT - USE TYP. 'X' GYPSUM BOARD AT ALL EXTERIOR BALCONIES, EXTERIOR STAIRES, EAVES, TRELLISES AND OTHER SILIMAR STRUCTURES

ELECTRIC ROLL DOWN SCREEN PER SPEC.

F.C. @ 1ST FLR
EL. 663.00

PREFINISHED METAL SIDING/FACIA TO MATCH METAL ROOF AND SIDING

DRIP SCREED

ICE AND WATER GUARD OVER SLIP SHEET

PREFINISHED S-CLEAT METAL PANEL TO MATCH ROOF

1/2" PLYWOOD SHEATHING

5/8" SINGLE LAYER GOLD BOND FIRE-SHIELD SHEATHING

FIBERGLASS BATT. INSULATION @ ROOF R-30 TYP.

2X RAFTERS PER STRUCTURAL DWGS.

2X BLOCKING

FAMILY ROOM
103

CONC. FOOTING PER STRUCTURAL DWGS.

CUSTOM ALUM. FLOOR REGISTER, COORDINATE SIZE AND LOCATION WITH MECHANICAL SUBCONTRACTOR

FIN. FLR. PER PLAN

2 LAYERS OF 3/4" PLYWOOD SHEATHING OVER VAPOR BARRIER

CONCRETE SLAB PER STRUCTURAL DWGS.

VOLCLAY VOLTEX DS BENTONITE WATERPROOFING SYSTEM

COMPACTED FILL

WOOD SIDING BEYOND

SLOT DRAIN SYSTEM BY ACO DRAIN

SEALED EXPOSED CONC. SLAB ON GRADE

F.F. @ FIRST FL. +0'-0"
663.00

F.F. @ 1ST FLR
EL. 653.00

1/2" EXPANSION JOINT

SLOPE

TERMINATION BAR TYP.

DRAIN SWD 10 BY JDR ENTERPRISES

details

left sliding glass elements allow for connection between exterior and interior spaces **right** construction section detail of poolside elevation

left space for relaxation right construction
detail sections of the main stairway

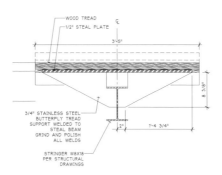

Tread Butterfly Support Detail
SCALE: 1 1/2" = 1'-0"

(7)

WOOD TREAD
1/2" STEAL PLATE

3'-5"

8 3/8"

3/4" STAINLESS STEEL
BUTTERFLY TREAD
SUPPORT WELDED TO
STEAL BEAM
GRIND AND POLISH
ALL WELDS

2"

1'-4 3/4"

STRINGER W8X18
PER STRUCTURAL
DRAWINGS

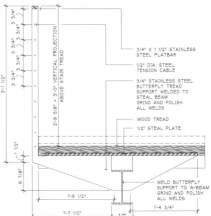

Railing Detail
SCALE: 1 1/2" = 1'-0"

(5)

3/4" X 1 1/2" STAINLESS
STEEL FLATBAR

1/2" DIA STEEL
TENSION CABLE

3/4" STAINLESS STEEL
BUTTERFLY TREAD
SUPPORT WELDED TO
STEAL BEAM
GRIND AND POLISH
ALL WELDS

WOOD TREAD
1/2" STEAL PLATE

WELD BUTTERFLY
SUPPORT TO W-BEAM
GRIND AND POLISH
ALL WELDS

3'-1 1/2"

2'-9 5/8" = 3'-0" VERTICAL PROJECTION
ABOVE STAIR TREAD

6 7/8"

1'-6 1/2"

1'-7 1/2"

1'-4 3/4"

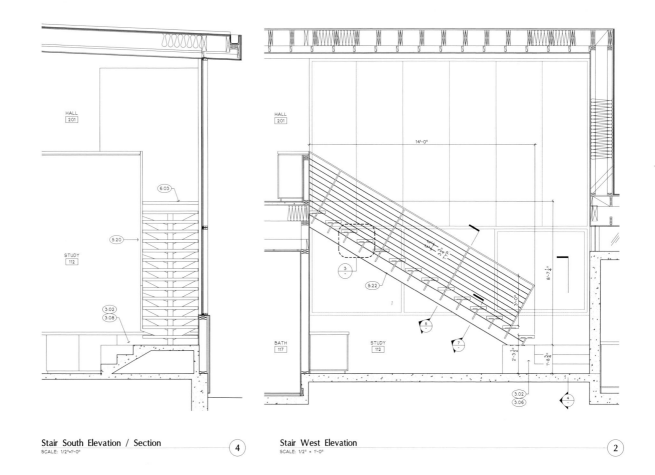

HALL
201

HALL
201

STUDY
112

6.03

5.20

3.02
3.08

14'-0"

8'-7¼"

BATH
117

STUDY
112

5.22

3.02
3.06

Stair South Elevation / Section
SCALE: 1/2"=1'-0"   (4)

Stair West Elevation
SCALE: 1/2" = 1'-0"   (2)

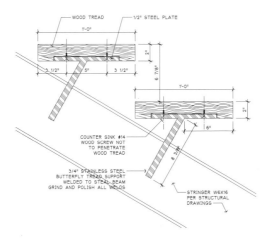

WOOD TREAD   1/2" STEEL PLATE

1'-0"

2"

3 1/2"   5"   3 1/2"

6 7/8"

1'-0"

2"

COUNTER SINK #14
WOOD SCREW NOT
TO PENETRATE
WOOD TREAD

6"

8 3/8"

3/4" STAINLESS STEEL
BUTTERFLY TREAD SUPPORT
WELDED TO STEEL BEAM
GRIND AND POLISH ALL WELDS

STRINGER W6X16
PER STRUCTURAL
DRAWINGS

Stair Tread Section Detail at Butterfly Support
SCALE: 3"=1'-0"   (3)

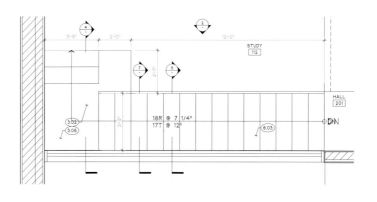

STUDY
112

HALL
201

3-5"   2'-0"   12'-0"

3.02
3.06

18R @ 7 1/4"
17T @ 12"

DN

6.03

Stair Enlarged Floor Plan
SCALE: 1/2" = 1'-0"   (1)

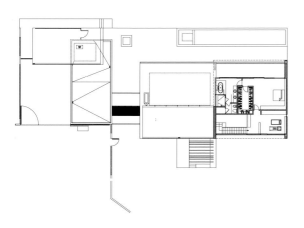

first floor

left kitchen and dining zone combines
with the covered terrace right each of the
residence's main spaces is clearly defined,
yet carefully delineated to flow into the
adjoining space

KELLY RESIDENCE

YEAR OF COMPLETION 2006
LOCATION Los Angeles, California
SIZE 5,000 square feet
PHOTOGRAPHY Richard Barnes,
except rear elevation by David Lena

Kelly Residence is an exploration of balance:
between solid vs. void, formal order vs. intimate
grace, private vs. public, and stoic vs. playful, all
relative to achieving a higher sense of spatial
freedom within an architectural home.

The Architects divided the use of the spaces
into public below (first floor) and private above
(second floor). The house has a parents' side and
a children's side, allowing each user their privacy
and sound control, with an umbilical cord, given
architectural form as a bridging element joining
the two parts.

The Kelly Residence is divided into four "boxes",
each finished in white plaster, and raised on
steel pilotis. Instead of being a complete four
sided object each "box" has a missing side which
is replaced by high-density wood panels coated
with phenolic resin which are extruded upward
from the first floor. The notion of free facade
is expressed with the nature of this façade's
materiality. The panels, manufactured by Trespa
from sustainable products, are installed as
a rain-screen. This façade is punctured with
stainless steel inserts, further articulating the
idea cladding panels are non load bearing.

Private bedrooms are up in the air, while on the
ground floor large expansive openings allow the
garden to "run" under the house. The interior
spaces are oriented to maximize views from the
house and draw the garden in. There is a strong
design language of solid versus void and formal
order versus amorphous patterning.

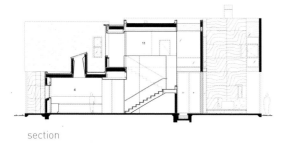

section

second floor

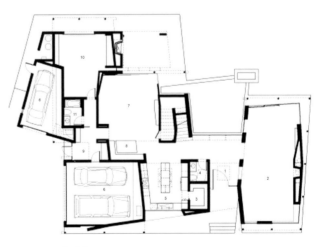

first floor

left exterior cladding panels were used
on the interior spaces to underscore
the architect's intention of using indoor/
outdoor places to form a spatial continuum

DAVIS RESIDENCE

YEAR OF COMPLETION 2007
LOCATION Toronto, Canada
SIZE 9,275 square feet (house),
3,225 square feet (basement)
PHOTOGRAPHY Tom Arban

The solid massing of the first floor is in response to the harsh Toronto winter and is clad in layers of stone and wood. As the façade lifts up and away from the grade it is clad in wood, detailed as a rain screen, which stands proud of the stone below it. The wood is set in front of the stone base, serving to layer the façade in a composition of plane and material. The second floor walls are free of the base in plan and follow the profile of the soaring roof. They are finished in white plaster to reinforce the concept of lightness as the house lifts to the sky. These walls end short of the roof, the result of which is spaces with upwards views to the densely wooded site. The green forest is brought inside. The roof soars above, light and ephemeral.

section

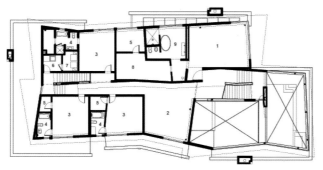

second floor

first floor

LEHRER RESIDENCE

YEAR OF COMPLETION 2010
LOCATION Malibu, California
SIZE 8,000 square feet

This house is a compound of several structures that create a tranquil courtyard with views to the ocean framed by the main house's outdoor two story living room. Parts of the ground floor of the main house are buried behind concrete retaining walls and covered with the lawn of the courtyard above. This allowed the gently sloping sight to be leveled to create an upper courtyard. This courtyard is a space to meditate the tranquility of the ocean horizon and the blue water of the swimming pool. The lawn in the courtyard undulates; symbolizing the ocean waves that role in. A lone sculpted skylight penetrates the lawn.

A gentle ramp along the side of the swimming pool connects the entry at the driveway to the main house below. A sequence of entry is created with axis that starts with views over the long view of the swimming pool, and then leaves, as the ramp moves down the side of the pool towards the main house.

In the distance, at the rear of the lot, is the guest house, perched on a knoll that was created to conceal the 4 car garage and hide the Pacific

Coast Highway behind. At the right, is the secondary bedroom wing that is raised over the undulating lawn.

The main structure is conceived as a roof that covers both outdoor and indoor living spaces. This roof frames the view from the entrance to the compound, emphasizing the horizontal of the ocean horizon. The master bedroom, at the right, looks over the ocean, over the loft like interior of the main living spaces and over the two story covered patio. The covered patio has the water of the swimming pool, seen through the glass end of the pool, as its backdrop. Its primary view is out towards the ocean.

The Lehrer residence on Malibu's Encinal Canyon Bluff over looking the Pacific Ocean really sums up all the themes of our Southern California lifestyle so important to our architecture. Here we have rooms with no doors, rooms with walls of glass, outdoor living spaces with soft filtered light, and an 80 foot long sliver of water that meets the horizon of the ocean and so typifies our Southern California lifestyle.

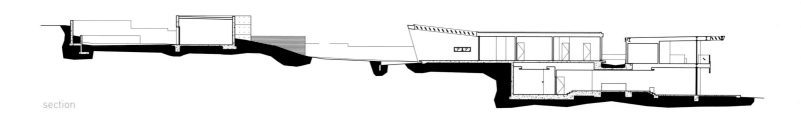

section

BARTON MYERS ASSOCIATES, INC

www.bartonmyers.com

Barton Myers

Ryan Ihly

Peter W. Rutti

Thomas Schneider

Barton Myers Associates (BMA) is an architecture and planning firm founded in Toronto in 1975. Barton Myers, FAIA moved to Los Angeles in the early 1980's to lead a distinguished team of designers in an urban design competition for Bunker Hill in downtown Los Angeles, and to teach at the UCLA Graduate School of Architecture and Urban Planning. Now based in Los Angeles, BMA currently works on an assortment of major commissions for public, private and institutional clients.

BMA is co-lead by long-standing Senior Associates Ryan Ihly, AIA, Peter W. Rutti, AIA and Thomas Schneider, AIA. These architects share a wealth of experience in the firm's areas of expertise and ensure that every project is executed to BMA's award-winning standards. The responsibility shared by BMA's architectural leadership ensures that Barton Myers is personally involved with every project through all phases of design and construction.

Barton Myers has earned an international reputation for excellence in architectural design and many of Barton Myers' projects have been pioneering efforts - his own industrial, off-the-shelf components house; the development of high-density urban infill; the sensitive restyling of existing buildings; and, the design of high quality cultural institutions throughout Canada and the United States.

From inception, BMA's commitment to design excellence has been recognized in awards for planning, architecture and interior design. Barton Myers received the American Institute of Architect's Los Angeles Chapter Gold Medal and a coveted Rudy Bruner Award for Urban Renewal in Newark for the New Jersey Performing Arts Center. In Canada, he was awarded the Governor General's Award for Architecture for Woodsworth College, the Seagram Museum and the Citadel Theatre, and the United States Institute of Theater Technology has honored the New Jersey Performing Arts Center, Cerritos Center for the Performing Arts, Portland Center for the Performing Arts, and Tempe Center for the Arts.

Barton Myers Associates is currently working on a number of projects nationwide. Scheduled to open in 2013, the DPAC Orlando Performing Arts Center is the largest performing venue being currently designed in the United States. Smaller in scale and closer to home, BMA is overseeing the design and construction phases on several projects, including residences and the headquarters for an independent film company.

RESIDENCE IN WEST LOS ANGELES

YEAR OF COMPLETION 2006
LOCATION Los Angeles, California
SIZE 5,000 square feet
PHOTOGRAPHY Ciro Coelho
ASSOCIATE-IN-CHARGE
Thomas Schneider, AIA
STRUCTURAL ENGINEER
Norman J. Epstein
LANDSCAPE DESIGN Katherine Glascock
GENERAL CONTRACTOR
Caputo Construction Corp

The West Los Angeles residence is an "elegant warehouse" in the tradition of Eames. It builds upon the Southern California tradition of seamless spatial integration of indoors and outdoors and continues explorations in steel housing in which industrial materials are used out of context.

The house is situated in a south-facing corner lot. The neighborhood is urban in character and contains a mix of single-family homes, small apartment buildings and a vibrant shopping and entertainment area. The design turns the house inward to create a protected precinct in the tradition of Los Angeles courtyard houses. Site walls of different heights and materials enclose the courtyard to the street side and provide brief glimpses to passersby of the interior space hidden behind the main gates.

The house is comprised of a group of three buildings all positioned around a central courtyard. A 500 sf garage and 700 sf games room are located on the western portion of the lot, the 3,000 sf main residence is centrally located, and a 400 sf guest house faces the eastern edge of the central courtyard. The three buildings form an ensemble that frame and enclose the intimate courtyard and lap-pool. The southeast facing courtyard takes full advantage of sunlight and encompasses spaces for different occasions including: a sun filled area for the lap pool; a covered, semi-protected patio for year-round outdoor dining; and covered porches for lounging and entertaining. The lap pool's circulation also serves to mask the sound of traffic and the nearby freeway.

The main building is an exposed structural steel frame, with a metal deck ceiling and concrete floors. The structures are open, loft spaces enclosed by glazed aluminum sectional doors, which can be opened and closed to varying degrees. North facing clerestory windows provide the house with constant, even light and allow for views of the sky and neighboring trees. Galvanized rolling shutters above the south-facing openings create a secondary envelope that provides additional sun control and insulation.

The house is equipped with roof-mounted photovoltaic panels that produce electricity, while the pool water is heated by south-facing solar collectors. The additional combination of optimally placed roof overhangs – which ensure summer shading and allow for the winter sun to warm the exposed concrete floors – with insulated windows and cross-ventilation makes the house very energy efficient. The house is built with an Energy Star rated "cool" roof and is in full compliance with the tough California Energy Efficiency Standards.

The landscape design pays special attention to the integration of indoor and outdoor space and is critical to the overall success of the architecture. Because the rooms are open to sky and light, the interior spaces are in constant conversation with the gardens and require an equally vital character and presence.

right view of courtyard and lap-pool

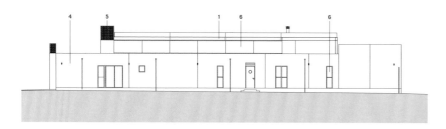

north elevation

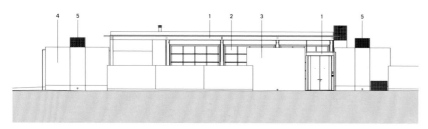

south elevation

1 exposed steel beams
2 overhead sectional doors
3 poured-in-place concrete
4 cement plaster
5 galvanized steel grating
6 clear glazing

right view from main entrance, guest
house is on the right

floor plan

1 entry
2 covered porches
3 guest house
4 kitchen
5 dining
6 living
7 master bedroom
8 master bathroom
9 bedroom
10 pantry
11 garage
12 games room
13 lap-pool

left main hallway with built-in storage, pantry is on the left. right, top kitchen and sitting room. bottom master bathroom. following page gardenwalls facing the street

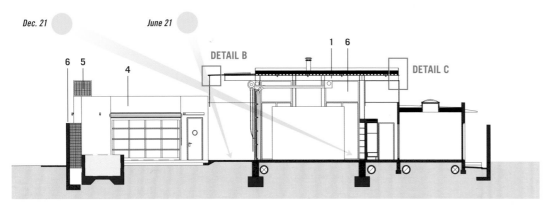

Dec. 21   *June 21*

DETAIL B

DETAIL C

1 exposed steel beams
2 overhead sectional doors
3 poured-in-place concrete
4 cement plaster
5 galvanized steel grating
6 clear glazing

section

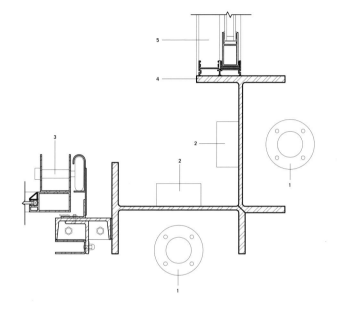

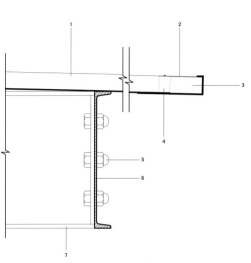

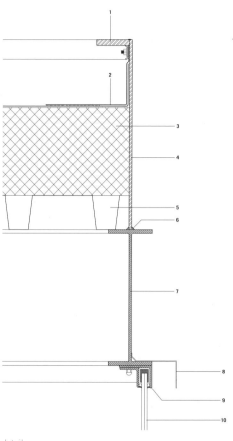

detail a/plan view

1 light fixture flush with finished floor
2 receptacles
3 overhead sectional door and shutter
4 steel columns welded at flanges
5 sliding glass door

detail b

1 galvanized steel deck
2 galvanized steel gutter
3 acorn bolt
4 steel channel
5 steel beam

detail c

1 steel plate
2 roofing membrane
3 insulation
4 galvanized steel deck
5 steel beam
6 drip
7 steel angles
8 1/2" clear tempered glass

BEKINS RESIDENCE

YEAR OF COMPLETION 2008
LOCATION Santa Barbara, California
SIZE 4,500 square feet
PHOTOGRAPHY Ciro Coelho
ASSOCIATE-IN-CHARGE
Thomas Schneider, AIA
STRUCTURAL ENGINEER Stephen Perlof
LANDSCAPE DESIGN Arcadia Studios
GENERAL CONTRACTOR
Caputo Construction Corp

Situated on a 10-acre, ocean-view property near Santa Barbara, the Bekins Residence continues Barton Myers' investigations in the blending of interior and exterior living spaces by utilizing industrial building materials in a residential context.

The 5,000 square feet residence is designed on a single floor level for a family of four. Conceived as a warehouse for living, the home's plan includes large live-in kitchen, dining and living rooms – each opening to a grand covered porch. A partial-height wall separates the private areas (bedrooms, bathrooms, etc.) from the shared living spaces. Exposed structural steel and concrete floors give the design a simple, industrial aesthetic. The building materials are accented by a muted palette of colors derived from the surrounding landscape.

Interior and exterior are seamlessly integrated throughout by a series of porches, courtyards and patios of different character and purposes. A protected, north-facing Zen garden frames the hillside and the Santa Barbara mountains, while the kitchen's eastern patio serves as the family's outdoor dining and barbecue area. The south-facing, covered porch and terrace are the home's focal point and main outdoor gathering space.

The historical gardens were designed by noted Landscape Architect Lockwood de Forest and include ancient olive trees surrounding an oval lawn that overlooks the Santa Barbara Channel Islands. Derrik Eichelberger of Arcadia Studios, restored the original gardens and designed the new landscaping features forming the interface between the historical gardens and the new building. Terraced slopes below the lawns are planted with avocado, citrus and other fruit trees.

The property was previously the site of "The Monastery" a rambling vernacular house built in 1935 by famed conductor Leopold Stokowski. In reverence to the site's noted figures, which also included Beryl Markham and Greta Garbo, two of original fireplaces were rebuilt as garden features. One, in the shape of the Hollywood Bowl shell, forms a fire pit facing both the house and the historical gardens, and serves as an outdoor lounge area. The second fireplace, in the form of a pipe organ, frames the kitchen's outdoor patio and provides warmth for outdoor dining.

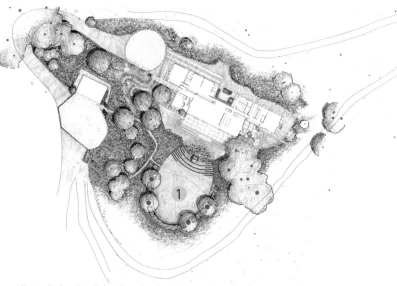

arcadia studios' updated site plan, showing the house
and historic lawn by Lockwood de Forest.

above main living spaces **right** kitchen and
sitting room

top main lobby view bottom view of the
studio theater and art gallery pavilions

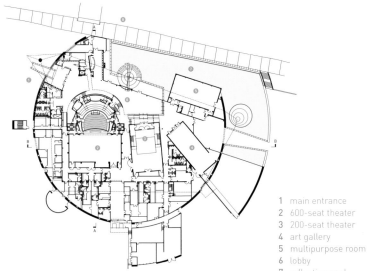

ground floor plan

balcony plan

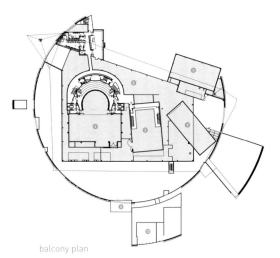

1 main entrance
2 600-seat theater
3 200-seat theater
4 art gallery
5 multipurpose room
6 lobby
7 reflecting pool
8 tempe town lake

TEMPE CENTER FOR THE ARTS

YEAR OF COMPLETION 2007
LOCATION Tempe, Arizona
SIZE 88,0000 square feet
PHOTOGRAPHY John Edward Linden:
01, 03, 04, 06; Michael Masengarb: 07, 08;
Peter Robertson: 02, 05;
ASSOCIATE-IN-CHARGE Peter Rutti, AIA
PARTNER ARCHITECT Architekton
ENGINEERING ARUP
LANDSCAPE DESIGN Design Workshop
GENERAL CONTRACTOR Okland
Construction

The Tempe Center for the Arts (TCA) is a unique collection of intimate venues within an iconic, protective envelope. Underneath the flight path of Phoenix Sky Harbor Airport, the sculptural shed roof not only provides the first level of acoustic protection, but also shelters its patrons and performers from the harsh desert sun. The roof is multi-referential, with inspiration from: monument valley; nearby Hayden butte; origami; and even stealth fighter design.

The roof's faceted form drapes over the independent 600-seat Proscenium Theater, including its fly tower, the 200-seat Studio Theater, the visual arts gallery and a common lobby. The individual venues are clustered to form and activate a lobby emulating a town square. The semi-circular, protective assemblage of Pueblo Bonito at Chaco canyon inspired the building's organization. Similar to Pueblo Bonito's south orientation adjacent to the trade route and once flowing river, TCA is oriented north adjacent to Tempe Town Lake with views to nearby and distant landforms that punctuate the valley.

TCA optimizes its location at the northwest gateway to Tempe with its 360 degree landmark architecture anchoring the west end of Tempe Town Lake. It is the contemporary element in the triptych of the geologic Hayden Butte and historic Hayden Flour mill. Acknowledging its location in the Sonoran desert, the architecture responds with a relatively opaque sculptural composition on the south, east and west orientations while becoming quite transparent on the north. Various locations around the building allude to how rainwater flows from the roof, similar to the way arroyos deliver rivers of rain across the desert floor.

01

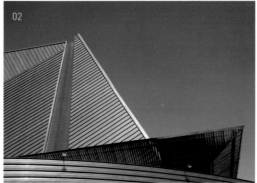

02

03

left view of the lake-side multi-purpose
room middle 200-seat studio theater
right 600-seat proscenium theater

1 sculpture garden
2 gallery solarium
3 art gallery
4 200-seat studio theater

5 lobby volume
6 main theater fly tover
10 administration

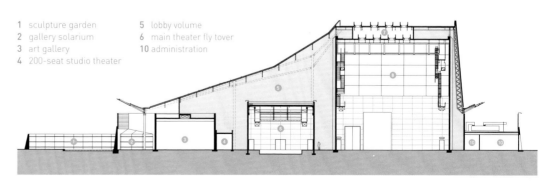

section

BELZBERG ARCHITECTS

www.belzbergarchitects.com

Hagy Belzberg

Belzberg Architects is a group of young designers guided by the experience and curiosity of Hagy Belzberg. The staff is energetic with an eclectic background of combined design experiences. The firm believes that their diverse educational backgrounds and apprehension toward fostering individualized working methodologies contributes to the uniqueness of each project and the firm's ability to handle the demands of any given project typology.

CONGA ROOM

YEAR OF COMPLETION 2008
LOCATION Los Angeles, California
SIZE 15,000 square feet
PHOTOGRAPHY Benny Chan (Fotoworks),
Hagy Belzberg
SUSPENDED ELEMENTS Spectrum Oak

The original Conga Room of Los Angeles acted as a destination for many Latin-Americans to dance and congregate in an environment sensitive to their specific culture. The new Conga Room at Nokia Center in downtown Los Angeles' new L.A. Live complex embraces the sensitivity of old toward Latin culture and is interpreted as architectural and space-defining elements. Encouraged by the client's desires for a ceiling which could reflect the vibrancy and dynamism of Latin culture, the architect utilized the idea of patterning the space throughout. The ceiling pattern consists of "pedals" and "flowers;" each panel representing a "pedal" and groupings of six "pedals" constituting a "flower." This base pattern was then manipulated in order to achieve an undulating pattern which moves and flows sinuous to the rhythms of the space. Simultaneously, the geometry of the panels allow for the mitigation of numerous and complex building infrastructure components specific to that of a live music venue such as lighting, mechanical and acoustic elements. Ultimately, the space isn't simply an aggregate of architectural panels which perform to a level satisfactory for that of a state of the art music venue. It is a space where each visitor is surrounded by patterned surfaces and culturally-inspired images which saturate the space and embolden the overall experience as Latin.

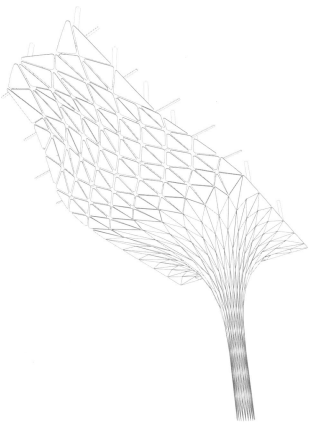

right the "tornado" pulls one from the lower level entrance to the club's main level

above right the "tornado" can be lit in varied hues to reflect the wished mood of any given event **right** conceptional visualization schemes for the "tornado"

Plan View of Tornado showing structural ribs

CNC milled structural ribs

CNC milled plywood petals

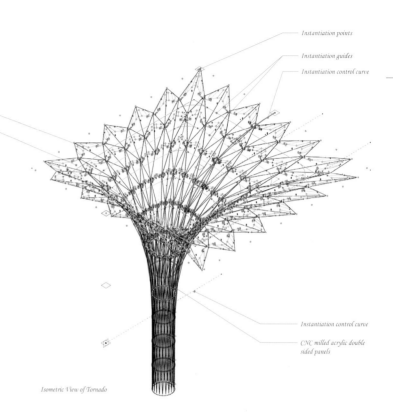

Instantiation points

Instantiation guides

Instantiation control curve

Instantiation control curve

CNC milled acrylic double sided panels

Isometric View of Tornado

Plan View of Tornado

below upon arrival on the main level, the
path continues to the entertainment zone,
which features a dance floor

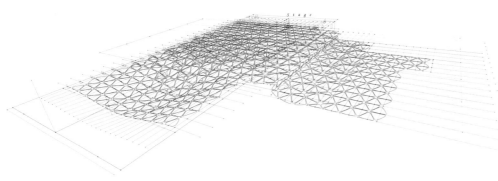

flower strap

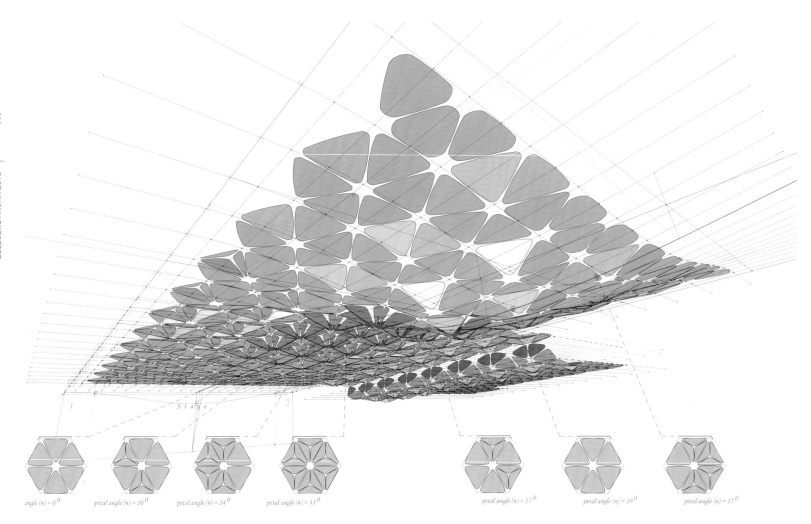

angle (n) = 0⁰   petal angle (n) = 10⁰   petal angle (n) = 24⁰   petal angle (n) = 31⁰   petal angle (n) = 17⁰   petal angle (n) = 10⁰   petal angle (u) = 17⁰

porosity gradient

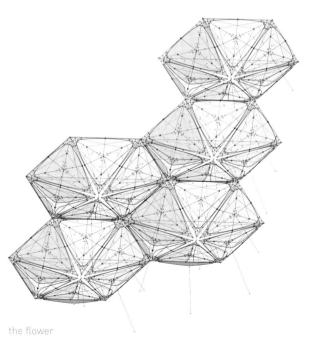

the flower

left, and above the ceilings of the club
space are composed of suspended panels.
the "flower" is combined in various
patterns to variegate the surface and
improve acoustic performance

BRENTWOOD RESIDENCE

YEAR OF COMPLETION 2007
LOCATION Los Angeles, California
SIZE 12,000 square feet
PHOTOGRAPHY Benny Chan (Fotoworks),
Art Gray, Hagy Belzberg
INTERIOR DESIGN MLK Studio/
Meg Joannides
CONTRACTOR Group F

The Brentwood Residence is located on a large picturesque lot in the foothills of the Santa Monica Mountains. Because the lot did not offer any immediate views from the buildable area of the property, the structures that comprise the project were designed to engage each other while focusing attention on the built and natural landscape within. The lot features a large California Oak tree on the rear half of the site which serves as the focal point of the formal procession through the project. To counteract the formal setup of the site plan the spatial organization has been setup to challenge the established axis without eroding it.

To achieve this, pathways have been intentionally designed to dissolve and reappear along the route. The line clearly divides the formal living area of the main house from the informal public spaces but it is counteracted by the complex interlocking geometry and asymmetrical volumes that make up the exterior.

As a homage to the palette of classic Mid-Century design, the house features a material composition of steel troweled plaster, gauged and stacked Pennsylvania Bluestone, and Mangaris wood siding.

left and right a network of indoor, covered outdoor, and exterior spaces weave together to provide a casual, yet gracious ambience

left folded planes wrap around to create a
unique spatial envelope
above a limited palette of materials was
skillfully employed to unite the spaces
right the path leading through the house
is consciously defined as a series of paths
that are interrupted, shifted, and redefined

perspective

SKYLINE RESIDENCE

YEAR OF COMPLETION 2007
LOCATION Hollywood, California
SIZE 6,000 square feet
PHOTOGRAPHY Benny Chan (Fotoworks),
Hagy Belzberg

Perched atop a ridgeline in the Hollywood
Hills, the presence of the Skyline Residence
represents an economical approach to creating
an environmentally sensitive building within a
limited budget. The pre-existing site presented
a challenge in terms of constructability as
the client presented the challenge of limited
allowable expenses.

Beyond incorporating sustainable building
product systems, the budgetary limitations
imposed on material choice forced the architect
to implement strategies for using resources in
close proximity to the site. Therefore, the general
concept adopted for this project stems from
"Carbon Neutral Economics," or the purchasing
of goods which are manufactured locally to save
carbon transportation emissions. In a low budget
architecture project where high-tech systems
such as photovoltaic panels, wind turbines
and recycled products are out of economical
reach, the Skyline Residence reverted back
to purchasing locally, minimized grading and
capitalizing on natural characteristics of the site.

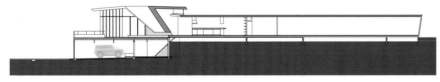

elevation

left this quintessential LA image stands in
the tradition of Pierre Königs Case Study
House #22 **right** open facades on the
valley side contrast with the veil of slats on
the back elevation

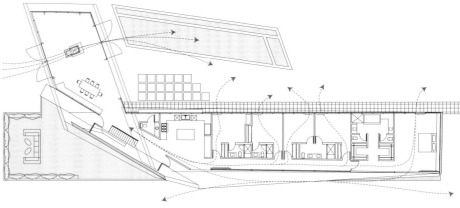

diagram

left grey and white surfaces inside at once
counter and complement the earthy tones
of the landscape above the home is sited
to take advantage of cooling winds

above folding facade planes define
unorthodox aperture-like openings that
emphasize the dramatic views

CLIVE WILKINSON ARCHITECTS

www.clivewilkinson.com

Clive Wilkinson

Clive Wilkinson established the firm in Los Angeles in 1991 after relocating to the West Coast from a successful career in London. His background includes thirty years of experience in a wide range of high profile creative design projects on four continents, most notably in creative office space, entertainment facilities, television stations and high tech office development projects, which have consistently won national and international design awards. Responsible for directing all design work, Clive initiates and develops conceptual design strategy in close collaboration with the Client team. Clive is a member of both the Royal Institute of British Architects and the American Institute of Architects; a member of the Interior Design Hall of Fame, and has held a Board Director position with the American Institute of Architects/ Los Angeles, 2004–2006. He was recently nominated a 2006 Master of Design by Fast Company magazine.

VCU ADCENTER

YEAR OF COMPLETION 2008
LOCATION Richmond, Virginia
SIZE 32,000 square feet
PHOTOGRAPHY Allen T. Jones

VCU Adcenter in Richmond, Virginia, is one of the foremost media, advertising and communications schools in North America. In an effort to expand and broaden the educational prospectus, a new building was planned. A vacant historic three-storey brick carriage house from 1890 provided the main school teaching space, and this is supplemented with a new 12,000 square feet three-storey 'service structure' located along side, which provides modern facilities and additional space on several levels, including seismic bracing of the old building.

Together, the structures house a school pioneering an advertising curriculum offering not only real-world business fundamentals and strategic branding, but hands-on understanding of the creative process and the experience of working with creative teams of students, teachers and professionals.

The project is an exercise in "interlacing" - a term describing the display of imagery on a computer screen in a non-contiguous manner. The interlace effect results in a low-resolution, pixilated version of a graphic in the foreground offering graphic massing while hinting to a more fine grain image, with higher resolution beyond. The image in the background gradually comes into focus slowly over time while more information is downloaded allowing the foreground image to reside and disappear. This method of using a graphic foreground to hint at a denser, textural background plays out throughout the project allowing the contemporary, graphic addition to act as a prelude to the primary structure – the historic artifact whose complexity is gradually understood overtime.

Acting as a catalyst, the new addition seeks to bring things together: old and new; student and faculty; academia and practice. Resisting the traditional academic hierarchy of student, faculty and administration, the project encourages a high level of social interaction between all users and all floor levels. Open communication is facilitated through the use of a series of small and large open "neighborhoods" such as the massive concrete gathering table in the basement and informal break-out areas throughout each floor.

While the central (entry) floor accommodates classrooms and acts as a communal gathering space, hosting public events, the basement floor is devoted to student workspace with adjacent media labs, and the top floor is given over to faculty space and seminar rooms. However, the intention is to have staff/student interaction dispersed throughout the building. The central floor is multi-purpose and flexible by insertion of a 50-person meeting room that folds up against the ceiling, and retractable acoustic curtains separating the 90-person lecture room. The old maple floors were refurbished, and new maple strip flooring and maple veneer was used for forming furniture on the Faculty floor.

left, and right the design experiments with contrasting, yet complementary building volumes, colors, and materials

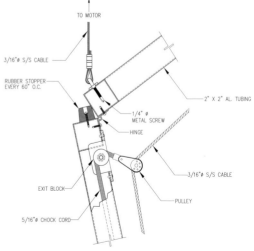

TO MOTOR

3/16"ø S/S CABLE

RUBBER STOPPER
EVERY 60" O.C.

2" X 2" AL. TUBING

1/4" ø
METAL SCREW

HINGE

3/16"ø S/S CABLE

EXIT BLOCK

PULLEY

5/16"ø CHOCK CORD

right upon entrance, a retractable tent-like
structure forms the focus of the foyer
space that also doubles as a place of
assembly for student events

details

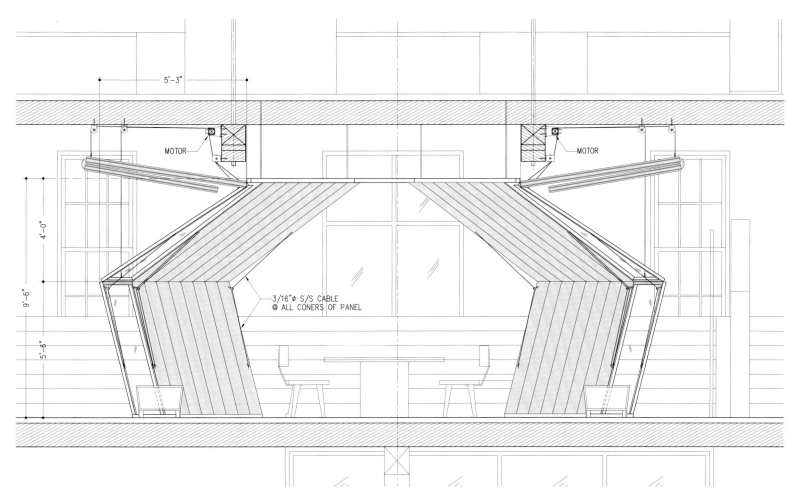

3/16"⌀ S/S CABLE
@ ALL CONERS OF PANEL

MOTOR

MOTOR

5'-3"

4'-0"

9'-6"

5'-6"

cross section

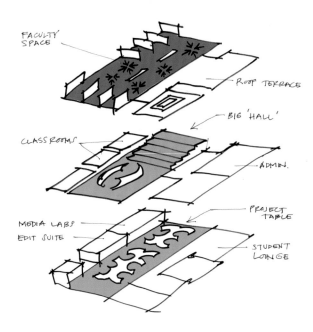

FACULTY SPACE

ROOF TERRACE

BIG 'HALL'

CLASSROOMS

ADMIN.

PROJECT TABLE

MEDIA LABS
EDIT SUITE

STUDENT LOUNGE

left learning spaces in the new wing are bright and friendly, diverse functions are inserted as underneath the characteristic historic beams of the original structure
right a multi-level circulation space acts as a spatial hinge between new and old

right a warm palette of oranges, yellows and greens reinterprets the vibrant colors of the local desert landscape

FIDM SAN DIEGO

YEAR OF COMPLETION 2008
LOCATION San Diego, California
SIZE 33,317 square feet
PHOTOGRAPHY Benny Chan (Fotoworks)

For over 35 years FIDM/Fashion Institute of Design and Merchandising has offered a specialized, private college education with emphasis on combining academic excellence and real world experience. In the latest installment of FIDM's unique creative learning environments, Clive Wilkinson Architects has designed a dynamic "learning landscape" for the San Diego Campus as part of an extended development of the FIDM brand in physical space. Together with sister campuses in Orange County, Los Angeles, and San Francisco the new architecture at FIDM has come to represent the college's reputation, brand, and philosophy towards education.

The college occupies the entire 3rd floor of a high-rise office building located in a newly revitalized area of downtown San Diego. CWA created a variegated internal landscape that is organized around the complex programmatic requirements of a school campus, all the while framing remarkable views of San Diego's skyline and an adjacent park. FIDM's new learning landscape is organized in three parts: a public entry zone, an educational zone and a zone for student support services and administration. A continuous path connects the different areas of the campus, taking one through specific areas such as reception, admissions, career guidance, financial services, classrooms, labs, student lounge and the library, each with its own unique spatial experience.

Upon arrival on the third floor, the entry zone immediately envelopes the visitor with rich color and material palette inspired by the native desert environment of the San Diego region. The campus is treated like a landscape, its functions integrated with design, and its parts connected through a holistic graphic design program. The warm palette of oranges, yellows and greens seen in the in the local desert vegetation compliment the rich blues of the clear desert sky. These saturated colors differentiate the "monuments" in the landscape from the warm muted background characterized by the large oak-paneled ceiling and sand colored quartz flooring in the public zone. The full height wall graphics of abstracted vegetation lend visual texture to the space, extending from the entry, through the reception and the central hallway, and culminating dramatically in the ceiling plane of the Financial Services area.

Unified by a brightly colored folded yellow ceiling and dark green carpet, the administration and student services zone is notable for its openness; glass fronted education, career planning and admissions offices along the perimeter of the building encourage interaction between staff and students. This glazing also serves to allow daylight to travel deep into the space, where lounge areas carved between offices invite use by students and staff alike.

The design of the classroom zone recognized from the outset that the school's creative and collaborative culture would not be well served by standard education planning. Where conventional education spaces treat classroom spaces as opaque boxes to be isolated from circulation, at FIDM's San Diego campus transparency between these zones is maximized with full length glass walls, and the circulation zone widens at intervals to create carved out open media spaces. Aware that academic life and social life each profit from the other, the Student Lounge space opens off of the classroom zone, offering a location for informal meeting to occur, accented by custom organic metal lanterns.

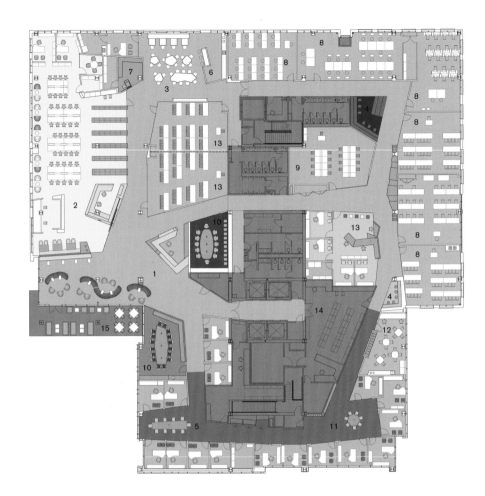

plan

1 reception
2 library
3 student lounge
4 computer lounge
5 admissions
6 pantry
7 store
8 classroom
9 computer lab
10 conference room
11 education and placement
12 faculty lounge
13 financial services
14 college service
15 terrace

left, above, and right a continuous path connects the various areas of the campus. leading through reception, admissions, offices, and the student lounge

JWT HEADQUARTERS, NEW YORK

YEAR OF COMPLETION 2008
LOCATION New York, New York
SIZE 250,000 square feet
PHOTOGRAPHY Eric Laignel

JWT, formerly J. Walter Thompson, is one of the oldest and largest advertising agencies in the world. While its credentials and client list were impeccable, the company needed to transform itself to meet the challenges of the new media world. Youthful new leadership at the New York headquarters determined to make that a complete physical, virtual and behavioral transformation. In June 2004, Clive Wilkinson Architects was appointed to design the transformation with workplace strategists, DEGW, assisting with client visioning, and HOK New York providing executive architect services. With a total population of 900 people, JWT occupied 250,000 SF in 5 floors of the office building at 466 Lexington Ave. The floors were sequentially gutted, remodeled and reoccupied in four construction phases over three years, with final completion occurring in February 2008.

From inception, it emerged that JWT was reframing its core vision about how it engaged with the public. Advertising would no longer focus on projecting messages to the consumer, but creating experiences which rewarded the public's time and attention. It's mission had become 'story telling'. To promote interaction, mobility and collaboration, the isolated divisions within JWT would be opened up and reconnected. The new space would be open architecture, with no private offices, and vertical movement between floors would be facilitated to unite the JWT community. Separate businesses, like the post-production facility of JWTwo, would be expressed as distinct but integrated companies, adding character to the space.

The architectural concept became a thematic thread: we used the tree as a metaphor for storytelling and extended it as organizing form and connective tissue between the individual branches of the agency. This 'narrative tree' links all floors and the trunk is the atrium void and staircase that connects all floors over the main entrance hall. The branches are ovoid shaped meeting rooms: either solid green cones, or acoustically padded green tents. The cones are angled, like branches stretching through floors. The sixteen different tents extend the metaphor further by each being incised using CNC machines with the first sentence of a famous novel. The words are cut into the fabric and the cut letters hang down – we called this effect 'falling words', and the cut letter shapes appear like leaves. The choice of content was a collaboration with JWT creatives - each sentence is incomplete in meaning, so the reader is free to extend its meaning.

left, and right the client reframed its core vision: advertising no longer focuses on projecting messages, but rather creates experiences that reward the public's time and attention

left, above, and right to promote interaction, mobility and collaboration, the divisions within JWT were opened up and connected

MAGUIRE ASSOCIATES

YEAR OF COMPLETION 2006
LOCATION Santa Monica, California
SIZE 14,400 square feet
PHOTOGRAPHY Benny Chan (Fotoworks)

In late summer 2005, Maguire Partners, a Los Angeles development company, approached Clive Wilkinson Architects with a request to relocate its Executive Offices from a glass tower in downtown LA to a radically new environment in a 14,400 square feet. penthouse space, one block away from Santa Monica Beach with dramatic waterfront views.

Inspired by Southern California's native beach culture and the site's natural surroundings, the main design vocabulary employs two different variations of curved shapes, expressing the extremes of the motion of water. Anchored at both ends of the space, the executive conference rooms are made up of edgy, shard-like slanting walls. Colored glass in dark and light shades is sandwiched in-between, creating a highly textured and faceted surface that resembles breaking surf. Throughout the floor in open workstation areas, more rounded overlapping low partitions evoke imagery of gentler rolling waves.

The two conference rooms and workstations in between are connected by a floating ceiling plane. The ceiling is a dynamic visual element that houses lighting and also visually conceals the mechanical ducting located above, while allowing the overall building envelope to be exposed beyond. The expression of motion and energy is also carried through in the detailing of the space. Millwork at the reception, pantry, and conference rooms serve as freestanding sculptural objects that are fully integrated in the same formal language.

Full size CNC-milled foam mock-ups were used as a design and construction tool on site to fine tune the highly sculptural design and ensure precise construction of the multiple unique complex curving forms. The foam pieces not only contributed to time and cost savings in construction, but served as a life-sized model for the Architect. The final wall shapes and locations were determined with these mock-ups in the field. The complex faceted and curved millwork elements, such as the resin-coated reception desk and conference room tables, were also produced using the same CNC technology. This technology enabled the execution of the project's highly complex and organic geometry.

left, and right the design vocabulary, inspired by beach culture, employs curved shapes that express the extremes of water in motion

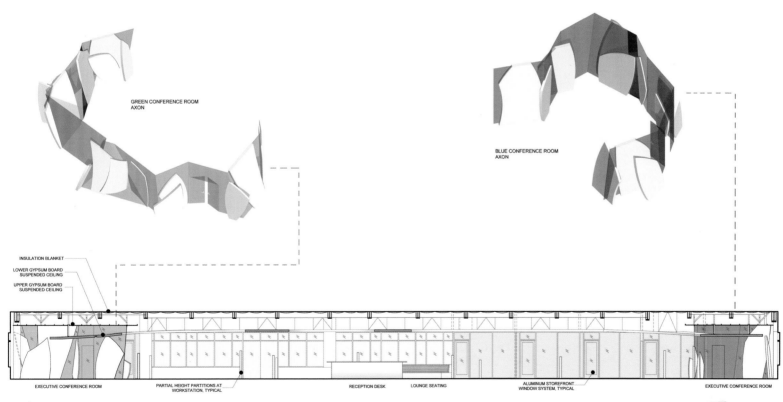

GREEN CONFERENCE ROOM
AXON

BLUE CONFERENCE ROOM
AXON

INSULATION BLANKET

LOWER GYPSUM BOARD
SUSPENDED CEILING

UPPER GYPSUM BOARD
SUSPENDED CEILING

EXECUTIVE CONFERENCE ROOM   PARTIAL HEIGHT PARTITIONS AT   RECEPTION DESK   LOUNGE SEATING   ALUMINUM STOREFRONT   EXECUTIVE CONFERENCE ROOM
WORKSTATION, TYPICAL   WINDOW SYSTEM, TYPICAL

section

DESIGNARC

www.designarc.net

Dion Mc Carthy and Mark Kirkhart

DesignARC is an innovative design firm comprised of progressive, like-minded thinkers who share a genuine desire to research, learn, and to apply newfound knowledge to the project at hand. Specializing in custom residential, commercial, hospitality and institutional design, with thriving studios in both Los Angeles and Santa Barbara, the company culture stresses collaboration among colleagues in the search for creative architectural solutions for its clients.

DesignARC has designed and seen through construction a decidedly diverse portfolio of architectural projects during the past thirty-five years, and has received over thirty design awards for Excellence in Architecture. The honored work includes many restaurant and hospitality projects in New York, San Francisco, Los Angeles and Santa Barbara, as well as numerous multi-family residential projects in Palm Springs, California.

Two projects were designed for the same client – an individual with a deeply humanistic affinity for music and the arts, and whose lifestyle articulates a certain aesthetic vision.

These homes represent the culmination of a long-standing and spirited collaboration between DesignARC and this special client. The result of the deep understanding and mutual creativity engendered by this collaboration has been distinctive homes – one for life in the city, and one for life at the beach – which are perfectly fitted to their respective environments. The homes are intended to complement one another other, and together offer particular and individualized places to realize the varied aspirations of a life fashioned around creative pursuits and artistic appreciation.

Photography by Ciro Coelho

BEL-AIR RESIDENCE

YEAR OF COMPLETION 2009
LOCATION Los Angeles, California
SIZE 7,200 square feet (main house),
1,500 square feet (guest house)
PHOTOGRAPHY Benny Chan (Fotoworks):
01, 02, 04, 05, 06, 08, 09, 10, 12;
Leif Wivelsted: 03, 07, 11

The Bel-Air Residence sits above Hollywood, along scenic Mulholland Drive, the storied thoroughfare that acts as a winding referee between the compact density of the San Fernando Valley, and the more ex-urban conditions of Los Angeles. In contrast to the client's weekend beach house, here the client envisioned a home that could share equally in the energy of the city, and the rustic qualities of canyon living. The resulting home is both minimal and refined—its abstract forms read against the wilder aspects of its nominally natural setting.

As a patron of music, and the arts, the client's creative interests suggested the overall design approach: A simple yet sophisticated backdrop for the presentation of recitals, and the display and appreciation of beautiful artifacts. The house avows a museum-like attitude—the rich, but restrained material palette draws from the colors and textures of the Santa Monica Mountains, and opposes natural with refined, polished with honed, quietly confirming a reverential aspect to this "temple on the hill".

The focus of the house is a dark and silent pool. Intended as a space of emptiness, the pool is an enigmatic statement—at once a source of origin for the house, as well as its apparent conclusion. The spatial aspects unfold from this moment, with the various rooms revolving around this essential void. The pool and its open rotunda echo the reservoir in the canyon below the house, while the ocean beyond ultimately underscores the house's strong commitment to water.

Simple stone walls, taut rooflines, and disciplined and minimal detailing allow the home to act as an armature for the client's personal expression of taste and creativity. In complement to the client's Mussel Shoals House, which suggests a relationship with the vast, and ever-widening horizon, the architectural resolution of the Bel-Air Residence emerges from the sheltered and enveloping emotion of the canyon.

left, and above along a ridge of the Hollywood hills, the site captures views of the Los Angeles basin, as well as the San Fernando Valley

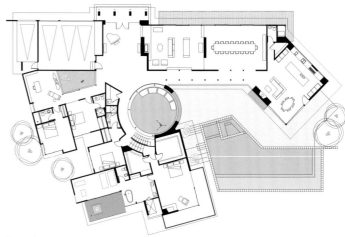

floor plan

left with a museum-like attitude, the material palette of the residence draws from the natural aspects of the site right the center of the house is a quiet pool, created by the intersection of the living and bedroom wings

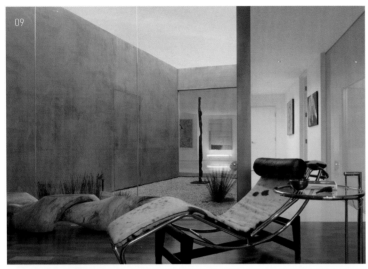

above in contrast to the outward looking attitude of
the other spaces of the house, the den looks onto an
interior court-offering a quiet, contemplative quality
right sculpture and works of art from the client's
collection enrich the various spaces of the house

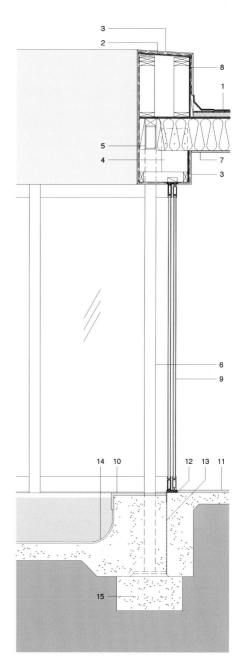

1 built-up roofing
2 membrane flashing over plywood
3 exterior cement plaster
4 wood gusset plate
5 curved tube steel beam
6 4" diameter tube steel column
7 gypsum board
8 curved plywood
9 curved sliding glass door
10 terrazzo coping
11 terrazzo flooring
12 metal sill pan
13 fluid applied waterproofing
14 pool plaster
15 column footing

drum section

MUSSEL SHOALS RESIDENCE

YEAR OF COMPLETION 2006
LOCATION Ventura, California
SIZE 2,800 square feet
PHOTOGRAPHY Benny Chan (Fotoworks)

The Mussel Shoals Residence is located at a critical juncture of the California coastline, between Los Angeles and Santa Barbara, near a legendary surf break. Designed as a weekend retreat from the demanding rigors of city life, the project responds to the significant constraints of a paucity of budget and a requirement to secure the house against storm and absence. The result is a confident and self-effacing home that defers to the repose and tranquility of the sea while providing a place of quiet respite for the client.

The restrained budget and need for security suggested a specific design approach: The creation of a homogeneous exterior, minimal in its aspect and material articulation, which would allow the color and texture of the ocean environment to be made legible and emphasized through the framework of this "shell." The introduction of rolling sunshades and storm doors complete the house's protective layering, fending off the depredations of sun, salt air, and rogue surfers, while allowing variability in living space based on weather conditions.

The arrival sequence begins at the adjacent highway and moves downward to the lower beach, passing through an entry courtyard created by the house's stepped section. This court, rendered as a terraced Zen garden, is designed as a calm but compressed space, which compels movement toward the ocean. The skyward emphasis created by simultaneous downward movement, coupled with the house's transparency in this direction highlights the endless line of the horizon and magnifies the vastness of the sea. The emphatic resolution

of the house's carapace contrasts with the soft textures of the garden, and introduces an asymmetric relationship with the ragged terrain of the rocky beach.

The intermediate level of the entry necessitates further descent to the home's main living area, thus preserving the skyward emphasis of view, while underlining the home's primary relationship with the sea and horizon. The master bedroom, located above the living area, shares in this relationship; one is invited to ponder the tranquility of the sea from this perch above the rocky shore.

A disciplined approach to design, minimal in its attitude, and based on an unsentimental framework, creates a home with a background posture to the site. The architectural resolution emerges from a recognition of the essential nature of the site, through the lens of design.

right the straightforward attitude of the house provides the framework that emphasizes the light and texture of the ocean environment

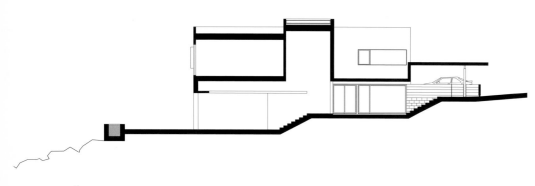

section

left and right the homogeneous quality of the
exterior "shell" wraps the minimalist spaces of
the interior

EHRLICH ARCHITECTS

www.s-ehrlich.com

Steven Ehrlich

Ehrlich Architects is internationally recognized for distinctive design, which extends the traditions of California modernism through an approach that fuses new technologies with cultural and environmental sensitivity. The firm has been recognized with prestigious accolades including eight National American Institute of Architects (AIA) awards, and was chosen the 2003 Firm of the Year by the American Institute of Architects, California Council.

Embracing the convergence of complex global factors that challenge today's architects, the firm has evolved a unique approach to architecture and planning called Multicultural Modernism™ (the title of a 2006 Retrospective Exhibition at the Palm Springs Art Museum and the firm's fifth monograph). Largely developed through the travels and experiences of founding Principal Steven Ehrlich (including a six-year sabbatical in Africa), Multicultural Modernism™ centers around architectural anthropology and incorporates four key elements: sensing place and listening to people; courtyards as an antidote to density and stress; the influence of Los Angeles, an "incubator of change"; and cross-cultural fusion. Multicultural Modernism™ is not a formula but a path towards an architecture that can respond sensibly, flexibly and with great exuberance to our increasingly urbanized, polyglot world, celebrating both global aspirations and local cultural uniqueness.

Ehrlich Architects' design philosophy also demonstrates a strong commitment to and implemen¬tation of sustainable strategies. The firm has successfully employed the LEED Green Building Rating System (including the LEED Gold certified Lantana Corporate Campus and the LEED Silver ASU School of Journalism), and the 700 Palms Residence was the awarded the 2009 Good Green Design Award. Each of the firm's commissions – whether institutional, civic, or residential – is designed with a straightforward approach to form and function that maximizes environmentally friendly materials and building methods.

Recent projects include the 235,000 sf design-build Walter Cronkite School of Journalism and the 285,000 sf School of Earth and Space Exploration, both for Arizona State University; the 75,000 sf Media Arts Building at the University of California, Irvine; the Performing and Media Arts Complex at Los Angeles Valley College; four residential towers in Taipei, Taiwan; the international design competition-winning scheme for the New Abuja City Gate in the capital city of Nigeria; and a house in Dubai.

700 PALMS RESIDENCE

YEAR OF COMPLETION 2005
LOCATION Venice, California
SIZE 3,000 square feet (main house),
1,200 square feet (guest house)
PHOTOGRAPHY Grey Crawford: 01, 02, 04,
08; Erhard Pfeiffer: 03, 05, 06, 09;
Julius Shulman & Juergen Nogai: 07

The objective for this eco-friendly residence in Venice, California was to: design a high-performance home that dissolves the barriers between indoors and outdoors; utilize raw, honest materials appropriate to the bohemian grittiness of the surrounding community; and have the smallest carbon footprint in balance with lifestyle.

Three garden courtyards embrace three 60-year-old trees. The courtyards afford privacy and enhance the well being of its occupants. The overall massing maximizes volume and natural light gains on the narrow lot (43 feet x 132 feet), yet displays sensitivity of scale to the eclectic neighborhood of beach bungalows. Exterior sunshades on an exoskeleton of steel control the heat gain from the Southwestern exposure. Flexible, transformative spaces were created through the use of extensive operable glass doors. The 16-foot high living-dining area opens up on three sides: to the lap pool on the west with sliding glass doors; to the north courtyard with pocketing glass doors; and to the garden and guest house to the south through pivoting glass doors. When open to the elements, the living area is transformed into an airy pavilion.

The house design takes full advantage of the local climate such that a net zero energy building is obtained. This was done by employing a highly efficient building envelope and incorporating passive solar gains. Radiant floors and solar thermal energy are utilized for space heating and domestic hot water heating. The house also relies on natural ventilation, thermal mass and operable shading to eliminate mechanical

cooling, despite the large glazing areas. Finally, by employing ultra-efficient appliances and lighting and by incorporating solar electric power for the remaining loads, the house achieves its goal for a net zero energy home.

The exterior water efficient landscape comprises three key elements. First, plants have been carefully selected to grow naturally in the local climate, adapting well to the site soil and site particular conditions. Moreover, plants are sparsely planted in order to reduce evapotranspiration. Second, water-efficient irrigation controls, including moisture sensors and timers, have been installed. Third, there is less than 10% of water impervious surfaces. The remaining soil surfaces are covered with gravel that reduces evapotranspiration and allows rain water falling directly, as well as rain water drained from the building roof, to percolate into the landscape. Thus, irrigation water is reduced to a minimum during the three- or four-month period of rain-fall at the project site, while the controls ensure that minimal potable water is used during that same period. It has been calculated that irrigation water is reduced by at least 34% from a baseline design, typical of the site neighborhood that utilizes turfgrass with traditional irrigation controls.

The chosen coating and maintenance-free exterior finish materials, including Cor-ten steel and TREX (a sustainable material made of recycled plastic bags and sawdust), weather naturally, while all interior surfaces rely on varying tactile materials such as carnauba-waxed carbon steel and plaster which are left unpainted.

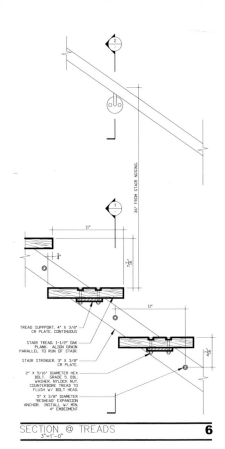

TREAD SUPPPORT. 4" X 3/8"
CR PLATE. CONTINUOUS

STAIR TREAD. 1-1/2" OAK
PLANK. ALIGN GRAIN
PARALLEL TO RUN OF STAIR.

STAIR STRINGER. 3" X 3/8"
CR PLATE.

2" X 5/16" DIAMETER HEX
BOLT. GRADE 5. DBL.
WASHER. NYLOCK NUT.
COUNTERBORE TREAD TO
FLUSH W/ BOLT HEAD.

5" X 3/8" DIAMETER
'REDHEAD' EXPANSION
ANCHOR. INSTALL W/ MIN.
4" EMBEDMENT

SECTION @ TREADS   6
3"=1'-0"

STAIR TREAD. 1-1/2" OAK
PLANK. ALIGN GRAIN
PARALLEL TO RUN OF STAIR.

STAIR STRINGER. 3" X 3/8"
CR PLATE.

RONSTAN 3/8" ADJUSTABLE
FORK FITTING. STAINLESS
STEEL. PART NO. RF158-06

1-½" X 1-½" X ½"
CR PLATE

3/4" LAMINATED GLASS OR
3/4" BIRCH PLYWOOD
GUARDRAIL. CONTINUOUS.

ELEVATION @ STRINGER   8
3"=1'-0"

09

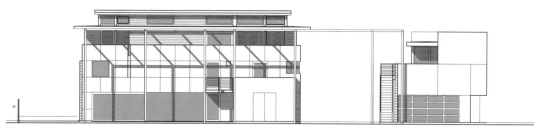

south elevation

left, and above the existing vegetation was
retained and is celebrated by the dramatic
placement of wall openings, many of which
can be completely opened

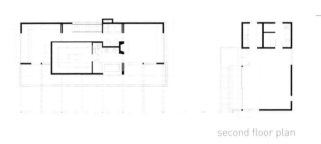

second floor plan

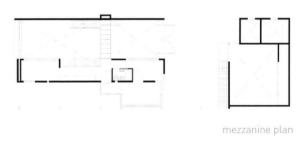

mezzanine plan

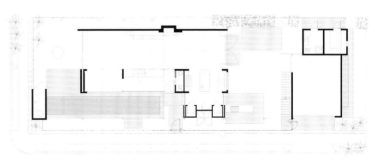

first floor plan

ZEIDLER RESIDENCE

YEAR OF COMPLETION 2008
LOCATION Aptos, California
SIZE 4,500 square feet
PHOTOGRAPHY Matthew Millman

Designed for a retired couple with grown children, the 4,500 square-foot house sits on a relatively flat corner lot at the top of a bluff overlooking the the Pacific Ocean. Interior and exterior living and entertainment spaces are arranged to maximize views, natural light, and ocean breezes within a subtle, sophisticated material palette.

The parti divides the program into two main structures on either side of a sheltered courtyard. On the ocean side, the two-and-a-half-story, one-bedroom main house accommodates the primary living spaces. A double-height living space provides generous art walls and features a burnished block fireplace and tall glass sliding doors that open the interior to the exterior spaces. A study is located at the mezzanine level and is oriented towards the view. The master wing has an efficient layout that terminates at a balcony oriented towards the panoramic view. The kitchen and dining room are separated from the living room by an oversized sliding glass partition. A full-sized roof deck has a built-in barbecue and fireplace and allows for various entertaining configurations to take advantage of the stunning sunset and white water views. A wine-tasting room and utility rooms occupy the full basement. All the levels are tied together by a compact but dramatic stainless steel and walnut staircase which incorporates display shelves for the owners' various collections.

The rear guest structure accommodates the garage and three separate living quarters for friends and family. The larger second level studio has a full kitchen and expansive deck with views towards the ocean. Together the main house and guest house enclose a landscaped courtyard with lap pool and built-in barbecue. A trellis with overhead panels encloses a walkway from the main house to the guest house. When the structures are open to the elements they form a complex of open air pavilions connected through the landscape. The front yard even incorporates a petanque court, a favorite pastime of the client.

The entire composition is tied together by a rich and elegant material palette that includes steel-troweled stucco, exposed concrete block, stainless steel railings, walnut millwork, cast glass partitions and Rheinzink.

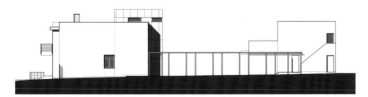

southeast elevation

northwest elevation

left a scheme of contrasts was deployed for the residences' orientation: closed walls toward the street, and generous openings facing the sea

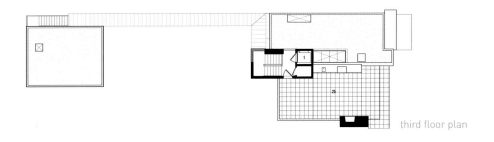

third floor plan

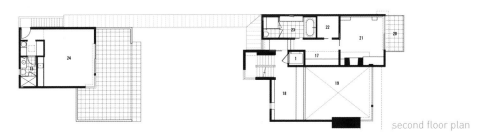

second floor plan

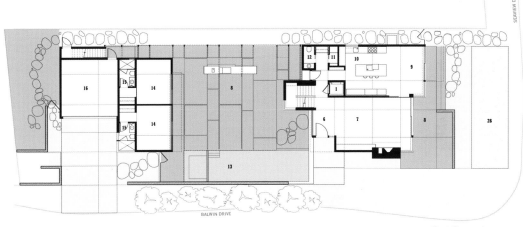

first floor plan

1 elevator
2 storage
3 wine room
4 laundry
5 mech
6 entry
7 family room
8 outdoor patio
9 dining room
10 kitchen
11 pantry
12 powder room
13 pool

14 guest room
15 bath
16 garage
17 dressing
18 mezzanine
19 open to below
20 balcony
21 master bedroom
22 closet
23 master bath
24 studio
25 roof deck
26 petanque court

basement plan

ASU WALTER CRONKITE SCHOOL OF JOURNALISM & MASS COMMUNICATION

YEAR OF COMPLETION 2008
LOCATION Phoenix, Arizona
SIZE 225,000 square feet
PHOTOGRAPHY Bill Timmerman

Located in downtown Phoenix, the new six-story, 225,000 square feet., 110-foot tall building has become an integral part of the fabric of ASU's energizing downtown campus and a harbinger of Phoenix's redevelopment.

Delivered in a design-build, fast-track method, work began on design in October 2006 and the school opened its doors in August 2008, 22 months later. School schedules and budgets were both met.

Ground floor retail spaces and ample shaded arcades foster outdoor seating and café life. The main entrance to the structure is under a three-story high "front porch" facing the civic space, and includes a large, scrolling, electronic news ticker highlighting the most current headlines. Immediately adjacent to one of the stops on the newly completed Phoenix Light Rail and numerous

bus stops, the Cronkite School allows students, teachers and professionals to arrive by public transportation. ·Parking capacity on the campus has been deliberately limited to encourage this. The building's main entry fronts onto 'Taylor Mall' – an urban green belt that runs the full length of the downtown campus. This fosters community connectivity that places student housing, the new downtown Phoenix Civic Space, Student Union and Arizona Center Mall all within easy walking distance. In addition, many of the School of Journalism's functions on upper levels, including the Cronkite News Service, are oriented toward and have open terraces overlooking Central Avenue, allowing the students and faculty to consistently be part of the bustle of downtown.

As truth and honesty are guiding principles to journalism – so are they to the design of the

above the ambitious project was completed in just 22 months from design to construction completion

building. The architecture is specifically expressive of function and materiality. The design is based on an economical 30-foot square exposed structural concrete column grid with post-tensioned concrete floor slabs. The exterior is clad with glass, masonry and multi-colored metal panels - the pattern of the panels is inspired by U.S. broadcast frequency spectrum allocations (the Radio Spectrum). The composition is kinetic and dynamic – symbolic of journalism and media's role in our society. The building's massing incorporates appropriate sun screens on each of the four facades; their specific architectural treatment reduces the heat loads and is one of many of the LEED Silver building's sustainable strategies. Burnished concrete block walls, ground and polished concrete floors and warm wood ceilings further express the forthright and direct nature of news delivery.

The Architect explains "We have brought a burst of color and life to an emerging district in downtown Phoenix. The building activates the street and instigates collaboration. The activity and energy inside the building is broadcast to the community and beyond."

The Cronkite School occupies all of the second and third floors and a portion of the fourth and sixth floors. The airy, multi-tiered First Amendment Forum is the heart of the school. By day, students gather spontaneously between classes, and in the evenings, the grand hall transforms into a public forum where students and industry leaders discuss the most critical issues facing today's news media. The First Amendment to the U.S. Constitution is a theme repeated throughout the building. Floor-to-ceiling versions of the Amendment are found in the lobbies of each floor, and quotes about

the importance of the Amendment to journalism encircle and embrace the central forum.

Half of the sixth floor has been custom tailored for the Cronkite News Watch. Both the newsroom and broadcast anchor desks are contained within one massive production space with views overlooking the city and beyond. Flanked by state-of-the-art control rooms and edit bays, Cronkite News Watch is in constant communication with itself and the community it serves. KAET Channel 8 Public TV also transmits live from their state-of-the-art studios on the sixth floor. This top floor location allows for long spans and high ceilings, required for the studios, and is constructed of a prefabricated lightweight steel structure. Satellite dishes from transmission are housed on the roof; they are specifically not screened and directly express the building's function as one of communication.

FREDERICK FISHER AND PARTNERS ARCHITECTS

www.fisherpartners.net

Frederick Fisher, David Ross and Joseph Coriaty

Frederick Fisher and Partners (FFP) is a leading architecture and planning firm serving a full spectrum of cultural, institutional, commercial and residential clients throughout the United States, Europe and Asia. Founded in 1980 by principal, Frederick Fisher, the award-winning firm began as a custom design practice, specializing in the arts and residential marketplace in Los Angeles. The long-term association of partners David Ross and Joseph Coriaty adds experience in larger building types and project management. Reflecting Fisher's interpretation of space, light and material, these projects became models for an architectural aesthetic that has won the firm international recognition for innovative and refined style.

Today, FFP provides a full range of architectural services – from programming, master planning, and design concept through construction documentation, entitlements and construction administration – to clients in the arts, education, residential and commercial sectors. With a full-time staff of 18 architects, designers and administrative personnel, the firm's signature is evidenced in more than 100 built projects across the nation and in France, Germany and Japan. The firm's extensive portfolio includes major commissions for museums and galleries, educational facilities, libraries, urban planning, community spaces, mixed-use developments, restaurants, live-work environments, as well as multi-family housing.

FFP is a firm dedicated to the betterment of the built environment through "green" architecture. As members of the U.S. Green Building Council with LEED Accredited design staff in house, FFP makes an effort to employ sustainable design methods and materials when possible in its architecture. Current green projects include the Sherrerd Hall for Princeton University, the Annenberg Center for Information Science and Technology at Caltech, the Annenberg Community Beach House at Santa Monica State Beach, and the Annenberg Center at Sunnylands.

Mr. Fisher's commitment to architecture is not limited to the production of physical work, as he remains invested in the philosophical and educational evolution of the profession. Such interests have encouraged him to stay involved with art & architectural education, acting as a professor for many universities around the United States, an artist collaborator and a lecturer at events around the world. This includes a seven year term as Environmental Design Department Chair at Otis College of Art and Design and current seat on The Board of Governors.

SANTA YNEZ RESIDENCE

YEAR OF COMPLETION 2006
LOCATION Santa Ynez, California
SIZE 7,000 square feet
PHOTOGRAPHY Benny Chan (Fotoworks)

A 20 acre site in the Santa Ynez Valley of California dominates the landscape with extensive views of the surrounding mountains and valleys. The natural environment has two distinct seasons consisting of hot summers and cold winters. A south easterly wind is common in the morning hours.

The owners, an artist and lawyer, requested a home that created a compound. The spaces to be included were an open living area, master bedroom suite, two guest bedrooms with a living space, an office, artist studio and lap pool. The 7000 square foot single–family residence is based on a grid of 25 squares. The firm's interest in the "square" and "box" along with the owner's square paintings generated the initial concepts for the home.

The 100 foot by 100 foot single-family residence is organized around a central courtyard that divides the building into three distinct "zones" with an area for living, sleeping and working. To take advantage of the warm climate during the summer months, three outdoor rooms extend the living space. This blurring of inside and outside is achieved with the use of large sliding glass panels. The interior courtyard protects the residents from harsh wind and sun while providing an alternative view of landscape, which is contemplative, serene and quiet. This contained exterior world is juxtaposed to the outer landscape of natural grasses, shrubs and trees. The residence clad entirely in corrugated Cor-ten steel has taken on a rich brown color as it oxidizes, complementing its earthy surroundings. Perforated Cor-ten steel is used for sun shading glass and covered areas adding a play of light across the homes surfaces. Large sliding and swinging steel gates enclose the home at night and while the owners travel.

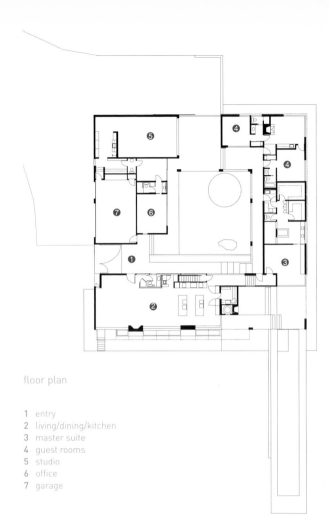

floor plan

1 entry
2 living/dining/kitchen
3 master suite
4 guest rooms
5 studio
6 office
7 garage

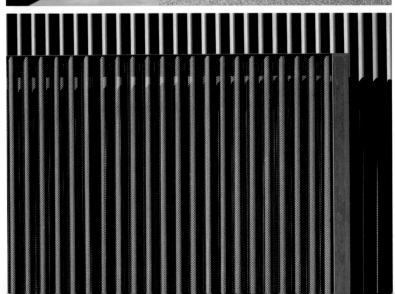

left, and above corrugated metal sheeting was used to sheath the entire structure. perforated sheets create a veil-like, translucent quality that gives the residence both an ephemeral, yet earth-bound feel

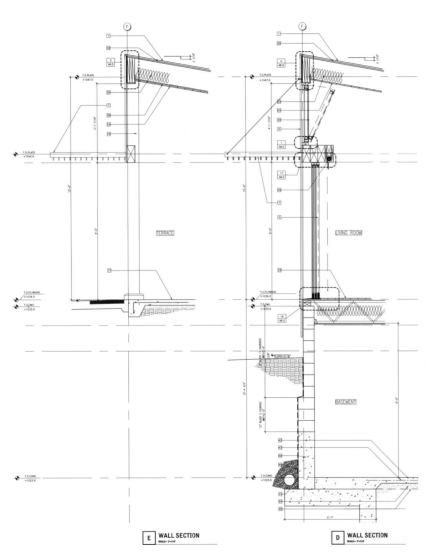

E | **WALL SECTION**
SCALE= 1"=1'-0"

D | **WALL SECTION**
SCALE= 1"=1'-0"

right deep wall niches allow for six sliding
panels to completely recess and achieve
a dramatic immersion of interiors and
exteriors

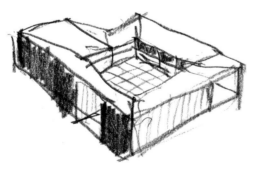

right the carefully modeled forms echo the rolling topography of the surrounding Californian hills

OCEANSIDE MUSEUM OF ART

YEAR OF COMPLETION 2008
LOCATION Oceanside, California
SIZE 16,000 square feet (addition);
26,000 square feet (total)
PHOTOGRAPHY Benny Chan (Fotoworks)

The Central Pavilion at the Oceanside Museum of Art was a design competition for a 16,000 square foot expansion. The new gallery wing is framed by the 5,000 square foot City Hall (originally designed by renowned architect Irving Gill in 1934), which currently houses the Museum, and the Fire Station (Gill, 1929), which will be renovated into an auditorium, administrative offices and School of Art in the future.

The program required the addition to accommodate expanded exhibition and education programs while maintaining existing exhibition galleries. The Central Pavilion was conceived of as a delicate insertion, deferential to the historic context of the site and city fabric, including an immediately adjacent Gill designed Fire Station. Following precedent set by the larger civic campus, a collection of buildings linked by outdoor plazas, the Central Pavilion is placed between existing buildings and set back from the street, respecting the formal integrity of the existing context and creating an outdoor plaza for sculpture and museum events. With an emphasis on proportion, simplicity and clarity of purpose, the new building's design response exemplifies the understated resonance of the Irving Gill buildings, qualities essential to the work of Frederick Fisher and Partners.

This project was awarded an Orchid Award in Architecture from the San Diego Architectural Foundation in 2008, with the jury calling the project "slick" and "cool," identifying the Central Pavilion as "one of the most sophisticated buildings in North County."

left, and right nestled netween two historic Irving Gill structures, the museum's forms speak of proportion, simplicity, and clarity of purpose

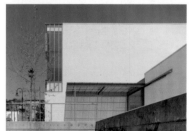

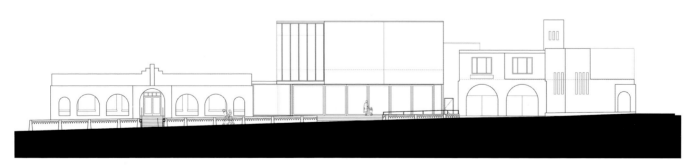

side elevation

left, and right the ground floor space for temporary exhibitions flows off the main stair as it wraps around the reception desk to access the main exhibition space on the upper level

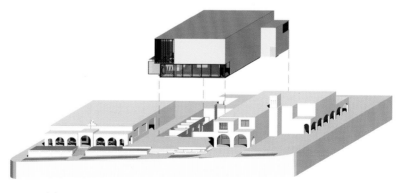

axonometric

THE ANNENBERG COMMUNITY BEACH HOUSE
AT SANTA MONICA STATE BEACH

YEAR OF COMPLETION 2009
LOCATION Santa Monica, California
SIZE 27,000 square feet (buildings),
5 acre (site)
PHOTOGRAPHY Grant Mudford
Photography

The Annenberg Community Beach House at Santa Monica State Beach is a multi-use public beach recreation facility. It occupies the site of the historic Marion Davies Beach House commissioned by William Randolph Hearst in 1927 and designed by William Flannery. The Davies/ Hearst five acre estate on Pacific Coast Highway included a one hundred room main house, a guest house, gardens, tennis courts and a pool. Only the Julia Morgan designed guest house and pool, both landmarks, remain and are restored.

The project is conceived as a series of indoor/ outdoor recreation and event spaces, both formal and informal, woven through the site. The new buildings and landscape elements of the project are designed to create a public gateway to the beach, an icon for the site's history and a framework for many kinds of community uses, returning the site to its former status as a landmark for the City and southern California.

The new public beach facility includes a pool house on the site of the original mansion to serve the historic pool area with changing rooms and a community room. A colonnade of white concrete columns recalls the location and scale of the mansion. An event room and terrace overlook the pool and provides views along the coast. The existing Guest House is renovated to support public meetings and the new Event House accommodates larger public and private events. A garden includes a sculptural installation by Roy McMakin, a fountain and palm trees. Amenities along the new boardwalk include a children's play area, a restaurant, gardens, a concession building, and beach volleyball courts.

The design process involved extensive community input and it is targeted for a LEED Gold rating. The project is a partnership between the Annenberg Foundation and the City of Santa Monica, which operates the facility.

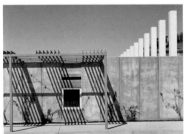

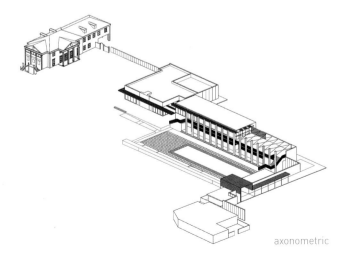

axonometric

left, and above the thin white columns of the colonade allude to the former Marion Davies Beach House that once stood here

THE WALTER AND LEONORE ANNENBERG CENTER
FOR INFORMATION SCIENCE AND TECHNOLOGY

YEAR OF COMPLETION 2009
LOCATION Caltech campus, Moore Walk, Pasadena, California
SIZE 46,000 square feet
PHOTOGRAPHY Benny Chan (Fotoworks)

The 46,000 square foot facility serves as home to participants of the IST Initiative, a program of interdisciplinary research that addresses the growth and impact of information science as it relates to all science and engineering practices. This is the first research and teaching activity in the country that investigates information from all angles: from the fundamental theoretical underpinnings of information to the science and engineering of novel information substrates, biological circuits and complex social systems. Participants in the IST Initiative migrate from all parts of the campus, representing all Colleges of Science and Engineering at Caltech. The aim of the facility is to foster collaboration, research and teaching intrinsic to this new academic discipline.

Caltech is a legacy campus with early 20th Century Mediterranean style buildings by Bertram Goodhue and Gordon Kaufman. The campus has a rich landscape which changes from formal arrangements of olive trees on one side to a more natural landscape of sycamores and eucalyptus around the Center's site. The Annenberg Center is sited at one end of a major campus pedestrian walkway. The campus Master Plan and the nature of the IST initiative called for a contemporary building. We developed a simple glass structure that met the surrounding frontages and height limit. A variety of green and clear glass blends with and reflects the surrounding landscape. Entrances are placed to engage both formal and informal campus circulation. Grand external stairways recall the Mediterranean prototypes on campus while providing for casual encounters and engaging the campus and building users.

The building was planned as an immediately accessible plaza of group teaching, learning and working spaces on the ground level supporting a two story research center. Glass walls make the ground level an active, connected environment. The upper two levels contain faculty and graduate student offices and studios, designed for the project teamwork which is at the core of Caltech's educational and research activities. These flexible studios open onto a two story light well that acts as a "town square", furnished for casual gathering, events and study. The upper levels are also interconnected by a two story "resident lounge" that functions as an updated faculty club with dramatic views of the San Gabriel Mountains and the campus walkway.

Sustainable building practices are a core requirement for the University. FFP integrated green materials and fixtures such as those made from certified wood & recycled content, low VOC paints and carpet, waterless urinals, and a white roof system. Stormwater controls were also incorporated into the site through the use of a bioswale and infiltration pit. A great focus was placed on the individual comfort of the professors that will have offices in the IST Center. To accommodate this in a sustainable fashion, FFP incorporated a chilled beam system in these work spaces, which is a localized radiant cooling and ventilation system with individual control that is cost and energy efficient. In addition, operable windows have been included to maximize thermal comfort and personal control. The project is on target to achieve a LEED Gold Rating.

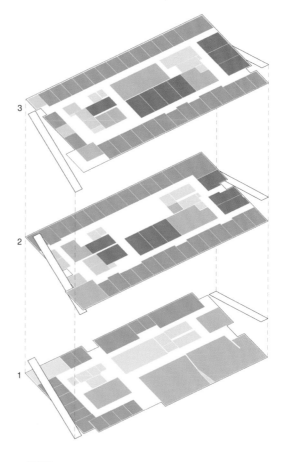

building support

public space

offices

studios

administration

top and bottom the design creates an accessible plaza for group teaching, learning, and working spaces on the ground floor that support a two story research center

THE CONTEMPORARY MUSEUM OF HONOLULU

YEAR OF COMPLETION 2009 (design)
LOCATION Honolulu, Hawaii
SIZE 16,000 square feet

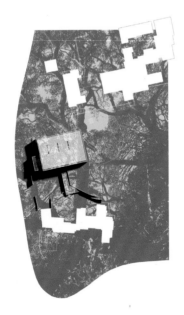

site plan

As the only institution in Hawaii dedicated to the exhibition of contemporary art, they requested a building that expressed their distinctive mission, to heighten awareness of contemporary art throughout the island region. To accommodate expanded exhibition and education programs they have a strong desire for a timeless pavilion, deferential but iconic, reflecting the dynamism and provocative nature of its contents and acting as a new symbol for the forward-looking institution.

Formerly the Spalding estate, the existing museum complex consists of two historic houses, designed by renowned Hawaiian Modernist, Vladimir Ossipoff, sited within James Hubbard-designed gardens. The bucolic, gently sloping site with its mature plantings and revered monkey pod trees is located in the Makiki Heights neighborhood of Honolulu. The site offers two distinct experiences, the first, a sheltered, residential-scaled, tropical refuge with meandering paths, meditation gardens and outdoor sculpture, the second, an expansive panorama, with landmark views of downtown Honolulu, Waikiki and Diamond Head.

To minimize any physical impact on the site and adjacent residential neighborhood, the new 16,000 gross square foot gallery building was sited within the outline of an existing tennis court, limited to a maximum height of 35' and conforms to a Conditional Use Permit.

Conceived as a looking glass that would echo views of the tree canopies and gardens, the building is cloaked in a prismatic layer of glass. The language of fabric; drape, cloak fold, and language of gems; cut, facet, fracture, explores reflectivity and refraction, moving the experience of surface beyond the reflection into the participatory realm of interaction (walking by, seeing in, seeing through, not seeing at all). Frit glass placed on fractured geometric planes manipulates perceived levels of transparency and reflectivity, producing a subtle and reserved presence that uniquely honors the pristine landscape.

An approach along a lush landscape path, through an entry vestibule, a contemporary reading of the traditional lanai, to a translucent lobby, initiates a sequence of spatial transitions through the galleries. Glimpses through art-filled exhibition spaces are punctuated by moments of landscape. Views of the site, captured and framed by the space of the gallery, complement the collection, creating a dialog between the container and the contained, between nature and art.

skin studies

Photography by Benny Chan

GRIFFIN ENRIGHT ARCHITECTS

www.griffinenrightarchitects.com

Margaret Griffin and John Enright

Griffin Enright Architects, established in 2000 by Margaret Griffin, AIA and John Enright, AIA, fuses interests in innovation and experimentation with a desire to explore cultural complexities relative to the built environment. Their versatile practice includes projects ranging from large-scale commercial and residential commissions to furniture design and gallery installations. Their work moves beyond the traditional scope of architectural practice, underscoring connections with the surrounding urban fabric and landscape by reinforcing existing conditions or creating new ones that allow architecture, urban context and landscape to be experienced in new ways. Griffin Enright's comprehensive approach to design depends on the simultaneous blurring and exploitation of distinctions between inside/outside, built form/landscape, site/urban context and theory/practice. The firm is the recipient of over thirty awards for design excellence including the 2006 American Architecture Award from the Chicago Athenaeum. The firm's work has also been published and exhibited extensively in national and international publications and exhibitions and their project 'Paradox Box' is part of the permanent collection at the MAK (Museum for Applied Art / Contemporary Art) in Vienna, Austria. In addition to guiding an emergent practice, Margaret and John are educators in design and technology at SCI_Arc and USC respectively.

KEEP OFF THE GRASS SCI-ARC EXHIBITION

YEAR OF COMPLETION 2004
LOCATION Temporary Installation at SCI-Arc, Los Angeles, California
SIZE 1,200 square feet
PHOTOGRAPHY Joshua White

Our firm was invited to participate in the Southern California Institute of Architecture's (SCI-Arc) gallery program to showcase our work. This temporary installation in the double-height gallery space is a critique on the environmental impact of Southern Californians' devotion to their perfectly manicured lawns. Our challenge was to expose the hidden environmental and societal costs of using this seemingly inexpensive, hybrid material - at once organic and manufactured - within the constraints imposed by an extremely lean budget of only $6,000.

Over 1,000 square feet of hydroponic grass, chosen for its thinness, was treated as a surface and formed into an undulating, hovering carpet suspended over the floor of the gallery, nearly filling the space. To underscore the plane as a floating piece, the entire structure was hung from steel cables attached to the gallery ceiling, leaving the ground beneath it free. Two parallel 12"-deep plywood beams provided the primary support for seventy 1" steel pipes placed a foot apart. The attachment of the pipes to the plywood beams was purposely separated so the plywood appeared to be floating slightly beneath the underside of the sod. At one point the sod was omitted and the structure of one beam exposed, allowing an unobstructed view of the support system.

Sobering statistics on the walls critiqued the pervasive use of grass in a desert environment. A long, horizontal strip of light was placed against the wall 3 1/2 feet above the floor, as a visual record of the volume of water needed to main the sod for one year. Pools of water placed beneath the grass, but beyond its reach, reflected

light aimed at perforations in the sod. The scale and placement of the sod in the room made it impossible to see the piece in its entirety except from a second story balcony. This promoted movement around the piece to see over and under it and also drew viewers upstairs. The undulating plane lowered at the entrance inviting the viewer into the space and as the undulations moved toward the back of the gallery a larger volume was defined by the underside of the roots and supporting structure.

The choice of sod refers to the original use of the site as an orchard and acknowledges the evolution of the property that SCI-Arc occupies today. The area developed over time, from an agrarian condition to an historic freight depot, (subsequently abandoned), to its current incarnation as an architectural school in an industrial part of downtown Los Angeles. Similarly, we designed the exhibit to transform over the course of the eight weeks. By deliberately not watering the grass, we triggered the entropic process, causing it to slowly decay, dry and shrink. The scent that resulted could be detected throughout the building, extending well beyond the gallery space. As the material diminished, the porosity increased, altering the quality of light coming through the perorations. The deterioration underscored our precarious relationship to landscape while reminding us of the disproportionate need even a small amount of sod has for water.

left, and right this exhibition, installed at SCI-ARC, focused on rethinking the impact of Southern Californian's devotion to manicured lawns .

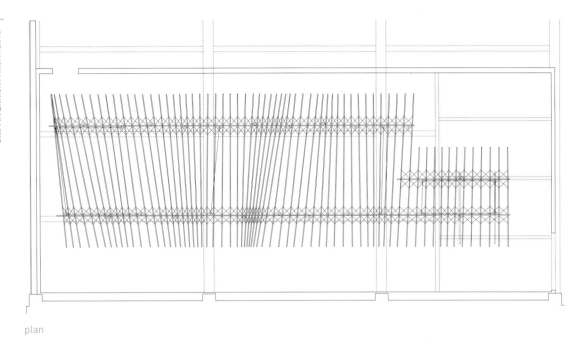

plan

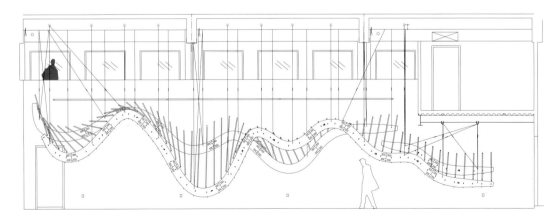

section

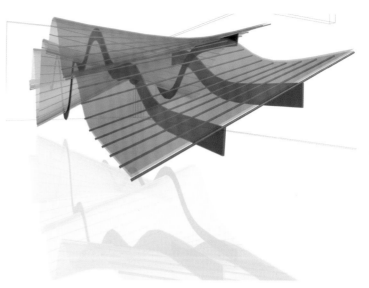

installation graphic

far left construction details of the
ondulating wave left the thought-
provoking installation was realized on a
limited budget

[WIDE]BAND – NOMADIC CAFÉ

YEAR OF COMPLETION 2006
LOCATION A+D Architecture and Design
Museum, Los Angeles
SIZE 850 square feet
PHOTOGRAPHY Benny Chan (Fotoworks)

[WIDE]BAND is a 750-square foot, portable project with the flexibility to accommodate a multiplicity of functions (more or less the architectural equivalent of a hermit crab shell). Originally designed as an installation for *NeoCon West*, it was subsequently moved to the A + D Museum in Los Angeles where it functioned as a café by day and as a bar/lounge space at night without altering the configuration. During an event held by the A + D Museum for the AIA National Conference, it was used as a venue for book signings.

The commission resulted from a competition sponsored by *Interior Design* magazine and *NeoCon West* to showcase an unusual mix of products by using unique approaches. Taking the brief one step further, we created a functional group gathering space for conference attendees to check email, sit and talk, or get a momentary respite. The name, [WIDE]BAND, alludes to the physical loop formed by the surfaces and to the broadband technology supporting the wireless Internet access provided.

The primary material, orange, 3/4" polycarbonate core panels *(Pep)* manufactured by 3Form, was chosen for its structural capacity to span large spaces and for its translucency, allowing the structure to be exceptionally thin and light. The panels are supported only by a skeleton of 1½" steel; in some places extending beyond the frame. Walls, floor, and ceiling are shaped by wrapping the panels in a continuous loop, culminating in the long table that then loops back, becoming an obstacle in the center of the room directing movement around and through the semi-transparent landscape. Physically, the table bisects the space, while at the same time it becomes a nexus for engagement, promoting the interaction of users with each other as they negotiate the space.

In addition to the polycarbonate core panels, we used a 3/4" eco-resin *(Ting Ting)* and ceramic tiles with a 1/2" offset, circular, raised projection in each. The mustard-colored tiles were placed randomly on the floor to generate a three-dimensional landscape, highlighting a visual connection to the circular structure of the Pep panels. At the front, three slumped-glass panels suspended on tension wire provide a distorted interior view. Nine-foot tall graphics on the wall spelling out [WIDE]BAND in skewed italics are revealed by painting the negative, interstitial spaces a light gray. The graphics form a visual backdrop to the looped landscape and are rendered visible only by their interaction with the loop.

The surface, lit from varying distances, glows in colors ranging from yellow to orange to red and ruby. Even in daylight, the translucent material yields different shades of orange. As the color travels along the loop, it creates an exaggerated, ambiguous sense of depth. The juxtaposition and integration of lighting, super-graphics and tiles with the panels animates the space with a sense of constant motion, energy and vitality. Shifting, uneven floor planes and changing table heights intensify this feeling.

top and bottom folded planes rise from the horizontal to vertical plane to create a sense of continuous space

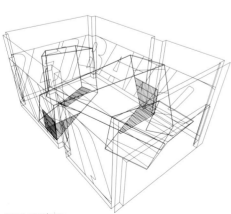
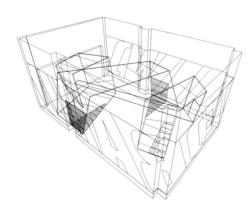
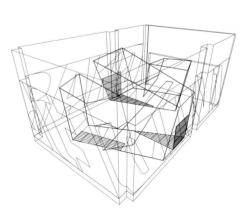

axonometrics

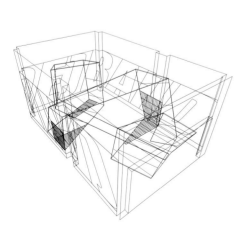

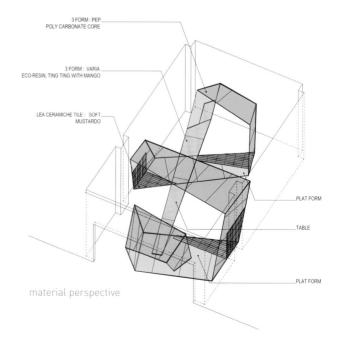

3 FORM : PEP
POLY CARBONATE CORE

3 FORM : VARIA
ECO-RESIN, TING TING WITH MANGO

LEA CERAMICHE TILE : SOFT
MUSTARDO

PLAT FORM

TABLE

PLAT FORM

material perspective

POINT DUME RESIDENCE

YEAR OF COMPLETION 2008
LOCATION Point Dume, Malibu
SIZE 6,000 squre feet
PHOTOGRAPHY Benny Chan (Fotoworks)

This house takes the typical paths of domestic movement and manipulates them to weave the exterior landscape and site into the house while enhancing natural airflows and views. An interest in the continuity of landscape, circulation, and the body's sequential movement through space has lead to an exploration of continuous spatial relationships in this residence. Smooth, sinuous surfaces delineate zones of space while maximizing the site's topography, views, and circulation.   Volumes are differentiated through a slicing of surfaces and materials, emphasizing the horizontal while allowing a multiplicity of spatial conditions to develop through the interaction of these forms, surfaces and volumes. These spatial intersections accumulate the more static elements of the house, while breaking down edges between inside and outside, allowing a more open and engaging relationship between the land and internal logics of the house.

The 60,000 square feet property and 6,350 square feet house is on the top of Point Dume in Malibu and is accessed from below by a driveway, an existing retaining wall bisects the site and moves along the geometry of an existing knoll. Panoramic views of the ocean are availed by the geometric morphologies of the residence. These major views delineated the shifts in geometry apparent in the angled "S" shape of the plan and created the sinuous sequence from the entry to the landscape and view that echoes the shoreline below creating a vacillation among differing distant views. Movement in the house bends from the entry to the living area and bends again towards the pool.

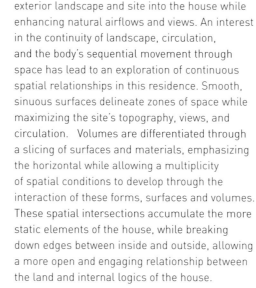

Entry occurs through a gap between the garage and guest bedroom volumes of the house. One descends into a narrow vertical hall below two curved clearstory windows that twists sinuously towards an emerging panoramic view of the ocean that is framed by the open horizontal living space. This fluid hallway becomes the nexus of the residence where sinuous movement among the public and private areas of the home is aggregated and intertwined by distinctive navigations of the curved hallway space. This main path of the house extends through the living area under an eco resin custom fabricated light box and extends to an out door terrace that curves around to the lap pool and a different view towards the Santa Monica coastline beyond.

The open living area has eleven-foot ceilings where kitchen, dining and living areas have a loft like feel. The living area literally extends to the exterior with two large sliding doors that afford eleven foot by twenty-two foot wide clear opening to the outside. An over scaled system of horizontal louvers extends along this edge of the residence to; control light, incorporate library shelving and become the railing system for the master bedroom terrace above. The second floor is peeled away from the louvered plane to simultaneously reorient to distant ocean views and create a private master bedroom terrace. At the far end of the master bedroom terrace a large a curved catwalk twists around an oculus like aperture allowing views to the out door terrace and pool below.

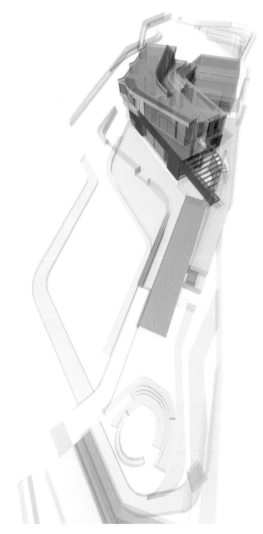

final linear diagram

far left entrance occurs from the north whereas the southern-facing elevation celebrates the view of the sea left the palette of materials selected for the interior employ dark floor surfaces that contrast with white wall and ceiling surfaces

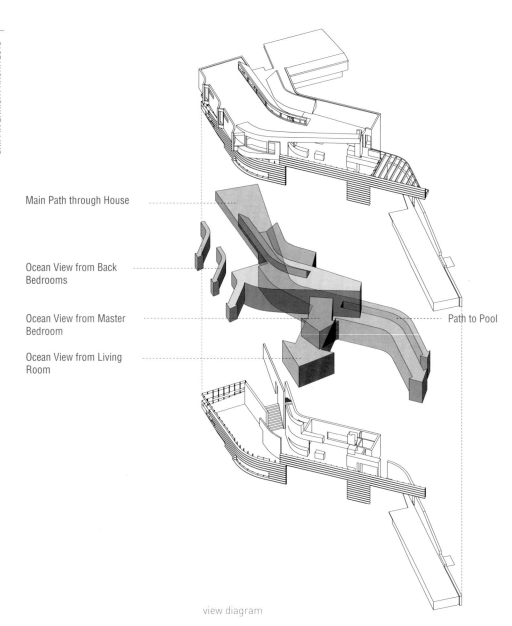

Main Path through House

Ocean View from Back
Bedrooms

Ocean View from Master
Bedroom

Path to Pool

Ocean View from Living
Room

view diagram

right a lighting installation of eco-resin
panels originates in the entrance hall, and
continues throughout the open living-
dining space

SCHINDLER'S PARADOX BOX

YEAR OF COMPLETION 2006 (design)
LOCATION West Hollywood, California
SIZE 29,500 square feet (total), 15,000
square feet (outdoor performance area),
2,000 square feet (gallery), 5,000 square
feet (public park), 7,500 square feet
(rooftop garden)

Proposal for MAK Center for Art &
Architecture, L.A., Winner of Vertical
Garden Competition, Model & Drawings
purchased by MAK Vienna for Permanent
Collection.

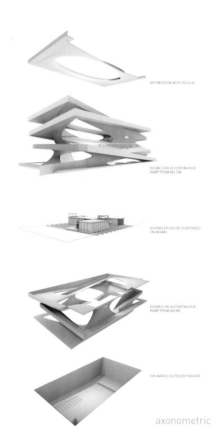

SKY MEADOW WITH OCULUS

DOUBLE-HELIX CONTINUOUS
RAMP FROM BELOW

SCHINDLER HOUSE SUSPENDED
ON BEAMS

DOUBLE-HELIX CONTINUOUS
RAMP FROM ABOVE

EXCAVATED OUTDOOR THEATER

axonometric

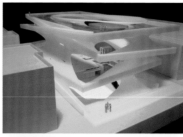

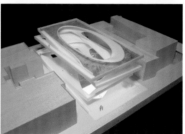

This project is a winning proposal for the Vertical
Garden Competition to re-envision the Schindler
house and its present-day context, sponsored by
the MAK center in LA and SCI_Arc. The Schindler
house no longer functions as originally intended,
but rather as a minor exhibition space/museum,
while the area surrounding the house reflects
development patterns that have evolved in Los
Angeles over the past eighty-four years. Once an
oasis in a sparsely developed suburb, the house
has become an island amid a sea of multi-family
residential buildings, boxed in from the three
primary property lines. In its present state, it
is an artifact of another time, of another Los
Angeles - outmoded, out-scaled, and outcast.

An innovative solution allows the house to be
kept intact as an artefact was explored, while
preserving the surrounding space for the public.
In order to develop a new notion of public access
to this unique place, the project begins by
excavating 45 feet below present grade to create
a new subterranean amphitheater, with the
house floating within the volume created beneath
a new rooftop garden. Precariously balanced and
liberated from the ground in much the same way
that it has been liberated and isolated from the
surrounding urban fabric over time, the Schindler
house would simultaneously be highlighted as
an artifact and re-constituted as a new public
amenity.

Double-helix ramps descend from grade to a
new open-air auditorium and ascend to a new
roof garden 45 feet above the house creating
a continuous, open, public circulation loop
surrounding the house, offering new views from
below, above, and the perimeter. The helices
are connected at grade on the north side of the

house, and reconnect at the roof garden and
the subterranean auditorium. The entwined
ramps create a common, continuous surface
that slips between them, emphasizing views
to the interior of the property, to Kings Road,
and the neighboring apartment buildings. The
continuous surface of the structure supporting
the ramps continues down to the subterranean
level independent of the perimeter soldier pile
retaining walls.

The roof garden negotiates between the
rectangular site and the profile of the house, and
relocates the original garden to the new urban
datum of the city's roof tops. The roof garden
becomes a sky-meadow, a nod to Schindler's
1920's context punctuated by an over-scaled
oculus to contrast glimpses of the residence
below with more distant views of the city afforded
from the rooftop landscape.

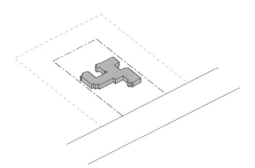

1922 - schindler house - radical
duplex residence in open bean field.

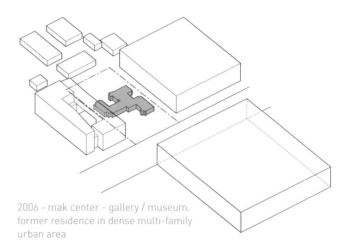

2006 - mak center - gallery / museum.
former residence in dense multi-family
urban area

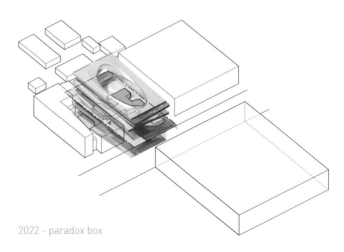

2022 - paradox box

JOHN FRIEDMAN ALICE KIMM ARCHITECTS

www.jfak.net

Alice Kimm and John Friedman

The work of John Friedman Alice Kimm Architects (JFAK) begins with the premise that architecture has the power to positively transform individual and collective lives, as well as the responsibility to both sustain and improve the environment.

Every JFAK project is dedicated to expressing its users' aspirations and identity through productive dialogue with the surrounding physical and cultural context, whether it be a chaotic urban environment, a rural setting, or the placeless interior of an existing structure. Light-filled interior spaces are organized to create meaningful adjacencies and unexpected views, as well as to encourage a range of activities – from individual contemplation to communal interaction and creative teamwork.

The size, type, or budget of a project is not important to JFAK. Rather, the firm takes on projects that involve a design challenge and the promise of developing an innovative solution. Wherever possible, JFAK employs new types of performative materials, often in concert with the most current design software and construction technologies. For JFAK, new digital techniques are not an end in themselves, but tools to explore new types of efficiencies, forms, textures, spaces, and branding identities. JFAK also applies the full range of sustainable strategies, whether they involve the most sophisticated engineering systems, simple passive techniques, or the choice of the most responsible materials. Casting its net as wide as possible, JFAK has engaged in collaborations with a host of talented artists, engineers, scientists, builders, and other specialists. Whether these individuals are JFAK clients, consultants, or advisers, they become partners in a shared vision, one of creating integrated and sustainable environments that inspire their users and better their lives.

GRADUATE AEROSPACE LABORATORIES,
CALIFORNIA INSTITUTE OF TECHNOLOGY (GALCIT)

YEAR OF COMPLETION 2008
LOCATION California Institute
of Technology, Pasadena, California
SIZE 18,000 square feet renovation
of a 55,000 square feet existing
concrete structure
PHOTOGRAPHY Benny Chan (Fotoworks)

Housed in a historically-protected structure
originally designed by Bertand Goodhue in 1921, the
Graduate Aerospace Laboratories at the California
Institute of Technology (GALCIT) has accomplished
some of the most revolutionary breakthroughs
in the history of aeronautics. This 33,000 square
foot renovation of the department's laboratories,
conference rooms, and common spaces
acknowledges these past achievements while also
suggesting the multitude of exciting directions for its
future.

To bring relevance and meaning to the project's
spaces, the design employs some of the same
concepts, processes, and sophisticated technologies
used in the department's widely varied and
interdisciplinary research. The results are joyful,
creative environments that encourage interaction,
teamwork, and the free flow of ideas.

Drawing on the idea of "flow," a concept central
to almost every facet of aeronautical engineering,
many of the project's forms were derived by
imagining the building as an "architectural wind
tunnel." The complex curves of the lobby ceiling
element, digitally designed and fabricated of PETG
thermoplastic with the most advanced software and
computer-controlled machines, is a prime example
of this strategy. The integration of subtle dimples
into its surface also acknowledges the crucial role
that materials research plays in the field – small
deformations like these have huge effects on
aerodynamic behavior.

The felt ceiling of the main conference room is a
direct representation of a seminal flow diagram by
Theodore von Karman, the founder of both GALCIT

and the Jet Propulsion Laboratory. Overall, the
project's design has provided an updated identity for
the department and served as a model for future
renovations on Caltech's campus.

Throughout the project, new glazed walls and
windows bring light into formerly dark laboratories
and classrooms, while also allowing views of
innovative research being performed inside them.
This heightened transparency has contributed to
an atmosphere of interdisciplinary collaboration
and cooperation. Many of these new glass walls
also incorporate vitrines that display meaningful
historical artifacts. The overall result is that GALCIT's
students and faculty are constantly inspired by the
department's past achievements, as well as the
scientists and engineers responsible for them.

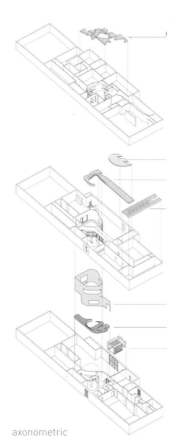

axonometric

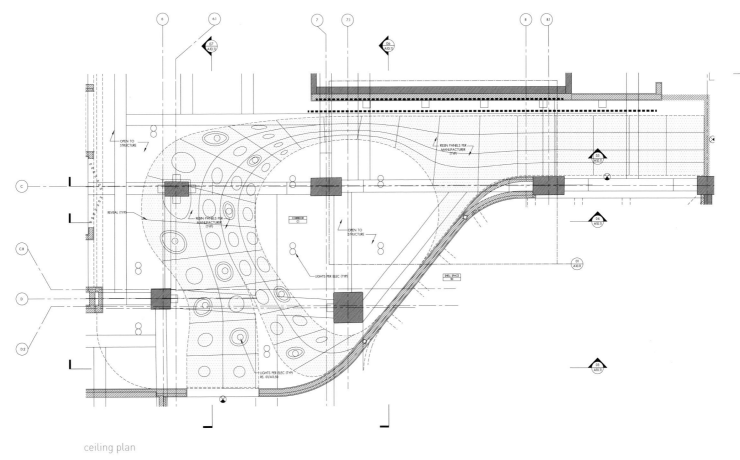

ceiling plan

top and bottom 3-form resin panels were moulded to form the suspended ceiling installation above ceiling plan

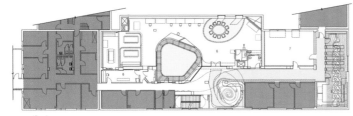

third floor plan

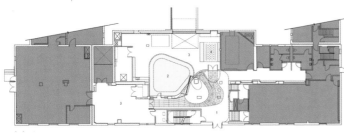

second floor plan

first floor plan

right, and below variegated interior spaces nestle within the massive walls of the existing structure

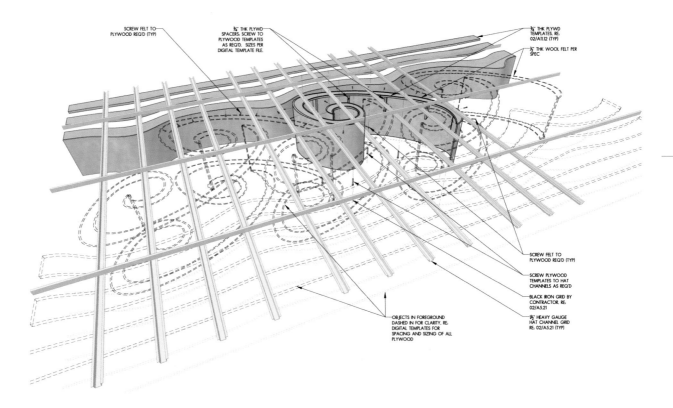

SCREW FELT TO
PLYWOOD REQ'D (TYP)

¾" THK PLYWD
SPACERS. SCREW TO
PLYWOOD TEMPLATES
AS REQ'D. SIZES PER
DIGITAL TEMPLATE FILE.

¾" THK PLYWD
TEMPLATES. RE:
02/A11.12 (TYP)

½" THK WOOL FELT PER
SPEC

SCREW FELT TO
PLYWOOD REQ'D (TYP)

SCREW PLYWOOD
TEMPLATES TO HAT
CHANNELS AS REQ'D

BLACK IRON GRID BY
CONTRACTOR. RE:
02/A5.21

1½" HEAVY GAUGE
HAT CHANNEL GRID
RE: 02/A5.21 (TYP)

OBJECTS IN FOREGROUND
DASHED IN FOR CLARITY, RE:
DIGITAL TEMPLATES FOR
SPACING AND SIZING OF ALL
PLYWOOD

a5 LOS ANGELES   165

bottom the felt ceiling of the main conference room is a direct represenattion of seminal flow diagram by Theodore van Karman, the founder of both Galcit and the Jet Propulsion Laboratory

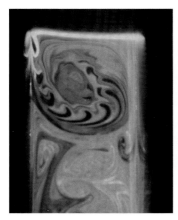

KING RESIDENCE

YEAR OF COMPLETION 2008
LOCATION Santa Monica, California
SIZE 4,300 square feet
PHOTOGRAPHY Benny Chan (Fotoworks)

The King Residence rejects the standard public front yard/private backyard typology, opting instead for a structure whose living spaces and bedrooms open onto a relatively large garden and patio that faces the public streets and surrounding houses. While this arrangement puts much of the family's communal and individual life on display, this is a positive feature for the Kings. The house's blurring of public/private reinforces the sense of community that they embrace and encourage.

By setting the house towards the rear of the site, the house does not crowd the intersection. Read in a more volumetric way, the house is a solid mass in which one corner has been carved away, revealing the house's inner life. But the structure can also be interpreted as series of planes, where angled walls that respond to the site's wedged shape also contribute a degree of privacy for the house's bedrooms. With a similar intent, the roof of the dining and "hangout" wing, angled to follow the gentle slope of the site, creates a sense of shelter for its inhabitants.

Primarily composed of renewable materials such as plaster and cement board, the general permeability of the house is reinforced by its green and gray cement board painting pattern, designed to echo the dappled light one sees when looking through a tree towards a sun-filled sky. The wood screens, made of vertically-oriented ipe, further help to dematerialize the structure's opaque walls.

Echoing the openness of the house to the neighborhood, the interior of the house is a series of free-flowing, continuous spaces that fosters a

supportive, interactive family lifestyle. Generous use of skylights creates constantly changing light conditions that activate the interior. Extensive vertical glazing reduces the need for artificial lighting and enables ocean breezes to naturally ventilate the entire house, which does not include an air-conditioning system.

right white walls and ceilings rise from
the horizontal floor plane surfaced in
wooden parquet
the residence steps intelligently back
from the street to allow unconventional
orientation both inside
and out

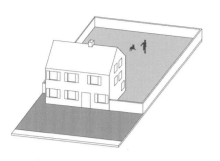

Typical Suburban Lot
-Small public front yard
-Large private rear yard
-Formal front facade
-Small windows
-Minimal public interaction
-Inactive

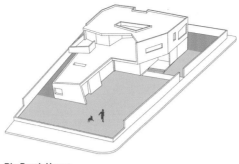

Big Porch House
-Large public front yard
-Small rear yard
-Relaxed / Playful front facade
-Large windows open to street
-Maximum public interaction
-Active / Inviting

1 foyer
2 office
3 bathroom
4 wine cellar
5 living room
6 kitchen
7 dining room
8 hang out room
9 powder room
10 laundry room
11 garage
12 fountain
13 patio
14 bedroom
15 master bedroom
16 master bathroom

SITE PLAN

0 5 10   20

site plan

GREEN DOT CHARTER HIGH SCHOOLS

YEAR OF COMPLETION 2008
LOCATION Los Angeles, California
SIZE 77,000 square feet
PHOTOGRAPHY Benny Chan (Fotoworks)

This 77,000 square foot project involves the transformation of two former manufacturing warehouses into a pair of high schools for the progressive Green Dot Charter School Organization. Located on the edge of a single family residential neighborhood in South Los Angeles (formerly known as South Central), these new facilities offer what has been unattainable in this historically underprivileged part of the Los Angeles - namely, the promise for a better future in the form of committed educators, effective teaching methods, and inspiring, uplifting environments.

Limited to 500 students, each school has its own separate administration, as well as its own architectural identity. Inhabiting the original brick warehouse, the school called "Animo Justice" utilizes warm, red and yellow hues and is entered from the south side of the shared exterior entry courtyard. In contrast, "Animo Ralph Bunche," the school housed in the tilt-up concrete structure,

uses a cooler, blue and green palette, and is accessed via a dramatic steel stair and second floor roof deck on the north side of the courtyard.

To accommodate the required floor area for two schools, as well as much needed exterior space, a second floor has been inserted into the higher, concrete building. While each school has its own circulation system, these have been designed to give independent access to a shared gym and library situated near the center of the combined facility.

Skylights are used extensively to assure that each classroom has access to natural light and a view of the sky. In some places, they provide light to the first floor spaces through shafts that run through the second floor. The project is the first LEED-certified charter school facility in Los Angeles.

two new schools each offer 500 students from
the historically underprivileged neighborhood
vital, light-filled learning spaces .

FIL GUADALAJARA

YEAR OF COMPLETION 2008
LOCATION Los Angeles, California
SIZE 77,000 square feet
PHOTOGRAPHY Benny Chan (Fotoworks)

This Guest of Honor Pavilion for the 2009 Feria Internacional del Libro de Guadalajara (FIL) in Mexico, honoring Los Angeles, created a public plaza for people to interact and trade ideas. An ephemeral, atmospheric environment, it was designed to communicate the spirit of this elusive, ever-changing City and to embody the spirit of *innovation* that suffuses much of L.A.'s culture, arts, and industries.

There were two signature elements. The first was a set of suspended, pneumatic "Idea Bubbles," originally inspired by the speech bubbles found in cartoons and designed using advanced computational tools. These bubbles formed the backdrop for ten specially commissioned short films. The second iconic element was a 100-foot long interactive "Author Wall," on which were

projected the names and biographies of 220+ writers whose work has illuminated Los Angeles over the years.

The use of projected, rather than printed, information created much less waste than is usual for an installation of this kind. In addition, all of the project's modular booths and book towers were gifted for reuse in Guadalajara's public libraries.

FITNESS AND ATHLETIC CENTER, CLAREMONT MCKENNA COLLEGE

YEAR OF COMPLETION Currently in Design Development. Construction projected for March 2011
LOCATION Claremont McKenna College, Claremont, California
SIZE 100,000 square feet

This 100,000 sf Fitness and Athletic Center at Claremont McKenna College includes a 2,000 seat arena for varsity games and special events, locker rooms, recreational facilities, and offices. It establishes a new communal center for the campus to encourage strong social ties, teamwork, and a sense of school spirit.

The project's compact form contributes to a dynamic, interactive environment and allows its large program to sit on a relatively tight site. The varsity gym sits at the geographic heart of the structure.

From different parts of the building, dramatic views can be had of the nearby San Bernardino Mountains, pool, track, and athletic fields. The generous use of glazed walls invites use of all facilities. Sustainable strategies include efficient mechanical systems, photovoltaic and solar hot water panels, maximum use of skylights combined with automated dimming systems, and adjustable solar shading.

The dynamic, sculptural form of the building suggests the athletic activities that go on inside of it. Its cladding of colored, perforated metal panels likewise alludes to the breathing, perspiring skin of an exercising person.

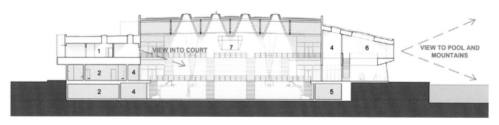

north/south elevation

VIEW INTO COURT

VIEW TO POOL AND MOUNTAINS

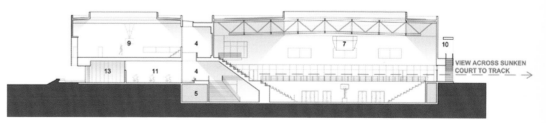

VIEW ACROSS SUNKEN COURT TO TRACK

above, and right the extensive program was skillfully fitted to the tight site by means of compact forms

east/west elevation

JOHNSTONMARKLEE

www.johnstonmarklee.com

Since its founding in 1998, Johnston Marklee's portfolio is distinguished by its conceptual approach to each project. Rather than adhere to a signature style, Johnston Marklee investigates issues of design, form, and technical resolution to create unique works of architecture. Principals Sharon Johnston and Mark Lee have developed their approach to projects varying in scale from master plans to contemporary buildings and temporary installations to distill the inherent complexity of each project into coherent, singular solutions.
The firm has a substantial architectural portfolio including a range of institutional, residential, and commercial commissions throughout the United States as well as in China, Argentina, Portugal, Switzerland, and Italy.

While maintaining a deep commitment to architecture history as well as the discipline's contemporary discourse, Johnston Marklee's creative process engages the respective knowledge and influence of collaborations
beyond those typical to architecture. Drawing upon an extensive network of professional experts in related fields, Johnston Marklee is widely recognized for culling the expertise of engineers, contemporary artists, graphic designers, writers, and photographers to broaden the breadth of design research. Johnston Marklee fosters collaboration in which the expertise of joining disciplines are sharpened, rather than blurred, maintaining permeable boundaries for greater results.

Principals Mark Lee and Sharon Johnston are equally engaged in academic and applied design research, and the firm fosters the vital links between these arenas in their practice. Johnston Marklee couples their conceptual approach to design with rigorous study of building and material methods, fabrication technologies, and construction techniques. The firm directs complex teams of collaborators where cross disciplinary practices yield unexpected results. Academic study focuses on critical reassessment of architectural and urban design history within the context of urban development and housing in border cities and culture-specific landscapes.

Mark Lee and Sharon Johnston

VIEW HOUSE

YEAR OF COMPLETION 2009
LOCATION Rosario, Argentina
SIZE 361 square meters
PHOTOGRAPHY Gustavo Frittegotto
IN PARTNERSHIP WITH Diego Arraigada
Arquitectos

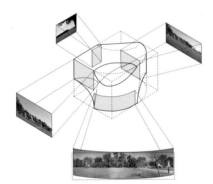

views

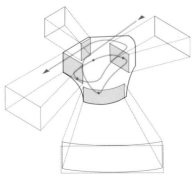

circulation

The View House is designed under conditions generated by both the potential and limitations of large suburban developments. Situated near Rosario on the rich landscape of the Argentine plains, the 3200 sq foot house occupies a 22,750 sq foot parcel in the Kentucky Club de Campo development. The design is driven by two conflicting desires: engaging the living experience of the house with the views of the surrounding landscape and preserving privacy from neighbors.

Planning demands and the unique position of the peripheral corner lot demanded a specific approach to the massing of the house and its engagement with the landscape. A compact massing strategy with a minimal footprint liberates and preserves the ground. By denying the traditional front, side, and rear yard designations, and instead intensifying the facade as a surface that continuously modulates the relationship of interior to exterior, the perception of the house unfolds through a sequence of oblique views where every surface of façade becomes primary. Boundaries between front and back, and building and site are eroded.

The formal and tectonic complexity of the house results from the repetition of four basic geometric subtractions from a primitive mass that create a dynamic exterior shape perceived simultaneously as embedded and lofted, cantilevered and slumped. In the interior, these operations define a continuous and modulated space that spirals upwards from the ground level to the roof terrace in a sequence of living areas. The four geometric subtractions have differentiated volumetric impressions on the inside of the house, each

of which, together with a contiguous aperture, results in an interior landscape of paired surfaces, views, and lighting effects.

The rotational strategy for the apertures results from the framing of desirable landscape features, the anticipation of neighboring developments and the choreography of internal circulation. The reduction of electric and HVAC demands by facilitating cross ventilation and natural light have also been taken into consideration. Varying in height, orientation, and depth, each framed opening captures a distinct view, providing alternating relationships between interior and exterior. The layering of subtractions and apertures also relates to the tectonic demands of the overall concrete shell. As a culmination of the internal circulation along a path of 360°, a flight of steps leads up to a panoramic roof deck, from which the expansive surrounding landscape can be perceived from a new height.

The rough concrete shell of the house was built using traditional local techniques and its form and finish retain the impression of the means and methods of its construction. In contrast, the interior of the house is smooth and polished in nature. Lightly hued terrazzo floors on the first floor are distinguished from the smooth plaster walls only by a degree of reflectivity and polish. The black window frames punctuate the views and define a contrast with the white interior atmosphere. In more intimate, private spaces, Lapacho wood covers the floors creating a new contrast with the walls and ceilings.

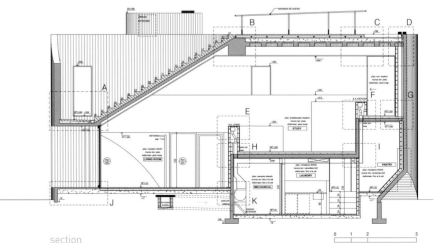

right at dusk, the residence seems to hover
on the Argentinian plain right construction
section details of the concrete structure

section

0 1 2 5

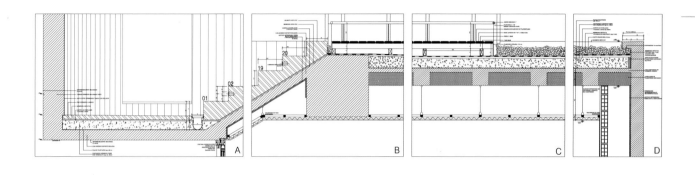

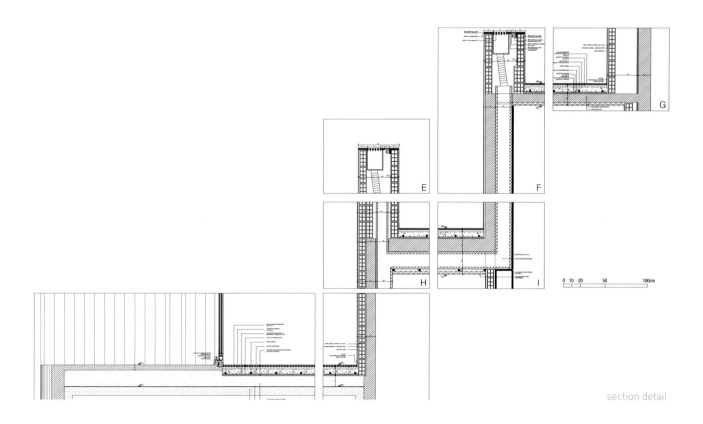

below the openings form precisely focused
apertures that frame select views out to
the landscape as one moves through the
spaces

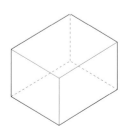
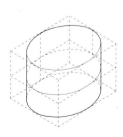
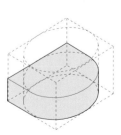
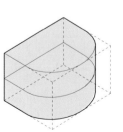
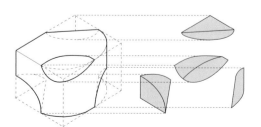

massing diagram

HELIOS HOUSE

YEAR OF COMPLETION 2007
LOCATION Los Angeles, California
SIZE 10,800 square feet (lot)
PHOTOGRAPHY Eric Staudenmaier
IN PARTNERSHIP WITH BIG at Ogilvy & Mather and Office dA

The legacy of gas station design is a rich history of innovative industrial architecture focused on column and long-span structures. This trajectory ranges from the elegant lightweight concrete shell structures of Felix Candela in Mexico to the attenuated mushroom canopy of Arne Jacobsen in Denmark. In the United States, Frank Lloyd Wright's 1956 gas station and the popular Googie roadside architecture form the cultural and historical context in which this project is situated.

Helios House uses architecture and design to reinvent the gas station experience. By restoring the fantasy and aspirations that gas station design once embodied, Helios House rediscovers the design potential of a structure that has dominated corner lots in the American landscape for much of the 20th century. It mines this history to conjure a vision for the future - one that melds bold design, inventive fabrication, and sustainable building practices with a multifaceted communication strategy to inspire a community that's eager to raise its environmental awareness.

Helios House is located in Los Angeles, at the intersection of Robertson and Olympic Boulevards – a major north/south, east/west crossroads. A conventional gas station was built on this site in the mid-1970s. An important goal of this project was to upcycle the original station in an environmentally conscious manner, by recycling old materials and installing sustainable and recyclable new materials.

Helios House transforms the site's existing features – the ground, canopy, cashier kiosk, back building (which lacked a public toilet), and two price signs – while incorporating green building features and messages into the project.

The design of the canopy is the most emblematic feature of Helios House. While conventional gas stations combine functionally distinct elements (canopy, columns, pay kiosk, and sign), this project develops a unique formal logic to integrate all of those elements into one seamless whole. Using a structural bay as a starting point, the cladding system unifies the relationship between column base, shaft, and capital with the canopy. The triangulated stainless steel panels reconcile complex, and sometimes contradictory, requirements of the site, program, codes, and zoning ordinances, and establish the site identity and core of the brand experience.

In keeping with the goal of sustainability, the fabrication and design systems were optimized to conserve labor costs and reduce material waste throughout the project. Developed with a design/build fabricator, the canopy incorporates 1,653 stainless steel panels into a prefabricated assembly system. Fastened together off-site, the canopy is comprised of 52 transportable components, which were erected on-site in four weeks. The efficiency and precision of these techniques tap into the potential of mass customization – using the controlled environment of a shop to calibrate modular components with unique geometric conditions, which facilitate efficient site installation.

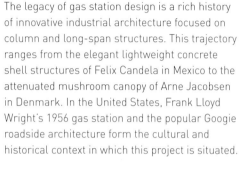

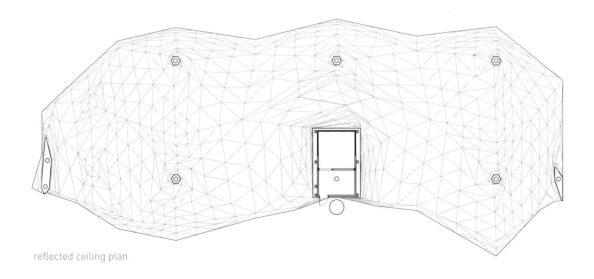

reflected ceiling plan

left, and right the angularly-tilted reptile-like surface panels wrap around to "ground" the ephemeral, hovering roof canopy with the terrain of Olympic Boulevard.

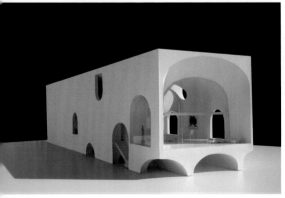

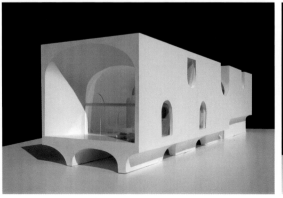

VAULT HOUSE

YEAR OF COMPLETION Design: 2009-
2010 / Start of Construction: 2010
LOCATION Oxnard, California
SIZE 4,200 square feet
PHOTOGRAPHY (Model shot by Johnston
Marklee)

Vault House is situated on a densely developed
Californian beach site and challenges the
standard prime, single-view typology for beach
front properties through complex layering of
transparent interior spaces.
With a series of stacked and unidirectional
vaults contained within a simple solid mass,
the parallel orientation of the rooms within
the house becomes a filter which extends the
expansive oceanfront view from the beachfront
façade to the street. Similar to the paradigm of a
shotgun-house, the singular direction of the vaults
maximizes the connection of all spaces within a
deep building, while incorporating the idealized
exterior landscape of the ocean and horizon.

With varied shapes, heights, and material finishes,
each individual vault defines an area in the house,
the combined effect of which creates a seriality of
interior spaces through a unified formal move. The
public spaces and master bedroom occupy the
portion of the house closest to the water, with
the garage and guest rooms situated towards the

back of the site. In the center of the house, an
inverse vault forms a courtyard, separating these
programmatic blocks and functioning as a main
entry court as well as a light box that allows light
and air to flow to all spaces within the structure.

Sectional shifts between the rooms are
emphasized as diverse vaulted forms intersect
and expose abrupt transitional moments. At these
intersections, fully operable glazing divides the
public spaces, Master Bedroom, and courtyard
allowing for a complete unification of the house
into one large space connected to the beach. In
contrast, openings on the facades perpendicular
to the direction of the vaults are articulated as
deep cutouts on the massive exterior box.

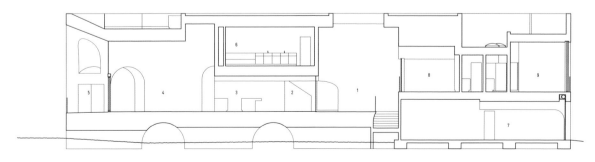

section

POGGIO GOLO WINERY

YEAR OF COMPLETION Design: 2008 –
2011 (Entitlements – Construction) / Start
of Construction: 2011
LOCATION Montepulciano, Italy
SIZE 1,200 square meters
PHOTOGRAPHY (Model shot by Johnston
Marklee)

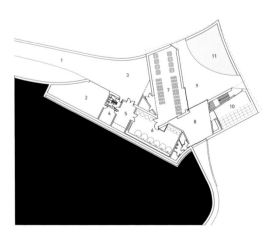

Poggio Golo winery is located outside of the
Tuscan town of Montepulciano and currently
houses a historical villa, guest houses, and limited
wine production facilities which will expand to
accommodate a winery with capacity to produce
50,400 bottles annually. The new buildings for
Poggio Golo winery (approximate 900 sq meters)
define a new boundary for the vineyard through
fortification of the existing hilltop villa and gardens.
The new wall which encircles and fortifies the
private precinct of the site is punctuated by a series
of buildings housing wine production, meetings
& wine tasting, and art spaces for exhibition and
studio production. These volumes, anchored to the
wall like pendants on a necklace, negotiate the

terrain by simultaneously embedding and emerging
from the surrounding topography. Their roofs form
a new contoured horizon from the hilltop patios,
while the building masses become visible when
descending into courtyard and gallery spaces,
where the silhouette of adjacent walls frames
distinct views of the surrounding site. A site specific
installation of the artist Daniel Buren, produced in
collaboration with the architects, is planned for the
winery courtyard.

The design is guided by the functional process of
wine making in relation to the specific topographic
contours of the site. Three wings extend from
a central intersecting space, and this tripartite

arrangement allows for fluid circulation and ease-of-access between production facilities. Projecting out from the hillside, two wings contain barrel and bottling facilities, along with tasting rooms. Sloping three meters downward from the property's hilltop towards the vineyards, they open to a central courtyard clad in travertine. Tucked into the hillside, a third wing houses fermentation rooms, mechanical facilities, and agricultural equipment storage. Along the courtyard, double-curved walls lean outward in section, while converging toward a common apex in plan. As these outer walls slope into a common point, they expose the central courtyard to panoramic views of the outlying landscape.

In response to climate control parameters for wine production and storage, Poggio Golo's design incorporates intuitively simple features to achieve the dual goal of maintaining specific temperature conditions while minimizing energy expenditure. With indirect exposure to sunlight, the winery's outward-extending wings feature large, inset windows that minimize electricity use in public spaces such as the tasting area, reception, and wine shop. The minimization of apertures in storage areas prevents barrels' exposure to sunlight and heat, factors adverse to the wine-making process. A shallow water feature within the courtyard cools air during the warm summer months.

A rusticated brick exterior resolves the formal opposition between the form of the winery and adjacent 17th-century villa. The brick application engages the region's architectural tradition, construction methods, and artisanship in the context of a contemporary building and landscape. Travertine slabs lining the courtyard, define an abstract, sculpted frame to view the surrounding landscape, which is reflected in the shallow pool at the apex of the patio.

HOUSE HOUSE

YEAR OF COMPLETION Design: 2008,
Construction Start: 2010
LOCATION Ordos, Inner Mongolia, China
SIZE 1,000 square meters
PHOTOGRAPHY (Model shot by Johnston
Marklee)

The design of House House emerges from an interest in finding the most elemental model for a house. As a type, the gable roofed shed is one that transcends cultures and civilization. The instant this house proliferates bears the seed for the basic model of settlement.

Considering pragmatic constraints, the siting of the house is driven by the need to situate a large building on a small lot with close proximity to adjacent structures. By situating the house obliquely to the lot and always exposing double facades to the main views, the primary image of House House is present at every angle but never the same. Clad with brick in its entirety, the design evokes the stability and stillness of a single building as well as the dynamism of its proliferation.

The internal organization of the house is driven by the notion of a double house, where public and private domains interlock around light filled voids. From the exterior, the house is divided in plan. Internally, the double use between public and private is divided in section.

The ground level contains the most public programs, the second level contains the semi-

public use, and the third level contains the most private rooms, where the interface with the roofline allows each room to become a house in itself. All levels of the house, including the basement, are connected by a light filled atrium stair.

The strategy for apertures results from the anticipation of the surrounding development and the choreography of internal moments, which migrate in plan and section concomitantly with circulation to erode traditional front/back and top/bottom planning organizations.

As one walks through the house, the apertures frame different views of the landscape and surrounding houses. On the exterior, the various positions and depths of the apertures serve to simultaneously dematerialize and reinforce the visual weight of the house.

Suspended between stasis and dynamism, introversion and extroversion, isolation and community, and past and future, House House breeds familiarity while suggesting the exceptional, reflecting the logic of the masterplan and the spirit of the development.

elevations

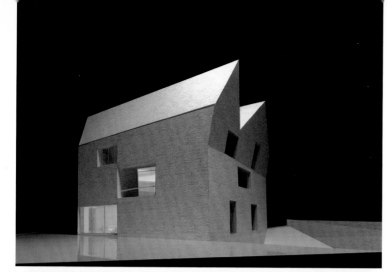

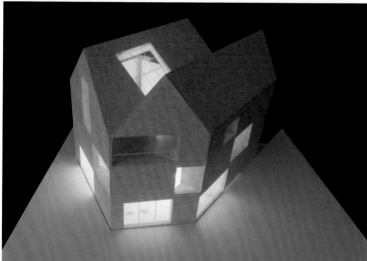

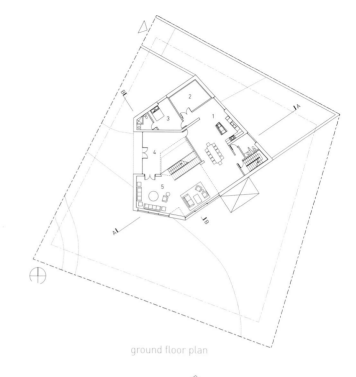

ground floor plan

second floor plan

third floor plan

KANNER ARCHITECTS

www.kannerarch.com

Stephen Kanner

Kanner Architects believes that every project is a special endeavor and that superior modern architecture is achieved by fulfilling our client's needs with thorough planning, cost-effective, cutting-edge, sustainable design, and sensitivity to all aspects of the site.

Whether projects are large or small, urban or rural, Kanner embraces the notion that buildings are meant to be functional, but must also be places of joy - open and accessible, timeless and inspirational. Every project must enhance the built environment.

Established in 1946, Kanner Architects will celebrate its 64th year of quality and innovative design work in Los Angeles in 2010. Stephen H. Kanner, FAIA, became president in 1998 and continues to lead the firm in its third generation. Stephen Kanner is the founder and remains chairman of the Architecture + Design (A+D) Museum in Los Angeles and was 2005 president of the Los Angeles Chapter of American Institute of Architects.

As a widely published and internationally recognized design firm, Kanner Architects has garnered over 50 design awards in recent years, most from the American Institute of Architects.

UNITED OIL GASOLINE STATION

KANNER ARCHITECTS

YEAR OF COMPLETION 2009
LOCATION Los Angeles, California
SIZE 20,600 square feet
PHOTOGRAPHY John Edward Linden

United Oil reinterprets the most ubiquitous fixture of roadside culture: the gas station and drive-thru carwash.

Situated on the southwest corner of La Brea and Slauson avenues in the Los Angeles neighborhood of Ladera Heights, this project seeks to breathe new life into a commercial intersection left ignored and in need of more thoughtful design. The project includes a 2,000 sq ft glass-encased mini-market, a car wash, and a pocket park on an acre site.

The sinuous and curvilinear metal roof structure, supported by dynamically flared steel columns, is the most prominent design feature. Taking cues from Los Angeles's most iconic urban infrastructure—the freeway—the canopy sweeps up to a point 30 feet above the pumps below while the station's concrete car ramp flows up and over the rear of the mini-market and back down into the carwash at the far west end of the site.

above in the tradition of Southern Californian roadside architecture, the soaring roof pulls drivers in to the station middle view towards the car-wash ramp right inner pump bay looking onto pedestrian entrance

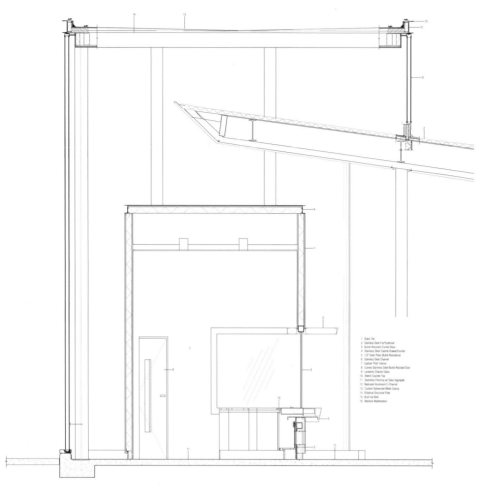

1. Glass Tile
2. Stainless Steel Fin/"Eyebrow"
3. Bullet-Resistant Curved Glass
4. Stainless Steel Cashier Drawer/Counter
5. 1/2" Steel Plate (Bullet Resistance)
6. Stainless Steel Channel
7. Cashier "Pod" Interior
8. Curved Stainless Steel Bullet-Resistant Door
9. Lambert's Channel Glass
10. Alkemi Counter Top
11. Seamless Flooring w/ Glass Aggregate
12. Radiused Aluminum C-Channel
13. Custom Galvanized Metal Coping
14. Elliptical Structural Plate
15. Built-Up Roof
16. Mortise Weatherdoor

section detail

left construction section detail of the
cashier's box. vibrant colors recall
Southern California's tradition of roadside
diners and gas stations

OAKLAND HOUSE

YEAR OF COMPLETION 2007
LOCATION Oakland, California
SIZE 4,200 square feet
PHOTOGRAPHY Tim Griffith

This Bay Area home situated on a down-sloping site in Oakland, California, was designed to capture the magnificent vistas spanning from the Bay Bridge to the Golden Gate. The clients wanted to create a dream home for their life as empty nesters, but still desired accommodations for their kids and other frequent guests. Thus, the four-bedroom home was planned as two volumes connected by a glass enclosed bridge.

The two-story lower structure is all about the view and open plan living. On the upper level, the kitchen, dining, and living rooms are open to one another. The master suite sits below, opening up to an outdoor terrace and infinity pool. The secondary volume, facing the street, has a glass carport, three guest rooms, and a recreation room.

Concrete floors, steel and glass window systems, and a mostly white composition define a minimalist composition. Color is introduced through a pale blue plaster, herringbone-toweled exterior scratch coat, landscaping, artwork, and borrowed dramatic views.

The building's bowed walls—an hourglass in plan—serve to create a visual compression, which has the effect of a volume being squeezed in the center and exploding to the view on the glazed façades.

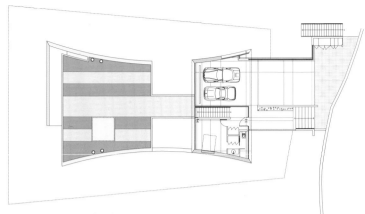

garage level

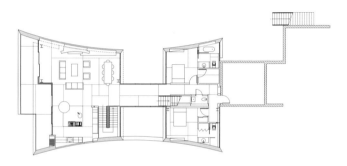

living level

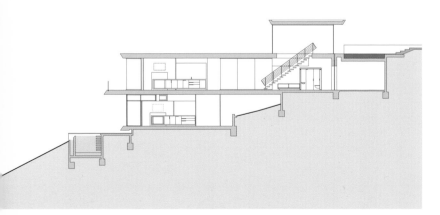

section

left, and above the spaces of this residence were deployed into two distinct building volumes connected by a glass stair bridge. living and entertainment spaces are contained in the valley-side mass, bedrooms and bathrooms are contained the street-facing wing

26TH STREET
LOW-INCOME HOUSING

YEAR OF COMPLETION 2007
LOCATION Santa Monica, California
SIZE 42,000 square feet
PHOTOGRAPHY John Edward Linden

26th Street Low-Income Housing is the product of an exhaustive community outreach mission. In addition to input from the city of Santa Monica and the community at large, the final design takes into account the region's mild climate, historical precedents of Southern California Modernist architecture, and the human scale of residents and pedestrians.

The design of the 44-unit apartment building incorporates dual-glazed and laminated windows along both street-facing sides to eliminate street noise. Drywells were dug beneath the project to collect and disperse stormwater runoff and minimize the project's impact on the city's storm sewer system. The project's 81 subterranean parking spaces—accessed from an alley to minimize traffic issues—exceed the minimum required.

Living spaces at 26th Street are organized in a linear fashion to facilitate cross-ventilation, a passive natural cooling technique that eliminates the need for energy-intensive rooftop air conditioning and mechanical equipment that disrupts views, makes noise, and can be seen from the street.

south elevation

above the central courtyard serves as
a place of gathering for tenants and
increases the sense of community of
this low-income housing development

floor plan

left, and right special care was taken to create light-filled generous spaces in spite of the limited budget. sustainable materials such as inexpensive, durable fiber cement exterior panels and low-energy lighting, non-toxic paints were implemented

Photography by Tessa Kappe

RAY KAPPE ARCHITECT

Ray Kappe

Ray Kappe, FAIA has been in architectural practice since 1953. Besides design, his career has included social and community advocacy, urban design and planning, and education. He has authored publications on environmental planning and urban design. He has completed energy and advanced technology research. He is an internationally known architect who has designed buildings which have been recognized with innumerable awards and publication. He was the first chairman of Architecture at California State Polytechnic University, Pomona. His involvement with education has also produced one the nation's most innovative and progressive schools, the Southern California Institute of Architecture, SCI-ARC. He was the founding Director in 1972, and in 1976 was awarded the CCAIA Excellence in Education Award. In 1990 he was the recipient of the Topaz Medallion, the highest award for excellence in architecture education in the United States presented by the American Institute of Architects and the Association of Collegiate Schools of Architecture.

Ray Kappe began his architectural practice in the early 50's committed to the ideals of the California lifestyle, which afforded the potential to live with nature. The design expression of the existing Southern California work beginning with Greene and Greene, Wright, Neutra and Schindler, and followed by Ain, Soriano, and Harris formed the basis for his own work. Architect Hayahiko Takase wrote in the Ray Kappe monograph by the Japanese magazine Toshi-Jutaku in March 1982 that, "Ray Kappe is one of the few successors of the 'Great Tradition of California Housing'. His work has similar characteristics to the preceding California masters such as open-mindedness, harmony with nature, clear systems, unostentatiousness and Japanese influence."

SANTA MONICA PREFAB RESIDENCE

YEAR OF COMPLETION 2006
LOCATION Santa Monica, California
SIZE approx. 3,000 square feet
PHOTOGRAPHY C.J. Berg, Grant Mudford

Erected in a densely settled neighborhood in Santa Monica California in just eight hours, the "exploded box" pre-fabricated design employs spatial characteristics such as double height spaces, level changes, openness, and glazed surfaces reminiscent of Kappe's earlier, conventionally-constructed residential projects.

Floor-to-ceiling sliding glass doors, glass walls, polygal (a multi-layered translucent plastic glazing material), and horizontal Forest Stewardship Certified (FSC) cedar siding were used to enclose the spaces. Additional outdoor living space is provided by decks that cantilever from the floor plates and are shaded by trellises. Freestanding wardrobe closets serve as space dividers, and bedrooms can be closed off with sliding partitions to allow the space to adapt to homeowners' changing needs. Following the contours of the land, Kappe created several additional levels that produce double height spaces, a mezzanine/loft space and walkways that overlook the lower levels, visually and spatially enlarging the house.

Kappe has long been environmentally sensitive and interested in multiple, affordable housing systems. In the early 1960's, rejecting the generally used "cut & fill" methods that scarred the hillsides, he developed a tower and bridging system that touched down lightly on the land. He then designed a modular, pre-fabricated student housing project for Sonoma California State University, for which he projected an off-site construction system. Since then, many of his custom homes, including his own house have been based upon the ideas he developed for that project.

This residence presented Kappe with the opportunity to explore these earlier ideas while utilizing the possibilities of present-day construction technologies. A range of new materials, reused materials, and innovative environmental systems were utilized in this project. Energy use is 80% more efficient than a conventional residence of similar size with much of the electricity being produced by on-site photovoltaic panels. Water is reclaimed for irrigation and the home was produced with 75% less construction waste than traditional home construction. Other features include: solar water heating and radiant heating in the floors, a native landscape and rooftop garden to divert storm water and alleviate the heat island effect of conventional black roofs, resource efficient appliances, LED lights that use a fraction of the power of conventional lights, an integrated storm water management system, which includes sub-surface irrigation, a 3500-gallon cistern and grey water recycling system to divert sink and shower water for irrigation, special fans that exhaust moisture from the bathrooms, a house fan that automatically vents hot-air, a 175 CFM fan in the garage tied into the garage door that automatically exhausts carbon monoxide from the garage; low-e Solarban60 glazing on the doors and windows and Polygal polycarbonate glazing that has better thermal properties than regular glass.

The residence was awarded the LEED® for Home Platinum in 2006 as the first home to achieve the highest classification of the Leadership in Environmental and Energy Efficient Design program.

left, and above trellis on terrace left below the fireplace serves as a focus in the living room right the residence adeptly straddles the hillside topography of the difficult site

MATERIAL ASSEMBLY

PASSIVE SOLAR SHADING

MOMENT FRAME

UTILITY CORE ASSEMBLY

CONCRETE FOUNDATINON

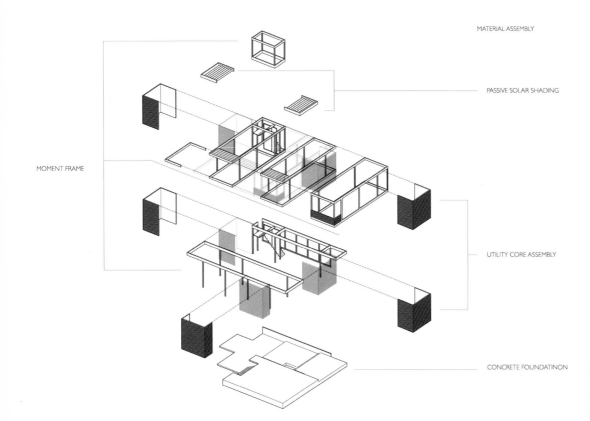

left exploded diagram showing modular
construction method above fabrication
and mounting process right prefab
construction details, sketch by Ray
Kappe

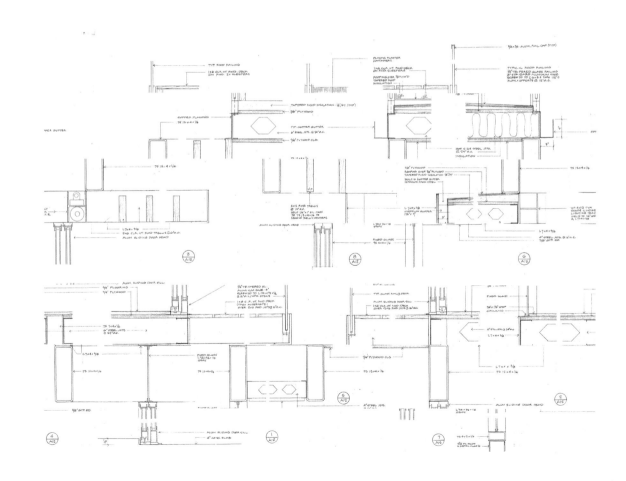

module key plan

site plan / first floor plan

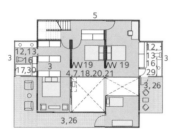

module key plan

second floor plan

ROOF STAIR MODULE

roof stair module

roof plan

left living room with upper gallery space
right media room, office space, bathroom

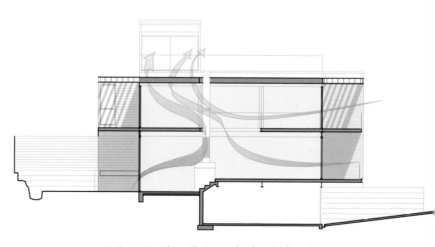

section: natural ventilation and solar shading diagram

top and bottom the living room, media
corner, kitchen, and dining zones all
interconnect to form the vital heart of
the residence right, below passive
cooling strategy

ROCHEDALE PREFAB RESIDENCE

YEAR OF COMPLETION 2007
PROJECT ARCHITECT FOR LIVINGHOMES
Finn Kappe
INTERIOR ARCHITECT Amy Sims
PHOTOGRAPHY Everett Fenton Gidley

The factory-manufactured Rochedale Residence was designed in departure from the Santa Monica Prefab Residence which included separate modules for the service units, a unifying steel module measuring 12'x12' in varying lengths was implemented. This modification was conceived to satisfy the fabricator's request to reduce costs and lessen fabrication complexity.

The two-story, 4,000 sq.ft. structure is composed of 11 prefabricated steel modules, weighing 50,000 pounds each, and lifted into place by crane. The installation of the house took just 2 ½ days.

The private bedrooms, bathrooms, and study/office rooms are grouped together on the ground floor. An open steel stair leads to the second, more glazed, level, where an open plan interconnects the living room, dining room, kitchen, and media room.

Consistent with Kappe's dedication to sustainable design, the property's previously existing house was deconstructed rather than demolished, reducing the amount of building materials sent to the landfill. The walls are framed with FSC certified wood and sheathed with reclaimed redwood milled from old military barracks buildings. The sliding glass doors and walls are glazed with insulated low-E glass. The home additionally features an Air-Floor forced hot air radiant heating and cooling system, LED lights that consume less energy than fluorescents and conventional light bulbs, and an Italian high-design Valcucine ecological kitchen.

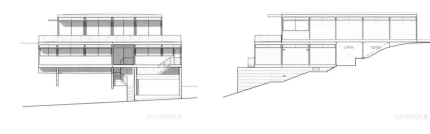

ELEVATION A

ELEVATION B

ELEVATION C

ELEVATION D

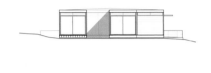

above kitchen and informal dining area
right formal dining area with view back
toward kitchen

SUNSET PLAZA RESIDENCE

YEAR OF COMPLETION 1957/2009
LOCATION Los Angeles, CA
SIZE 2,300 square feet
BUILDER Hinerfeld-Ward Construction
LANDSCAPE Mia Lehrer
PHOTOGRAPHY David Lena

The Sunset Plaza residence was originally built in 1957 in a canyon area north of Sunset Boulevard as a 1,900 sq. ft. in the then predominant "post-and-beam" vein. The new owner approached the home's original architect with the intention of enhancing and even bettering the original design. Kappe met the challenge with a holistic approach for restoring, updating, and expanding his original design that is characterized throughout by careful attention to detail.

Enlarging the master bedroom, and adding a bath, dressing room, and a new bedroom, allowed the home to expand by 468 sq. ft. With the remodeling, replacing an existing swimming pool with a lap pool, and completely re-landscaping the site, Kappe succeeded in creating a new ensemble that resounds with the modesty and simplicity of the former structure, while at the same time further defining the tenets of Southern California living that have always been formative in his work.

left the original 1957 residence received a 468 square foot addition, and the landscape design was modified to include a lap pool

left, and above great attention was lavished on the precise detailing, with the goal of intensifying the clear lines of the original post-and-beam house .

LEAN ARCH

www.leanarch.com

James Meyer

The Architectural Design/Build practice of LEAN ARCH, Inc. was established in the summer of 2000 and officially incorporated in August 2001. Founder James Meyer describes the office as a Design/Build collaborative focusing mostly on residential, commercial and civic-oriented architecture, but as also having worked on a variety of projects ranging from furniture and product design to corporate branding, packaging and graphics. Founded on the principles of modernism, the firm strongly believes that architecture and the built environment has the ability to improve people's lives – their physical surroundings, their appreciation of nature, their understanding of the arts, and their relationships with one another. The firm is committed to offering ideas that address the specific needs of a client while remaining conscious of the physical and psychological impact a work will have on both nature and the human-made environment.

LEAN ARCH is a full-service firm offering Architectural Design and Construction Services. The office prides itself on the quality and extent of service provided to clients. All projects, regardless of scale, are given the same level of attention – "right down to the doorknobs." A variety of techniques are used in the presentation of design ideas. These may range from sketches on paper to more realistic computer generated 3D models and animations. From the conceptual or schematic phase, through construction, LEAN ARCH works closely with clients, consultants and contractors to make sure that what has been designed is what will be constructed. Objectives have always been met by keeping in mind the idea that people must work together to solve a problem. More ideas, better solutions...

From the beginning, LEAN ARCH has strove to move beyond the realm of "paper architecture." The firm's priority has always been to see their work through to completion. In their words, Architecture is about people, and the realization of the project is the only way in which one may critique the effectiveness of the design. Dealing with executed works enables the firm to assess their impact on both users and critics, and to ultimately become better and more effective designers and builders. It is this dedication to the work and the rigor in which it is executed that has earned respect and appreciation from a growing number of clients, consultants and contractors,

KUHLHAUS 02

YEAR OF COMPLETION 2008
LOCATION Manhattan Beach, California
SIZE 4,080 square feet
PHOTOGRAPHY Claudio Santini: 03, 04,
05, 06, 07, 08, 09, 10;
Culver Van Buren: 01, 02

This single family residence located in the Gaslight District of Manhattan Beach seeks to redefine the modern home by carefully addressing concerns relating to energy consumption, land-use and the environment. The solar powered home features 4 bedrooms with 4 bathrooms, powder room, kitchen by Valcucine, open living and dining areas, family room, recreation room with a wet bar, walk-in wine cellar, and laundry room. The open plan and large glass sliding pocket doors create both visual and physical continuity between the interior and exterior. Outdoor patio and deck space adjacent to the kitchen, the living and family rooms, and the master bedroom enhance the quality of each space and allow for flexibility in their use. A perforated metal stair, metal panel siding, radiant floor heating and a 4.3 KW array of solar panels on the roof are a nod to "industrial chic".

right the minimalist aesthetic of the exteriors stands out pleasantly in the visually cluttered, beachside community of Manhattan Beach

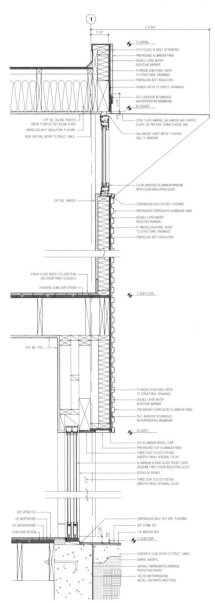

① 3'-0 3/4"

3 1/2"

T/ COPING

2 PLY CLASS 'A' BUILT-UP ROOFING
PREFINISHED ALUMINUM PANEL
DOUBLE LAYER WATER
RESISTANT BARRIER
PLYWOOD SHEATHING, REFER
TO STRUCTURAL DRAWINGS
FIBERGLASS BATT INSULATION
HEADER, REFER TO STRUCT DRAWINGS

SELF-ADHESIVE BITUMINOUS
WATERPROOFING MEMBRANE
BY HEADER

GYP. BD. CEILING, PAINTED
REFER TO REFLECTED CEILING PLANS
FIBERGLASS BATT INSULATION, R-30 MIN.
ROOF RAFTERS, REFER TO STRUCT. DWGS.

STEEL PLATE AWNING, GALVANIZED AND PAINTED
SLOPE 1/8" PER FOOT DOWN TO EDGE, MIN.
GALVANIZED SHEET METAL FLASHING
SEAL TO WINDOW

CLEAR ANODIZED ALUMINUM WINDOW
WITH CLEAR INSULATING GLASS

GYP. BD., PAINTED

CONTINUOUS GALV. SHT. MTL. FLASHING
PREFINISHED CORRUGATED ALUMINUM PANEL
DOUBLE LAYER WATER
RESISTANT BARRIER
PLYWOOD SHEATHING, REFER
TO STRUCTURAL DRAWINGS
FIBERGLASS BATT INSULATION

FINISH FLOOR, REFER TO FLOOR PLAN
AND ROOM FINISH SCHEDULE
HYDRONIC SUBFLOOR SYSTEM

T/ SUB FLOOR

GYP. BD., PTD.

PLYWOOD SHEATHING, REFER
TO STRUCTURAL DRAWINGS
DOUBLE LAYER WATER
RESISTANT BARRIER
PREFINISHED CORRUGATED ALUMINUM PANEL
SELF-ADHESIVE BITUMINOUS
WATERPROOFING MEMBRANE

B/ SOFFIT

3/4" ALUMINUM REVEAL / DRIP
PREFINISHED FLAT ALUMINUM PANEL
THREE COAT STUCCO SYSTEM
SMOOTH FINISH, INTEGRAL COLOR
ALUMINUM SLIDING GLASS POCKET DOOR
ASSEMBLY WITH CLEAR INSULATE GLASS
EXTENT OF POCKET
THREE COAT STUCCO SYSTEM
SMOOTH FINISH, INTEGRAL COLOR

3/8" STONE TILE
1/4" MORTAR BED
1/4" BACKER BOARD
SUBFLOOR SYSTEM

CONTINUOUS GALV. SHT. MTL. FLASHING
3/8" STONE TILE
1/4" MORTAR BED
T/ SUBFLOOR

CONCRETE SLAB, REFER TO STRUCT. DWGS.
GRAVEL BACKFILL
ASPHALT IMPREGNATED DRAINAGE
PROTECTION BOARD
VOLTEX WATERPROOFING
INSTALL PER MFR'S DIRECTIONS

section details

05

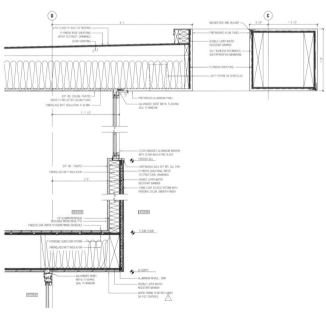

section details

left, and above the succinct exterior
details unite a carefully chosen palette
of austere materials: corrugated metal,
concrete fiber board sheathing, and prefinished aluminum panels

basement level

first floor

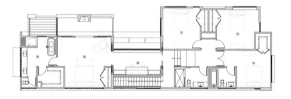

second floor

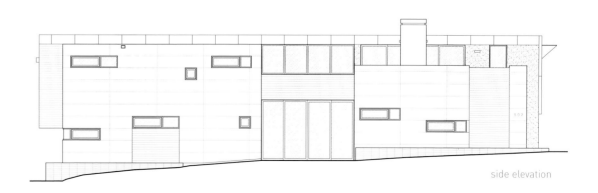

side elevation

WILD OAK RESIDENCE

YEAR OF COMPLETION 2008
LOCATION Los Angeles, California
SIZE 3,680 square feet (including garage)
PHOTOGRAPHY Annika Lundvall: 01, 05, 06, 07, 08; Claudio Santini: 02, 03, 04

Seemingly poised to take flight, this Los Feliz residence features a private bridge at the main entrance and cantilevered living spaces. Telescoping steel decks extend beyond the building face, providing additional vantage points from which to enjoy the abundant views of the city and canyons below. The machine-like steel structure is delicately clad with anodized aluminum and stucco panels which seem to peel away to embrace the stair and bridge. Walls of glass on the north and west elevations visually connect the interior with the surrounding natural landscape and highlight the 'Hollywood' sign situated across the adjacent canyon. The terraced patio, sundeck and deep blue pool are encircled by clusters of agave and forests of bamboo, punctuated by the dramatically cantilevered cabana and guesthouse.

right anthracite-colored flooring surfaces
provide a gracious basis from which the
white walls and extensively glazed walls
effortlessly arise

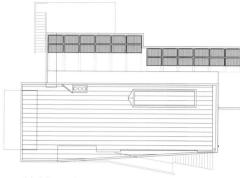

third floor plan

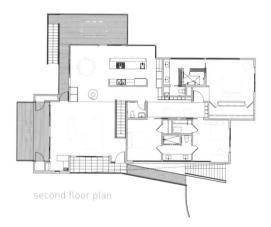

second floor plan

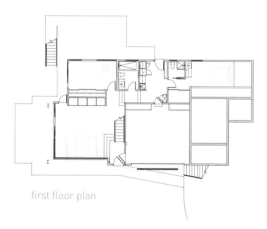

first floor plan

KUHLHAUS 01

YEAR OF COMPLETION 2007
LOCATION Manhattan Beach, California
SIZE 2,200 square feet (including garage)
PHOTOGRAPHY John MacLean

A counter-attack on the developer supplied housing stock where the norm for the single family residence is driven by the mentality that "bigger is better"; Kuhlhaus 01 experiments with redefining the prototype for housing in the area. Located on a half lot with a floor area of under 1800 SF, the three bedroom, three bath residence incorporates an open design with flexible living spaces to mitigate the smaller floor plates. Expanses of floor to ceiling glass provide breathtaking 270-degree views of the Pacific Ocean. The project also integrates a 2 KW array of photovoltaic modules that will supply 100% of required electricity for the home.

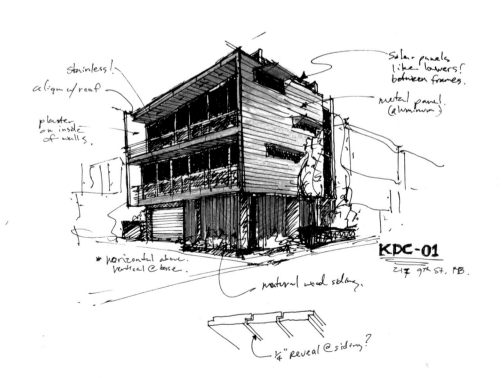

left, above the open living/kitchen/dining zone flows around the suspended fireplace
left, below the bedroom opens directly to a relaxing tub right the spaces open dramatically toward the ocean view

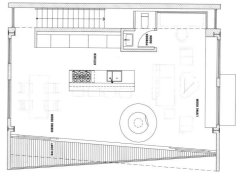

second floor plan

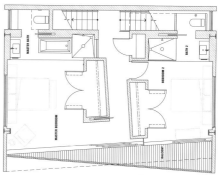

first floor plan

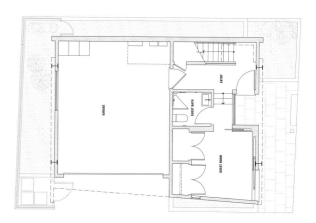

basement plan

LEHRER ARCHITECTS

Michael B. Lehrer

www.lehrerarchitects.com

Lehrer Architects LA has won over major 50 design awards since 1996, including honor awards from the national, state, and local chapters of The American Institute of Architects. His Studio was bestowed the Institute Honor Award for Interior Architecture in 2008, the top annual award for architecture in the United States, as well as top awards from the International Interior Design Association, the AIA California Council, AIA LA, the Los Angeles Business Council, Contract Magazine, and Builder Magazine, among others. In 2004, his James M. Wood Community Center received the Business Week/Architectural Record Award from the AIA; the AIA Housing Award was given to Norton-Towers-On-the-Court; and Temple Bat Yahm received The Interfaith Forum on Religion, Art, and Architecture / Faith and Form Magazine / AIA Award. In 2001, the Downtown Drop-In Center won the Institute Honor Award of the American Institute of Architects, as well.

The recently completed Water + Life Museums in Hemet, designed with Mark Gangi, AIA, has been certified by the United States Green Building Council as the first LEED™ Platinum museum in the world. The $35 Million Phase I project, including buildings and landscape, is an energy efficiency showcase, featuring a 550 kilowatt photovoltaic rooftop installation. The Museums have won Honor Awards from AIA California Council, Los Angeles and Pasadena Foothill Chapters, among others. Metropolitan Home magazine included it among its "Design 100, Best Designs in the World for 2008". The Chicago Athenaeum: Museum of Architecture and Design and The European Centre for Architecture Art Design and Urban Studies and Metropolitan Arts awarded them the American Architecture Award in 2008 and the Green Good Design Award in 2009. They have also won the Beyond Green 2007 High Performance Building Award from the Sustainable Building Industry Council, and the Pacific Coast Builder's Conference, Gold Nugget Award for the Best Sustainable Commercial Buildings.

Michael's work has been widely published nationally and internationally and he is regularly called upon to comment about design matters in national and local broadcast media, print, panels and symposia to explain the public interest from the architect's perspective. This includes Architectural Digest, Architectural Record, Business Week, Azure, Builder Magazine, Metropolitan Home, NPR's Weekend Edition, All Things Considered, KCRW's Which Way L.A.?, The LA Times, The New York Times, The Chicago Tribune, Hong Kong's avant garde Hinge Magazine, among many others.

MUSEUM OF WATER AND LIFE

YEAR OF COMPLETION 2007
LOCATION Hemet, California
SIZE 70,000 square feet on 15 acres
DESIGN PARTNER Mark Gangi, AIA
PHOTOGRAPHY Benny Chan (Fotoworks)

The challenge here was to design an engaging museum campus that celebrates the link between Southern California's water infrastructure and the evolution of life. Phase 1 of the campus includes two museums, laboratories, classrooms, administrative offices, support facilities, gift shop, café, and interpretive/educational landscape. Phase 2 includes outdoor amphitheatre, front and courtyard water features, two auditoriums, and canal.

A crisp, modern design concept envelops the 17-acre campus, whose indoor and outdoor spaces mingle within the framework of airy floor plans and endless window walls. The two sister museums—The Center for Water Education and Western Center for Archaeology and Paleontology—are striking mélanges of metal and glass at the eastern entrance to Diamond Valley Lake.

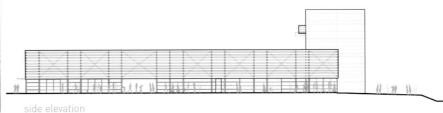

side elevation

above the stoic tower elements of the
approach elevation recall archaic architectural
forms while at the same time employing
contemporary materials and technologies
right shaded colonnades frame the entrance
plaza from which both museum wings are
accessed

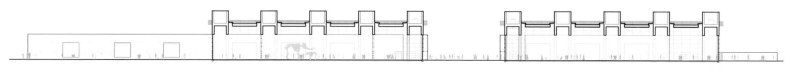

north south section

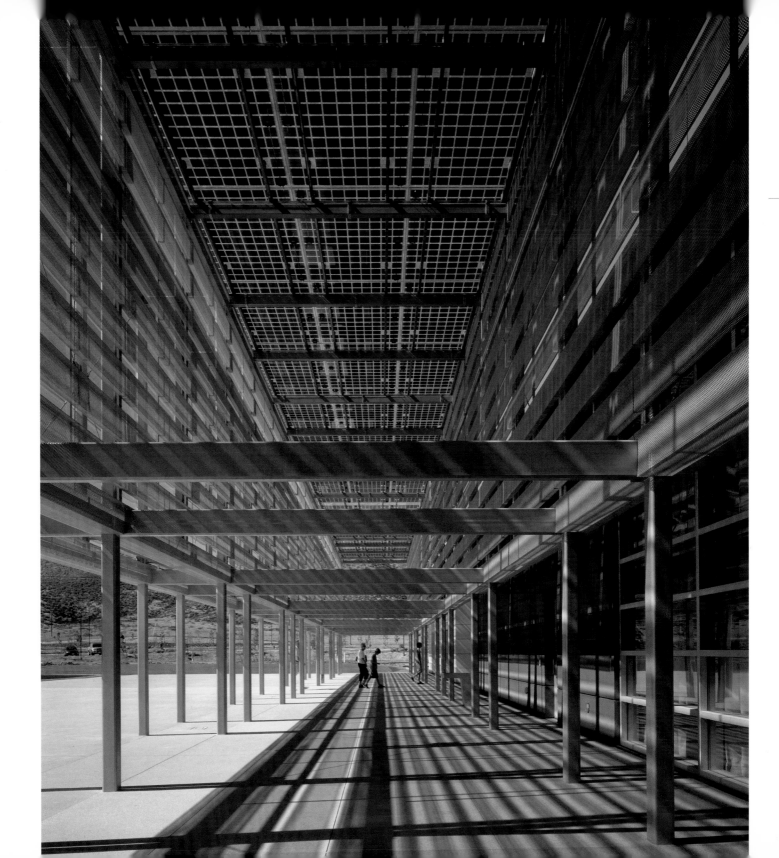

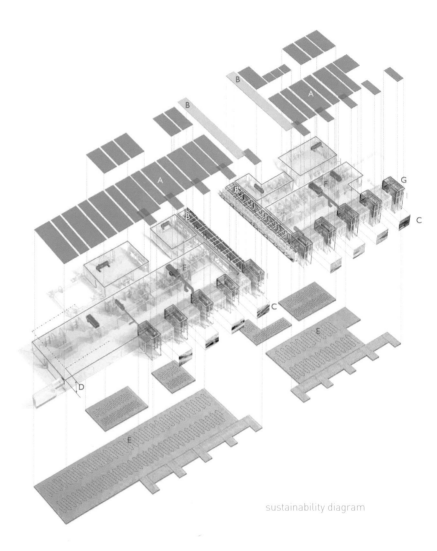

sustainability diagram

A **PHOTOVOLTAICS + INSULATION**
A rooftop photovoltaic array of 3,000 panels produces 540 kilowatts. It also shades the roof and will prolong the life of the rof covering by about 25%. The system will provide a projected savings over buildings lifespan of about $13 million.

B **PHOTOVOLTAICS + SHADING DEVICE**
Special photovoltaic panels - square silicon wafers in clear glass - produce shade as dappled light over formal loggia (B')

C **SHADING DEVICE**
Translucent banners shade the east facade to mitigate heat radiation.

D **DISTANCE BETWEEN PV AND ROOF**
The distance between the roof and the photovoltaic panels works as a climate zone to keep the roof from overheating.

E **RADIANT HEATING + COOLING**
A radiant heating and coolign floor system is found throughout the building.

F **MINIMAL FORCED AIR UNITS**
Minimal forced air units work in conjunction with radiant heating/cooling.

G **INSULATION**
Thick wall insulation mitigates cooling loss to exterior.

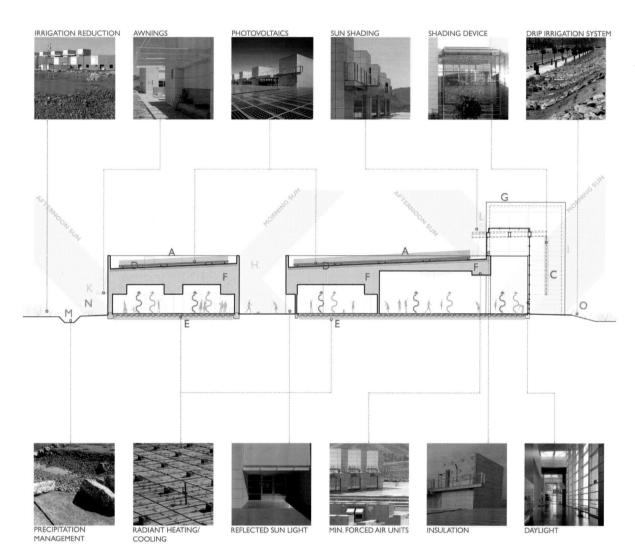

IRRIGATION REDUCTION AWNINGS PHOTOVOLTAICS SUN SHADING SHADING DEVICE DRIP IRRIGATION SYSTEM

PRECIPITATION MANAGEMENT   RADIANT HEATING/COOLING   REFLECTED SUN LIGHT   MIN. FORCED AIR UNITS   INSULATION   DAYLIGHT

H REGLECTED SUN LIGHT
   Reflected sun light provides ambient natural light in offices while overhangs reduce solar heat gain.

I DAYLIGHT
   High-performance glass curtain wall contributes to 75% of building being daylit.

K AWNINGS
   Awnings on west facade protect from afternoon sun.

L SUN SHADING
   Roof overhang and catwalk provide sun shading for western clerestory

M IRRIGATION REDUCTION
   A radiant heating and cooling floor system is found throughout the building.

N DRIP IRRIGATION SYSTEM
   Native rocks and grasses are sustained by a state-of-the-art drip irrigation system using reclaimed water

F PREVIPITATION MANAGEMENT
   On site precipitation management via rocky swales recreate natures braided streams.

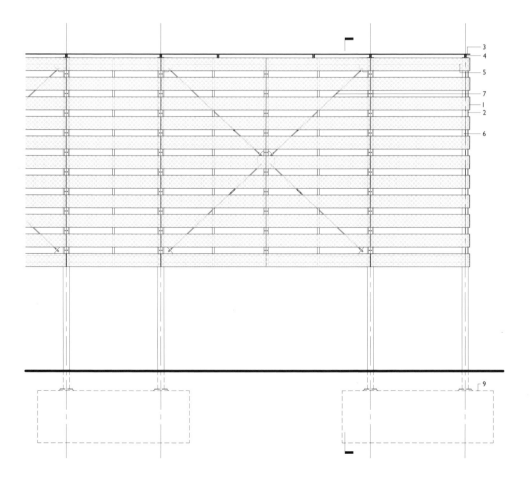

1 12" PERFORATED METAL SLATS WITH 1 1/2" RETURN TOP AND BOTTOM - ATTACH TO ALUMINUM CHANNEL W/ SELF-TAPPING SCREWS @ EA. END

2 2" x 2" x 1/8" THICK ALUMINUM CHANNEL EXTRUSION - ATTACH TO TUBE STEEL W/ SELF-TAPPING SCREWS @ 2'-0" O.C. VERT.

3 1/4" LAMINATED CLEAR BUILDING INTEGRATED PHOTOVOLTAIC PANELS W/ RUBBER H-GASKETS BETWEEN PANELS - ATTACH TO UNISTRUT RAILS W/ BOLTS & RUBBER WASHERS

4 P1001 UNISTRUT RAILS - ATTACH TO TUBE STEEL W/ SELF-TAPPING SCREWS

5 4" x 6" x 3/16" PAINTED TUBE STEEL BEAM

6 6" x 6" x 1/4" PAINTED TUBE STEEL COLUMN

7 1/2" DIA. ROD BRACING W/ CLEVIS AT EACH END FOR ATTACHMENT TO 1/2" THICK GUSSET PLATES

8 EXTERIOR UPLIGHTING - ATTACH TO TUBE STEEL BEAM FACE & CONCEAL CONDUIT INSIDE BEAM

9 4'-0" THICK CONCRETE FOOTINGS

10 4" THICK CONCRETE COURTYARD PAVING

11 4" ARCHITECTURAL GRAVEL

LEHRER ARCHITECTS OFFICE

YEAR OF COMPLETION 2005
LOCATION Los Angeles, California
SIZE 7,300 square feet
PHOTOGRAPHY Benny Chan (Fotoworks)

An existing buiding was readapted into a working space of light, air, and transparency. The project included succinct interventions, such as blowing out the southern wall, creating 4'x8' work surfaces of white-painted solid core doors, finishing floors with epoxy, installing off-the-shelf storage systems, painting a dramatic red line along the floor to resolve the trapezoidal shape of the space, and creating a strategic landscape design. The total cost of $20 per square foot encompasses the mechanical/electrical/data/ telephone infrastructure, garden, and build-out of all work surfaces.

Although the office would specifically house architects, the architects designed a multipurpose working space that simply and clearly honors the rudiments of work: vast work surfaces, massive natural light, seamless connections to the landscape and fresh air, generous storage, and clearly individuated workstations that add up to a coherent, palpable group.

Upon entering the office, process and product become one. The visitor is immediately drawn into the architecture—which is about the beauty of making architecture. The space succeeds as an open, collaborative working lab for creative design.

In addition to the creation of meaningful architecture, the office is host to community events, drawing classes, and municipal design reviews. The innovative design of this adaptive-reuse project has garnered a long list of accolades and awards including the 2008 Institute Honor Award for Interior Architecture from the national organization of The American Institute of Architects.

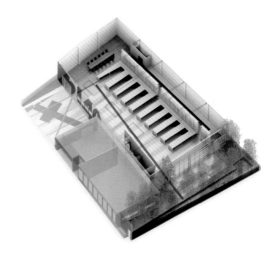

SANTA MONICA CANYON RESIDENCE

YEAR OF COMPLETION 2010
LOCATION Santa Monica, California
SIZE 13,000 square feet on 1 acre

The Canyon Residence is a long-term collaboration between architect and client. Originally conceived as a dining-room addition to an existing single-family home, the project has evolved throughout the course of many years of design and refinement to encompass an entirely new, ground-up residence.

Situated in a shady canyon, the project site and the client's desire to preserve key aspects of the wooded landscape have had a considerable influence on the building design.

A number of significant trees dot the site (including a 100-foot-tall California Sycamore), thereby limiting the extent of the building footprint, while the client's extensive garden stretches the length of the rear property.

Working within these constraints while taking advantage of the expansive site and garden, the architects organized the building around two planes: the horizontal plinth of the garden patio that extends the private garden into the living spaces of the ground floor; and the vertical datum wall or spine that connects and organizes the various parts of the building program.

Spaces that abut and traverse the spine create openings within the wall, framing views and vistas of the site and garden.

Just as the project has been a true working relationship with the client, the residence has served as a working tool for Lehrer Architects to explore ideas, materials, and complex building systems. Currently under construction, the steel-frame structure will be clad in 1/8"- thick stainless-steel rain-screen panels with expanses of sliding glass walls to open out to the garden and walkable skylights to open up to the sky.

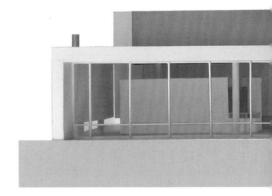

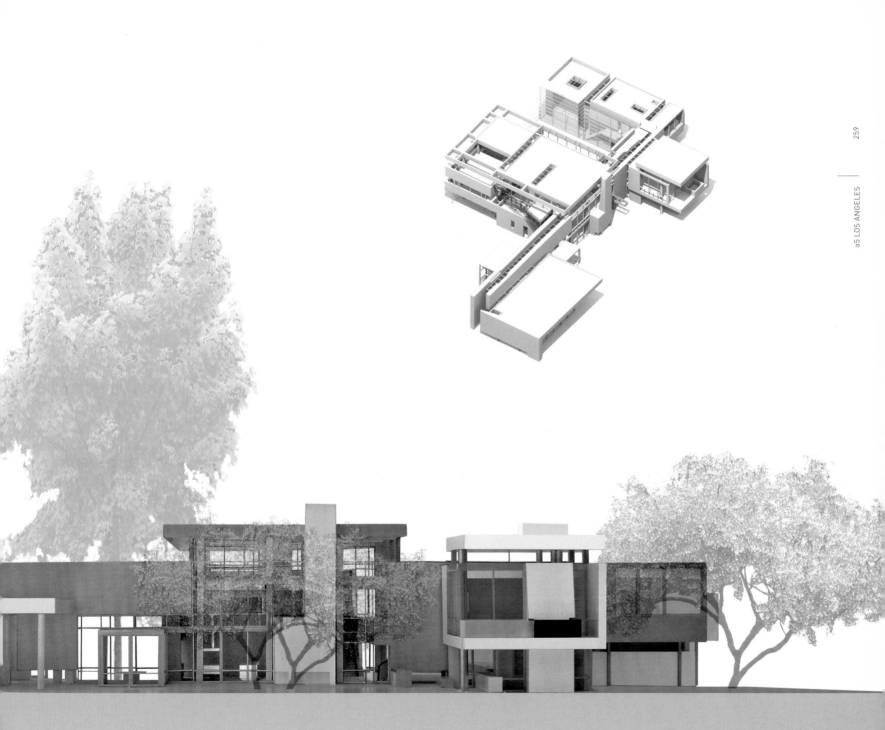

MARMOL RADZINER

www.marmol-radziner.com

Leo Marmol and Ron Radziner

Leo Marmol, FAIA, and Ron Radziner, FAIA, formed their partnership in 1989, launching a unique design-build practice led by architects. Since its inception, the Los Angeles-based firm has developed a growing reputation for its innovative design approach, research and precision in applying construction standards. The firm's unique business practice and commitment to design excellence was rewarded with the honor of being named the American Institute of Architects California Council's 2004 Firm of the Year. In 2007, both Marmol and Radziner were elevated to the prestigious College of the Fellows of the American Institute of Architects.

By adopting the role of the traditional "master builder", the company integrates design services with a range of construction capabilities. The central tenet of the company is design excellence, achieved through careful control of every step in the design and construction process, as well as active collaboration with clients. The firm's projects strive to provide a unique architectural identity and build connections between indoor and outdoor spaces.

Today, a breadth of projects distinguishes the firm, from small, intimately scaled residential projects to large public and community urban proposals. Residential projects include those for Tom Ford, Creative Director of Gucci and Yves Saint Laurent in Los Angeles, London, Paris and Santa Fe, fashion designer John Ward and jewelry designer Chan Luu in Rustic Canyon, and a private residence Altamira Ranch in Rancho Palos Verdes. The practice's commercial and civic projects include The Accelerated School in South Central Los Angeles, TreePeople Center for Community Forestry, TBWA\Chiat\Day ad agency's San Francisco offices, and the Costume National fashion retail store, Los Angeles.

The firm has developed a particular design-build expertise in restoring modern architectural icons in Southern California. Established as a leader in the field of architectural restoration, the firm's work includes the Kaufmann House in Palm Springs, originally designed by legendary architect Richard Neutra in 1946. For the firm's meticulous restoration, it was honored with awards from the American Institute of Architects and The California Preservation Foundation.

PALMS RESIDENCE

YEAR OF COMPLETION 2008
LOCATION Venice, California
SIZE 2,800 square feet (14 modules)
PHOTOGRAPHY David Lena

The Palms Residence is located on a narrow, urban lot in Venice, CA. The home looks inward, incorporating covered decks and a small courtyard space, giving the structure a sense of privacy despite its location on an infill lot. Comprised of 14 modules, the 2800 square foot house includes 3 bedrooms, 2.5 baths, a living room/dining room, a double height kitchen with an operable skylight, an office, and 700 additional square feet of outdoor living space. Large expanses of glass on the southern side of the structure fill the home with natural light and connect the interior and exterior spaces.

The home includes custom walnut casework in the living room and kitchen, concrete floors on the first floor, and eco-timber hickory floors on the second floor. The bed rooms have built-in beds and additional casework.

The exterior of the home is finished with cedar siding. A series of screening techniques, including landscaping, fencing, and louvered panels provide shelter from the street while retaining the open feel of the home.

The home includes a variety of green features including, a recycled steel frame, Structural Insulated Panels (SIPS), Triple-Pane insulating glass, eco-friendly materials, Energy Star-rated appliances, and natural cooling features. The home was produced in the MRP factory, substantially reducing the environmental impact of its construction.

left the street elevation imbues modest elegance right prefabricated modules were delivered to site and hoisted into place in just a few hours

left delivery and mounting of the prefabricated steel modules
right construction detail illustrating the connection joints between the modules at rooftop, first, and ground levels

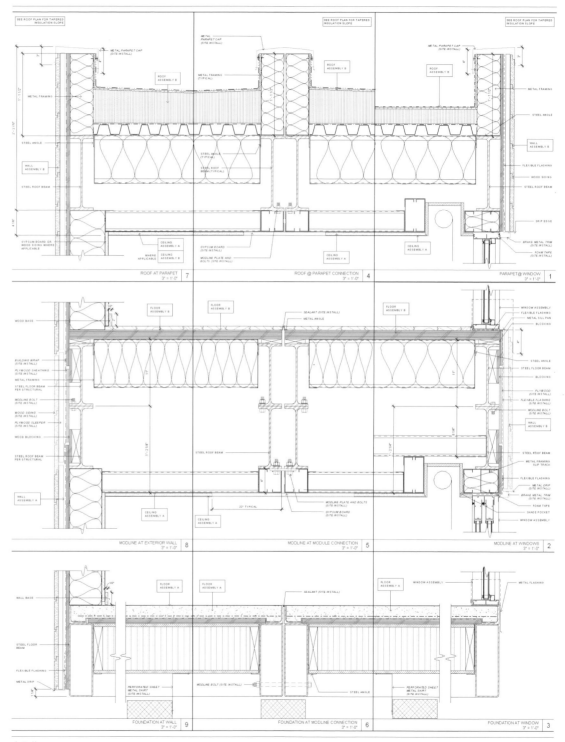

SEE ROOF PLAN FOR TAPERED INSULATION SLOPE

SEE ROOF PLAN FOR TAPERED INSULATION SLOPE

SEE ROOF PLAN FOR TAPERED INSULATION SLOPE

METAL PARAPET CAP (SITE INSTALL)

METAL PARAPET CAP (SITE INSTALL)

METAL PARAPET CAP (SITE INSTALL)

ROOF ASSEMBLY B

METAL FRAMING (TYPICAL)

ROOF ASSEMBLY B

ROOF ASSEMBLY B

METAL FRAMING

METAL FRAMING

STEEL ANGLE

WALL ASSEMBLY B

STEEL ANGLE

STEEL ANGLE (TYPICAL)

WALL ASSEMBLY B

FLEXIBLE FLASHING

STEEL ROOF BEAM (TYPICAL)

WOOD SIDING

STEEL ROOF BEAM

STEEL ROOF BEAM

DRIP EDGE

GYPSUM BOARD OR WOOD SIDING WHERE APPLICABLE

CEILING ASSEMBLY A

GYPSUM BOARD (SITE INSTALL)

CEILING ASSEMBLY A

BRAKE METAL TRIM (SITE INSTALL)

WHERE APPLICABLE

CEILING ASSEMBLY B

MODLINE PLATE AND BOLTS (SITE INSTALL)

CEILING ASSEMBLY A

FOAM TAPE (SITE INSTALL)

| ROOF AT PARAPET 7 | ROOF @ PARAPET CONNECTION 4 | PARAPET @ WINDOW 1 |
| 3" = 1'-0" | 3" = 1'-0" | 3" = 1'-0" |

WOOD BASE

FLOOR ASSEMBLY B

FLOOR ASSEMBLY B

SEALANT (SITE INSTALL)

FLOOR ASSEMBLY B

WINDOW ASSEMBLY

METAL ANGLE

FLEXIBLE FLASHING

METAL SILL PAN

BLOCKING

BUILDING WRAP (SITE INSTALL)

PLYWOOD SHEATHING (SITE INSTALL)

METAL FRAMING

STEEL FLOOR BEAM PER STRUCTURAL

MODLINE BOLT (SITE INSTALL)

WOOD SIDING (SITE INSTALL)

PLYWOOD SLEEPER (SITE INSTALL)

WOOD BLOCKING

STEEL ANGLE

STEEL FLOOR BEAM

BLOCKING

PLYWOOD (SITE INSTALL)

FLEXIBLE FLASHING

MODLINE BOLT (SITE INSTALL)

WALL ASSEMBLY B

STEEL ROOF BEAM PER STRUCTURAL

STEEL ROOF BEAM

STEEL ROOF BEAM

METAL FRAMING SLIP TRACK

FLEXIBLE FLASHING

METAL DRIP (SITE INSTALL)

WALL ASSEMBLY A

MODLINE PLATE AND BOLTS (SITE INSTALL)

22" TYPICAL

GYPSUM BOARD (SITE INSTALL)

CEILING ASSEMBLY A

CEILING ASSEMBLY A

BRAKE METAL TRIM (SITE INSTALL)

FOAM TAPE

SHADE POCKET

WINDOW ASSEMBLY

| MODLINE AT EXTERIOR WALL 8 | MODLINE AT MODULE CONNECTION 5 | MODLINE AT WINDOWS 2 |
| 3" = 1'-0" | 3" = 1'-0" | 3" = 1'-0" |

WALL BASE

FLOOR ASSEMBLY A

FLOOR ASSEMBLY A

SEALANT (SITE INSTALL)

FLOOR ASSEMBLY A

WINDOW ASSEMBLY

METAL FLASHING

STEEL FLOOR BEAM

FLEXIBLE FLASHING

METAL DRIP

PERFORATED SHEET METAL SKIRT (SITE INSTALL)

MODLINE BOLT (SITE INSTALL)

STEEL ANGLE

PERFORATED SHEET METAL SKIRT (SITE INSTALL)

| FOUNDATION AT WALL 9 | FOUNDATION AT MODLINE CONNECTION 6 | FOUNDATION AT WINDOW 3 |
| 3" = 1'-0" | 3" = 1'-0" | 3" = 1'-0" |

details

KITCHEN

LAUNDRY

WASHROOM

LIVING ROOM

OUTDOOR
LIVING

CARPORT

DINING ROOM

first floor plan

MASTER
WASHROOM

BEDROOM

BEDROOM

MASTER
BEDROOM

OFFICE

OUTDOOR
LIVING

second floor plan

far left the cabinetry details throughout provide a common aesthetic and functional thread for the diverse spaces left the ground floor recess and covered terrace on the upper level create appreciated indoor/outdoor spaces

VIENNA WAY RESIDENCE

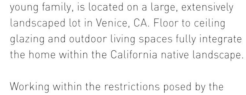

YEAR OF COMPLETION 2007
LOCATION Venice, California
SIZE 4,554 square feet
PHOTOGRAPHY Joe Fletcher

The Vienna Way residence, designed for a young family, is located on a large, extensively landscaped lot in Venice, CA. Floor to ceiling glazing and outdoor living spaces fully integrate the home within the California native landscape.

Working within the restrictions posed by the narrow site, the design divides the lot into thirds, with the two main volumes placed on the exterior edges of the property, bridged by a sunken kitchen in the center. The one-story structure to the south houses a great room that combines formal living and dining areas. The structure begins in the front of the property and flows into an outdoor dining patio. A large expanse of glass along the east provides a visual and spatial link to the pool area.

The northern structure runs from the back of the property forward, also leading to an outdoor living area, and contains more casual, private spaces, including a family room and an office on

the first floor and bedrooms on the second floor. Glazing along the second-story hallway offers views of the green roof (above the kitchen) and tree tops below.

The kitchen acts as the hub of the residence, connecting the public and private areas and providing views of the pool, side yard and rear property. From the exterior, the kitchen is shaped by a bronze box that emphasizes its significance and provides contrast to the plaster façade found on the main volumes of the residence.

In addition to bridging the two main volumes, the kitchen is the center of a water-related area that starts in front with a swimming pool and flows through the kitchen and over its green roof, and continues in the backyard's riparian landscape planted with rushes, reeds, and sycamore trees. These plantings give way to a large play yard filled with buffalo grass and surrounded by Oak trees and other California native plants.

left the juxtaposed building masses of this residence are united by the pool, that serves as lap pool, reflecting pond, and passive cooling element

left a decisive palette of natural materials
was used throughout the residence, in
keeping with Southern California modern
tradition wood was used not only for
cabinets, shelves, and wall panels, but also
as a ceiling sheathing material

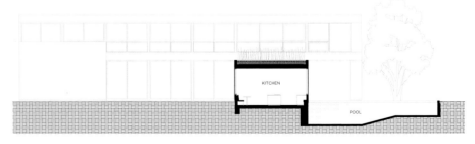

KITCHEN

POOL

east-west section

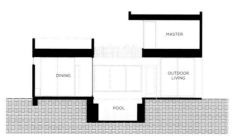

north section

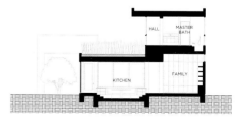

south section

THE ACCELERATED SCHOOL (TAS)

YEAR OF COMPLETION 2004
LOCATION South Los Angeles, California
SIZE 131,000 square feet
PHOTOGRAPHY Benny Chan (Fotoworks)

In 1993 two young teachers, working in the Los Angeles Unified School District, saw firsthand the need for a stronger public education initiative. Together they created the vision of The Accelerated School (TAS), located in South Central Los Angeles. Through new charter school legislation and the commitment to better education, the school opened its doors for 50 pre-school children in the fall of 1994. For three years the school operated in the social hall of a local church, having to store all of its classroom furniture, equipment, and fixtures in a storage closet every Friday to make room for the church's weekend activities.

Six years after the instigation of TAS, the fledgling idea has become an expanding reality. The school now has a permanent residence thanks in part to the donation of a site by clothing designer, Carole Little and her business partner Leonard Rabinowitz.

The Accelerated School currently has an enrollment of over 200 students in Kindergarten through eighth grade, with a waiting list for perspective students over 1,000. The vision of the co-founders to expand to a pre-K to 12 institution is currently taking shape with the design of an 110,000 square foot facility by Marmol Radziner + Associates. The new facility will add three new buildings, providing classrooms, administrative, community, and outdoor recreation spaces for the projected 870 students and the community. Envisioned as much more than a school for multiple age groups, The Accelerated School re-defines inner-city education as a means to re-build urban communities in Los Angeles.

The Accelerated School serves as a model for new urban schools in Los Angeles, departing from typical urban school designs that require more acreage. Rather than single story buildings, a concept reflective of 1950s suburban planning standards, TAS is a series of medium-rise structures interconnected by covered circulation paths. Generous outdoor terrace spaces, exterior circulation, and translucent materials take advantage of the temperate Southern California climate and ensure an abundance of natural light.

Maximizing Available Land

Like most urban schools, a significant characteristic of The Accelerated School site is the lack of available open play and athletic spaces. In response to the confines of the site, TAS utilizes an "every space counts" philosophy. Every horizontal surface of the school is treated as an opportunity for walking, playing, or teaching. For example, all exterior circulation occurs on roof surfaces, and the basketball and volleyball courts are within the interior of the gymnasium, and on the roof. Access to the extensive roof areas requires an unusual number of staircases. Rather than hide the stairs in dark, interior shafts, they are sculptural additions integrated with the façade, thus serving a dual purpose of form and function.

The "every space counts" approach defines the whole building as a potential classroom. Different types of spaces, from extra-wide hallways, to terraces, to roofs, are envisioned as places for impromptu -or planned- gatherings for learning. A roof terrace may house science projects or provide a platform for viewing weather conditions; an exterior courtyard may be used for art class.

Providing A Center for the Community
Located on the corner of Martin Luther King Boulevard, The Accelerated School has the presence of a civic building. The design locates community spaces on the ground level to provide controlled access during school hours, after school hours and on weekends. Spaces such as the library, the gymnasium, the auditorium, and a health clinic are accessible and located in close proximity to school entrances and exits. Coupled with the desire to provide public access is an equally important concern with security. Controlled ground floor access and visible circulation corridors allow the School to serve the surrounding community while protecting students' safety.

A Holistic Approach to Education

A unique aspect of the Accelerated School is the combination of multiple age groups and learning levels into one educational institution. The co-founders are committed to providing long-term education to their pupils and the community. They believe that the strong community commitment produces stronger, smarter, and more community-oriented citizens. In addition, parental involvment is encouraged, and three hours of volunteer time per month is mandatory.

The architecture reflects this holistic approach to grade level education. The new building is anchored by the gymnasium on one end, and the Cal State Los Angeles Professional Development Center on the other end. Located at the corner intersection of Martin Luther King Boulevard and Main Street, the library and multi-purpose room acts as the pivot point for the two arms of the new building. Classrooms are organized in series of clusters for each grade level, with the high school and elementary school in opposite wings of the building. Shared spaces such as the music room, multi-purpose room, elementary art room, library and gymnasium are all located on the ground floor. The middle school and high school are located on the upper levels. For virtually every group of classrooms, there exists an exterior gathering space that creates an identity for each age group and provides an alternative teaching space. Teachers at The Accelerated School often hold class outdoors to relate lessons of environment, community and context to their students. These exterior areas allow multiple classes to interact and enjoy the outdoors.

A Public and Private Partnership

The Accelerated School is the only public charter school within LAUSD to operate on funding from private and public partnerships. It is also the first school in Los Angeles to combine charter status with the Accelerated School model, the national model of education created by Dr. Henry Levin of Stanford University.

Funding for TAS is divided in nearly equal parts by state bond proceeds, local bond proceeds, and private contributions from organizations such as Washington Mutual, Wells Fargo Bank, and the Weingart Foundation, among others. In addition, The Accelerated School has developed strong ties to the higher education system in Southern California, which also provides financial assistance. For example, the Cal State Los Angeles Charter School of Education will provide oversight and additional funding while maintaining administrative offices and a Development Center at the TAS site.

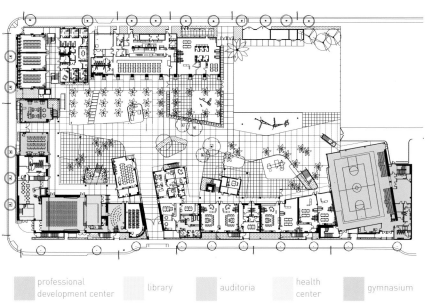

| | professional development center | | library | | auditoria | | health center | | gymnasium |

ground floor plan/spaces shared with community

far left the street-side elevation is characterized by fire stairs, and acts a a buffer to the classrooms behind it **left** the courtyard-side circulation network serves as a communicative space during recess **above** the floor plan illustrates how spaces were wrapped around the common courtyard to create a sense of community

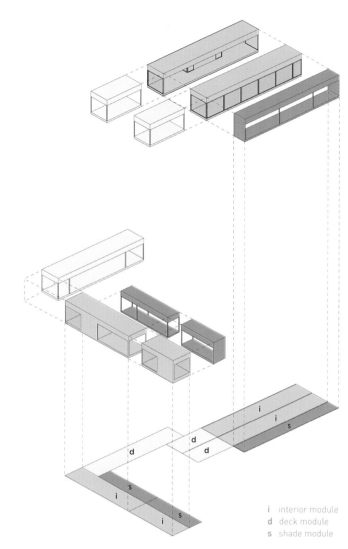

i interior module
d deck module
s shade module

axonometric

left, and right the prototypical Californian experience of desert living, established with legendary post-war homes of Palm Springs residences, was successfully readapted here to integrate contemporary prefab technologies

DESERT HOUSE

YEAR OF COMPLETION 2005
LOCATION Desert Hot Springs, California
SIZE 2,100 square feet (interior), 2,450 square feet (covered decks), 5 acres (site)
PHOTOGRAPHY Benny Chan

Marmol Radziner Prefab's prototype prefab home is oriented to best capture views of San Jacinto peak and the surrounding mountains. Located on a five-acre site in Desert Hot Springs, California, the house extends through the landscape with covered outdoor living areas, which double the 2000 square-foot interior spaces. A detached carport allows the owners to "leave the car behind" as they approach their home.

Designed for managing principal Leo Marmol, FAIA and his wife Alisa Becket, the house employs four prefabricated house modules and six prefabricated deck modules. Sheltered living spaces blend the indoors with the outdoors, simultaneously extending and connecting the house to the north wing, which holds a guest house and studio space. By forming an "L", the home creates a protected environment that includes a pool and fire pit.

The home is built with prefabricated technologies in a factory out of three basics types of modules: interior modules comprising the living spaces, exterior modules defining covered outdoor living areas, and sunshade modules providing protection from the sun. Using steel framing, twelve foot wide modules extend up to sixty four feet in length. The modules employ different types of cladding, including metal, wood, or glass, or are simply left open to the surrounding landscape. The steel moment frame construction is sustainable and durable, while allowing for maximum flexibility in creating large expanses of open space and glass.

The modules were fabricated in the factory and shipped to the site including many pre-installed finishes, such as the custom wood cabinets and polished concrete floors. The modules were

then craned on to the foundation, with minimal work remaining to complete the installation. As a prototype home, this house provided valuable design, fabrication, and installation lessons for the development of the Marmol Radziner Prefab's new line of modern prefab homes.

Just as the spaces of the home embrace nature, so too do the designs and methods of fabrication. The factory-made modules employ renewable and environmentally friendly materials. For example, the home is made from recycled steel rather than non-sustainable wood framing as the primary structural system. The home derives its electrical power from solar panels located on the roof above the bedroom. Deep overhangs shade the house from the harsh summer sun, and hidden pockets hold window shades that provide additional protection from the sun. In colder months, concrete floors absorb solar energy during the day and release the stored heat at night, helping to make the home sustainable. To increase insulation from the extensive fenestration, the home uses triple-pane, low-e, argon-filled insulating glass for the windows and glass doors. Because factory-construction provides greater precision in cutting materials and increases the ability to save and reuse excess material, the construction of the home created create significantly less waste than a home built on site.

Seeking to compliment the modern aesthetic of the architecture and the rustic beauty of the desert surroundings, the interior design reflects great esteem for nature and obscures distinctions between indoor and outdoor living spaces. By combining vintage, contemporary, and custom pieces, the home has a feel of understated elegance that highlights a connection to the earth.

MINARC

**Tryggvi Thorsteinsson
and Erla Dögg Ingjaldsdóttir**

www.minarc.com

Minarc is an award-winning Santa Monica-based design studio that specializes in modern, innovative, and sustainable architecture and design. Principals Erla Dögg Ingjaldsdóttir, Assoc. IIDA & AIA, and Tryggvi Thorsteinsson, Assoc. AIA, hail from Iceland, and take inspiration from the pure, austere beauty of their home country for all of their projects.

Founded by the duo in 1999, Minarc (the name is a play on "minimalism in architecture") has grown from a staff of two to over a dozen. Projects range from new construction to renovations; residential as well as commercial. All projects share an emphasis on blurring the line between indoors and out through the use of abundant natural light, outdoor living spaces, and framed views of nature. Innovation in use of materials is another hallmark of Minarc's designs. Warm, natural materials such as walnut, birch, and ipé are combined with cement panels, pebble stones, and recycled tires.

Fashion design by Helga Solrun

RAINBOW HOUSE

YEAR OF COMPLETION 2009
LOCATION Santa Monica, California
SIZE 3,900 square feet
PHOTOGRAPHY David Lena

This residence is a re-purposed 5-unit apartment building converted to a single-family residence by remodeling less than 50% of the existing structure. The simple, eco-conscious design focuses on functionality and creating a healthy family environment. The design elements are oriented to take optimum advantage of natural light and cross ventilation. Maximum use of natural light also helps to cut down electrical cost. An interior/exterior courtyard allows for natural ventilation as do the master sliding window and living room sliders.

The wood beams in the courtyard atrium were constructed using salvaged wood from original structure. The residence was constructed wholly without paint, tile, carpet, or AC/HV. Solar thermal radiant floor heating and solar thermal domestic water heating were utilized throughout. A heated patio and fireplace for outdoor dining maximizes indoor/outdoor living. The courtyard veranda and hammock chairs off the playroom further connect the indoors and outdoors. The floor materials are interconnected in an unobtrusive and whimsical manner to increase floor plan flow and spaciousness.

second floor plan

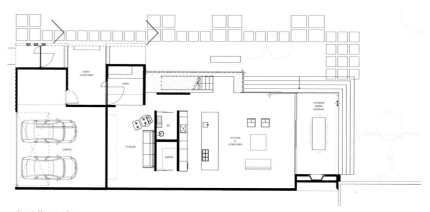

first floor plan

far left non-toxic materials and used furniture are foreseen throughout left view from entrance atrium into the main living level above the stair hovers above the floor cutout filled with blue pebbles that evoke water

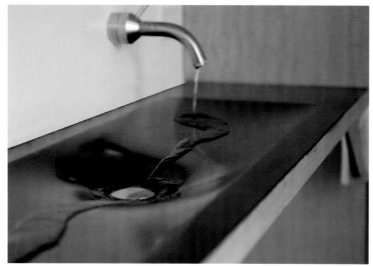

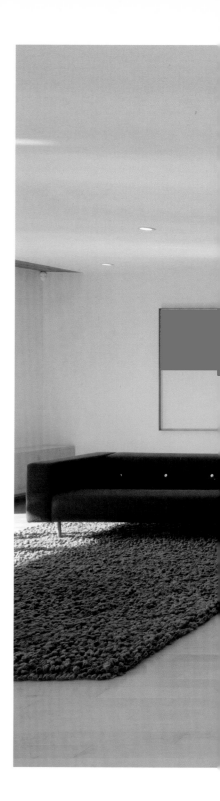

above master bathroom with custom-built
sink installation constructed of recycled
rubber right the cube-like kitchen island
incorporates built-in chairs

MINARC HOUSE

YEAR OF COMPLETION 2007
LOCATION West Los Angeles, California
SIZE 2600 square feet
PHOTOGRAPHY Ralf Seeburger, Brandon
Klein

This simple, eco-conscious design is focused on functionality and creating a family environment. The house is oriented on the site for optimum advantage of natural light and cross ventilation. A maximum use of natural light to cut down electrical cost. There was no use of chemicals, carpets, tiles or paint. Exterior panels of the home contain 30% recycled materials.

The design and use of color inspired by dramatic landscape to create contrasting stimulating interior. The orange (volcanic) kitchen island creates a multi-functional gathering point in the heart of the house. The blue (liquid rubber) staircase (waterfall) combines elements of strength and infinity. The use of black lava creates visual contrast and enhances the exteriors.

Material manufactured from recycled tires is used on kitchen cabinetry and kitchen chairs, creating an elegant kitchen unaffected by normal wear and tear of family life. Pebble stones on master bedroom balcony floor absorb the warmth of the sun creating a healthy reflexology surface beneficial for walking. There is also an outdoor sleeping area meant to encourage a healthy lifestyle.

second floor plan

first floor plan

left the living/dining space flows out to the covered exterior terrace, built in chairs are integrated into the kitchen island
right open stair treads rise to the parent's bedroom level, where an exterior sleeping terrace directly adjoins the master bedroom

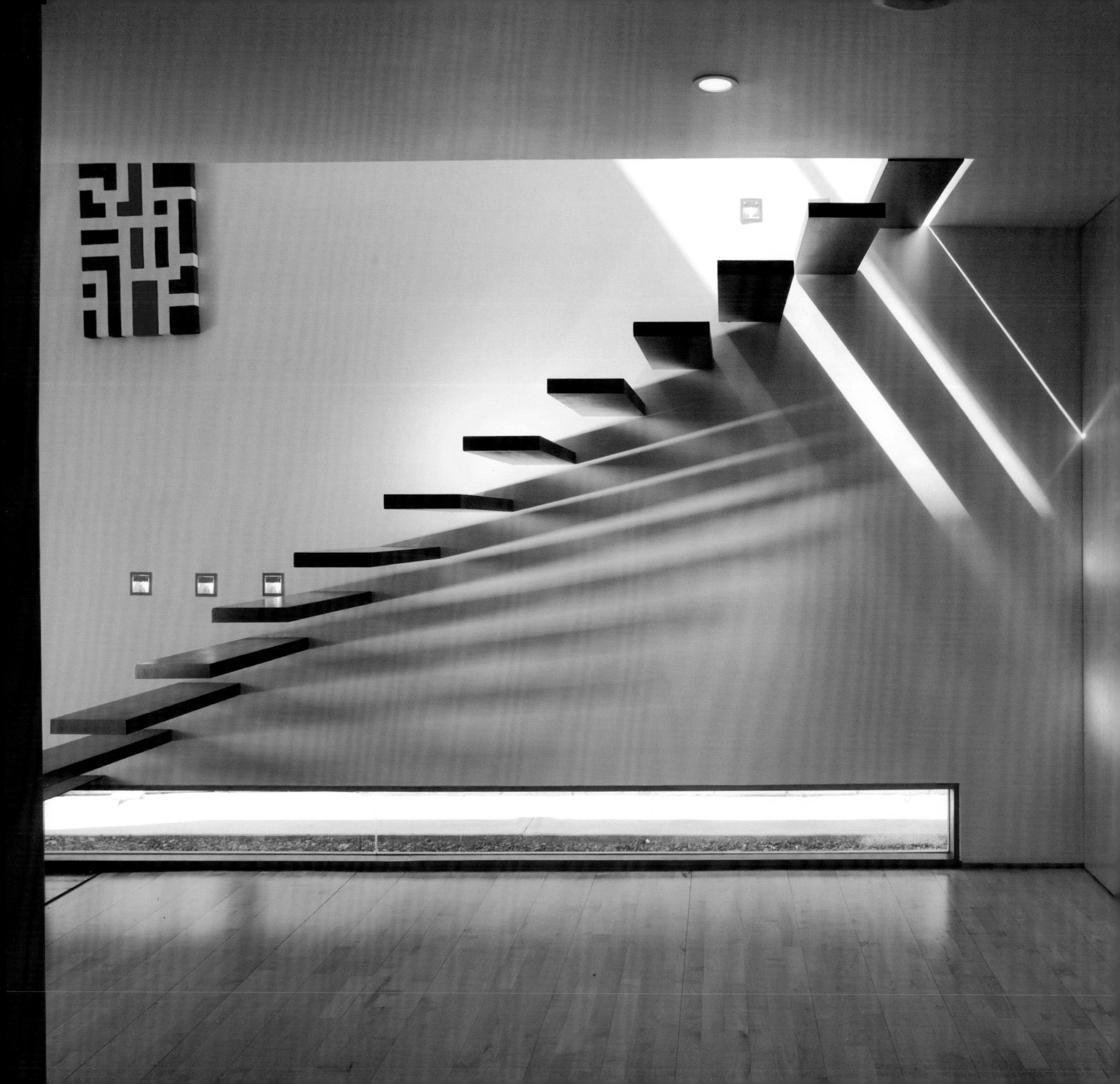

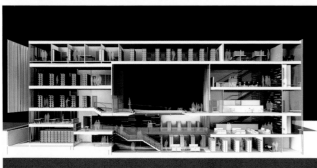

section

The building masses of this visionary library design were purposefully counterpoised to create a dynamic tension similar to the polarity of natural elements formative to Iceland, such as fire and ice

YEAR OF COMPLETION 2009 (design)
LOCATION Hafnarfjördur, Iceland
SIZE 33,500 square feet

Designed to expand and remodel the current public library in Reykjavik, Iceland, this project tries to become an important city landmark. The proposed design adheres to the established program which required expanding the Library from 1000 to over 3000 square meters, providing a wide variety of new services like: cafeteria, digital Information room, archived collection, music library and classrooms. The design rescues as much as possible from the Existent library, and envelops it with two new skins. The project integrates the surrounding community, framing views Of the town and the surrounding neighborhood, and attracts the society to engage in public activities like movie Screenings at the park. The library makes allusion to the city's official icon -the lighthouse- with its translucent walls That illuminate the city at night and allow panoramic views across town.

PATRICK TIGHE ARCHITECTURE

www.tighearchitecture.com

Patrick Tighe

Tighe Architecture is committed to creating an authentic, contemporary Architecture informed by technology, sustainability and building innovation. The work is not of style but of process – a process driven by influences such as site, environment, budget, society, and culture. Since the inception of Tighe Architecture, a strong and diverse body of projects has been realized that include city developed affordable housing, commercial, mixed use projects, civic art, installations and residences. The firm advocates a collaborative approach and has developed an extensive network of highly skilled consultants, artisans, and trades people.

Sustainability is an integral component in all the work as evidenced by The Sierra Bonita Mixed use Affordable Housing project for people living with disabilities. The building is now under construction and serves as a pilot for the City of West Hollywood's newly implemented Green Building Ordinance. Recently, Patrick Tighe Architecture completed the US headquarters for the UK based Moving Picture Company, (a division of Technicolor) located in downtown Santa Monica. Projects are now in development in Morocco, Asia and the Middle East.

Tighe Architecture has gained recognition for unique solutions that re-evaluate the way people inhabit their environments. The Firm has won several National AIA Honor Awards, American Architecture Awards, a progressive Architecture Award, Los Angeles Architecture Awards other awards include local AIA Honors. The work of Tighe Architecture has been published extensively appearing in Architectural Record, Architectural Digest, The LA Times Magazine, Interior Design, LA Architect, Form and Newsweek. The work has also been included in numerous architectural book compilations.

Projects have been realized in New York, Texas, Maine, Massachusetts, and many of the culturally diverse communities within the greater Los Angeles area. Tighe Architecture is located in Santa Monica, California.

MOVING PICTURE COMPANY

YEAR OF COMPLETION 2009
LOCATION Santa Monica, California
SIZE 8,700 square feet
PHOTOGRAPHY Art Gray Photography

The 7,800 square feet visual effects post-production facility is located within a generic office building in downtown Santa Monica, California. The Moving Picture Company is a UK based visual effects post production company, a forerunner in the visual effects and animation fields for the feature film, advertising, music and television industries. The facility serves as the United States Headquarters.

The company is highly regarded for its work in the field of color manipulation in film. With this in mind, the project explores the notion of light as it relates to color. The forms and patterns developed are produced using studies of light. Light is analyzed and modeled three dimensionally. Frames from the animation are chosen and layered to organize spatial qualities and movement throughout the office environment.

An organic, sinuous spine weaves its way through the suite. An appendaged soffit grows from the serpentine walls and serves as an armature for cable trays, mechanical and electrical systems. Light portals pierce the organic forms and are equipped with programmable LED lighting. Patterns derived from the animated studies are emblazoned onto the laser cut walls and circumscribe the interior.

Movement is expressed throughout the space in many ways. The lighting scheme reinforces the notion of movement. Groupings of LED lights penetrate the serpentine wall and emit color. The aluminum pieces are custom fabricated to house the LED fixtures. The housings are flush with the outside (public) face of the wall and protrude into the private rooms. The fixtures add texture and create a more intimate scale to the larger context. The lighting is programmable, offering various intensities and color options. The otherwise colorless scheme is ever changing as per the client's wishes.

Grading rooms, Edit bays, Conference rooms, open and closed offices, client areas, production spaces, entertaining areas, tape vault, mechanical rooms, machine rooms, exterior terraces and support spaces make up the program of the facility.

far left since the working and production spaces require no natural lighting, circulation occurs around the periphery of the urban fit out floor plan left, top the roof terrace offers views of the nearby Pacific and downtown Santa Monica

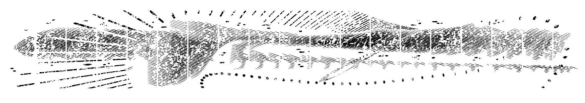

plan

above, and right graphic motives
abstracted from film work executed by
the client were projected onto metal
sunscreen panels and routed with CNC
technology

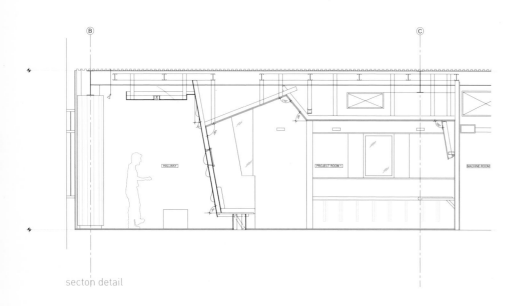

secton detail

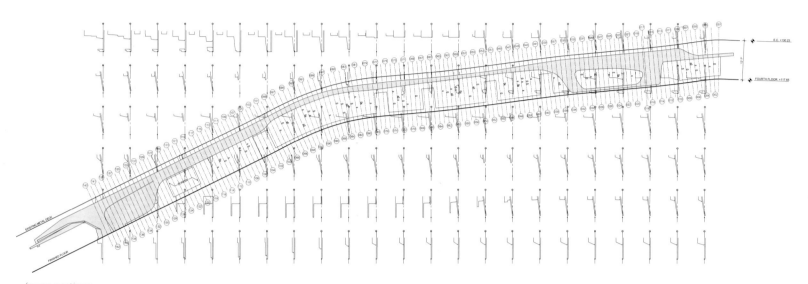

frame sections

left, and above the building contractor
convincingly met the challenge of precisely
forming the undulating wall and ceiling
surfaces where no two sections along the
length of the spatial installation are the
same

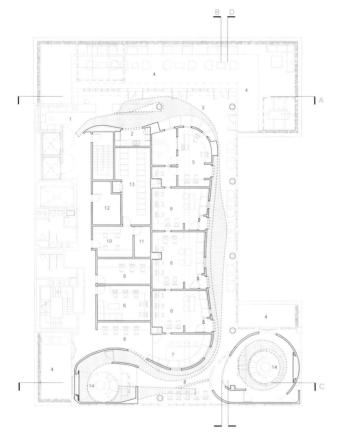

1 lobby
2 kitchen
3 common area
4 terrace
5 office
6 project room
7 conference room
8 open office
9 edit room
10 tape op room
11 scan
12 film/tape vault
13 machine room
14 grading room

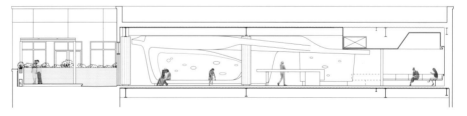

section

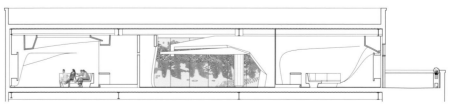

left the interior film production spaces
are accessed by an irregularly flowing
circulation spine above a niche carved
out of the interior core serves as a spatial
focus for the reception area

section

TIGERTAIL RESIDENCE

YEAR OF COMPLETION 2008
LOCATION Los Angeles, California
SIZE 3,500 square feet
PHOTOGRAPHY Art Gray Photography

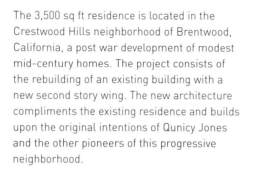

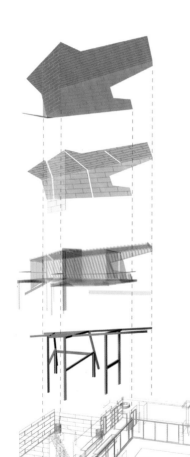

The 3,500 sq ft residence is located in the Crestwood Hills neighborhood of Brentwood, California, a post war development of modest mid-century homes. The project consists of the rebuilding of an existing building with a new second story wing. The new architecture compliments the existing residence and builds upon the original intentions of Qunicy Jones and the other pioneers of this progressive neighborhood.

The architecture is a direct result of the various conditions inherent within the site. The peculiar geometry of the second story volume is a result of the existing site conditions and the current building setback regulations. Openings to the views and the need for solid walls for shear and privacy were also factors that defined the building envelope.

The building is low and unassuming at the street and in keeping with the scale of the neighboring homes. The residence opens to the courtyard with walls of glass. A series of bent, steel moment frames straddle the existing one story structure and are expressed in the new architecture. The folded planes of the walls and

roof are an extension of the rolling topography of the hillside site. The folded planes are sheathed with interlocking metal panels. The interior is clad with wood, blurring the distinction between wall, ceiling and floor. Views are framed as the building projects outward to the city, the ocean and the neighboring Getty Center in the distance.

left, and right protective walls shield the bedoom toward the street and frame the aperture for the glazed wall that opens on to a view of the Crestwood Hills neighbourhood with many 50s homes by A. Quincy Jones, and the nearby Getty Center by Richard Meier

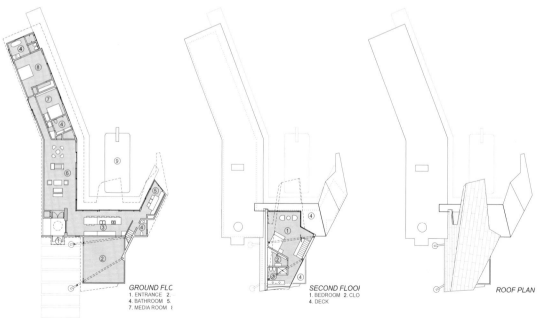

GROUND FLC
1. ENTRANCE 2.
4. BATHROOM 5.
7. MEDIA ROOM ¦

SECOND FLOOI
1. BEDROOM 2. CLO
4. DECK

ROOF PLAN

ground floor plan

second floor plan

roof plan

MOROCCO RESIDENCE

YEAR OF COMPLETION 2010 (design),
Construction begin 2011
LOCATION Skhirat, Morocco
SIZE 15,000 square feet

Located where the desert meets the Atlantic Ocean at the Northern tip of Africa, the Villa Skhirat is a sustainable, site-specific series of building components strategically placed within the spectacular seaside Moroccan landscape. The building is a continuation of the strata of the site. The natural forms of the reinforced concrete branch-like structure are expressed as strands that become surfaces. The structural filigree allows for Mosaics of light that emblazon the interior surfaces. The patterning of light changes throughout the day and from season to season.

The site is a 43 hectare parcel on the Moroccan coast located outside the town of Skhirat, 200 miles north of Casablanca. A stretch of dune separates the desert landscape from the ocean. The building pad is a plateau perched high above the coastline overlooking the rocky coast and

sandy beaches all seen within the 270 degree panoramic view. The Villa is a private residence. The program consists of a public reception hall, dining and media halls, the main residence, private guest quarters, parking structure, staff quarters, service areas, pool house, as well as the private living quarters. The building is a reinforced concrete frame with concrete floor plates. The building envelope consists of various surfaces both transparent and solid.

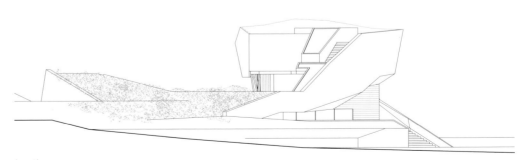

elevation

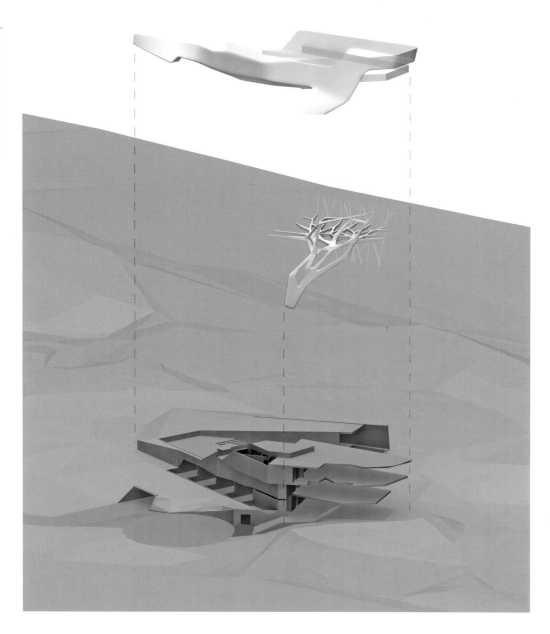

left, and right the natural forms of the reinforced concrete branch-like structure are expressed as strands that become surfaces

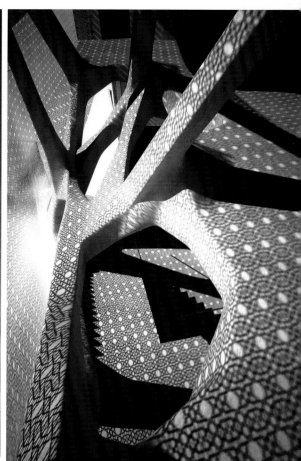

SIERRA BONITA AFFORDABLE HOUSING

YEAR OF COMPLETION 2010
LOCATION West Hollywood, California
SIZE 42,000 square feet

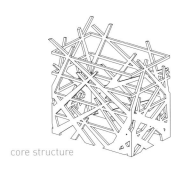

core structure

The Sierra Bonita Mixed Use Affordable Housing project is being constructed by the City of West Hollywood to address an affordable housing shortage for tenants living with disabilities. The mixed use program brings higher density into the urban core of the city. Locating the project within the central urban fabric of the community ensures that residents have direct access to local businesses and services. Multiple public transportation options are directly accessible on the busy transit corridor of Santa Monica Boulevard minimizing the need for private transportation.

The building demonstrates one of the city's core values of environmental responsibility and its commitment to green building and sustainable design by serving as the pilot project for the City of West Hollywood's new Green Building Ordinance.

The Sierra Bonita project takes advantage of the City of West Hollywood's mixed use development incentive and the State of California's affordable housing initiative. Through these two programs the project realized a 0.5 increase in FAR (floor/area ratio) bringing the project maximum FAR to 2.5. These incentives also allowed an additional story with a corresponding fifteen foot increase in height bringing the maximum building height to fifty feet and allowed for five stories.

The building contains 42 one bedroom residential units each of approximately 620 square feet. Commercial / Retail space is located along Santa Monica Boulevard at the ground level. Parking is provided at grade for retail use and for visitors.

Resident parking is located in the subterranean parking level. The living units are oriented along the north south axis. An outdoor courtyard provides a garden for residents from which access to the units is provided. Each apartment has its own private outdoor space (80 sq ft) with designated storage room. Common areas exist for the residents as well as for public use.

Sierra Bonita serves as the pilot project for the City of West Hollywood's green ordinance, which was passed in 2007. The arrangement of the proposed architectural scheme facilitates an environmentally conscious approach to the building services design. Passive solar design strategies are used and include: north south orientation for the living units; locating and orienting the building to control solar cooling loads; shaping and orienting the building for exposure to prevailing winds; designing windows to maximize daylight; minimizing west-facing glazing and designing units to maximize natural ventilation. A photovoltaic panel system is integrated into the façade and roof of the building that will supply most of the peak load electricity demand. The panels are integral to the building envelope and the unused solar electricity will be delivered to the grid. The building meets or exceeds all of the green ordinance requirements. Seventy-five percent of the construction and demolition waste will be recycled during construction.

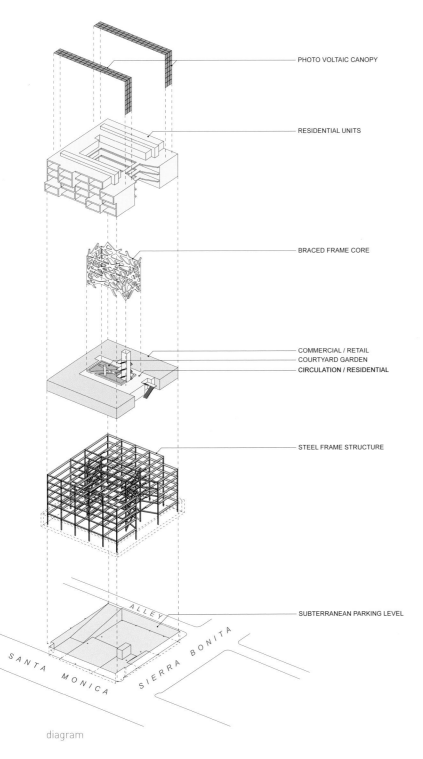

PHOTO VOLTAIC CANOPY

RESIDENTIAL UNITS

BRACED FRAME CORE

COMMERCIAL / RETAIL
COURTYARD GARDEN
CIRCULATION / RESIDENTIAL

STEEL FRAME STRUCTURE

SUBTERRANEAN PARKING LEVEL

ALLEY

SANTA MONICA   SIERRA BONITA

diagram

far left spatial abstraction of the
perforations for the core structure
left, diagram of the formative spatial
components below view on Santa
Monica Boulevard, courtyard circulation
impression

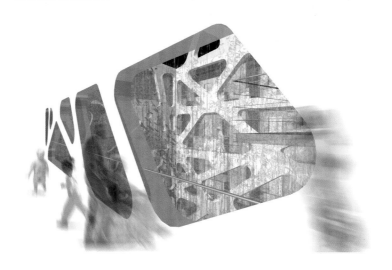

RANDALL STOUT ARCHITECTS, INC

www.stoutarc.com

Randall Stout

Randall Stout Architects, Inc. (RSA) is a Los Angeles-based architectural, interiors, planning, and urban design firm, with award winning national and international projects. Founded more than a decade ago, RSA has designed numerous buildings that are recognized as prominent architectural icons within and beyond their respective communities. Not only do they aesthetically embody the ethics and values of the clients they serve, but they also engage the public with uplifting forms and spaces that incite curiosity and respect.

RSA takes great care in creating forms that are inviting and artistic without being static. Light, shadow, form, and materials all contribute to shaping a dynamic architecture that heightens one's awareness of space and sense of discovery; the sequences of rooms and views emphasizes the experience of the building rather than the display of form. Users are not a passive audience on a stage but actors in their own unfolding space.

Although RSA's work is unquestionably contemporary in nature, it does not have a singular style. Instead, each project expresses the uniqueness of its each site, regional context, and client objectives. These expressions tend toward abstraction, allowing individual interpretation and meaning. Collectively, RSA buildings contain a narrative that expresses optimism about our culture, technology, and arts, evidencing their place in the 21st century.

Recognizing the interdependence of design innovation and functionality, RSA fields a highly talented team that methodically pursues creative design solutions. The materials used to realize these goals are often not exotic. With a proven expertise in executing complex and specialized projects, Randall Stout and the design team prefer to work in a "matter-of-fact" manner, using familiar building materials with excellent life-cycle value, crafting them in ways that make the ordinary extraordinary.

RSA also understands the importance of architecture's role in the global environment. The team includes LEED accredited architects who are active with the California Council Sustainability Task Force and the AIA's Committee on the Environment and are focused on sustainability and environmental responsibility. RSA projects have been recognized for both design and environmental excellence and have received top sustainability awards in the United States and Europe including an AIA/COTE "Top Ten Green" Award and the SOLTEC 98 Award for "Innovation in Technology".

TAUBMAN MUSEUM OF ART

YEAR OF COMPLETION 2008
LOCATION Roanoke, Virginia
SIZE 82,000 square feet
PHOTOGRAPHY Timothy Hursley

To accommodate rapid growth in its collections and programs, the Art Museum of Western Virginia commissioned Los Angeles-based architect Randall Stout, principal of the firm of Randall Stout Architects, Inc., to design a new 82,000 square feet building commensurate with its ambition to become a gateway arts institution in western Virginia and its area of the United States. Located at one of Roanoke's most visible and historic downtown intersections, the new Museum is the first major purpose-built museum ever constructed in the city.

The building, with forms and materials chosen to pay homage to the famed Blue Ridge and Appalachian Mountain surroundings, quadrupled the size of the Art Museum's previous facilities at Center in the Square. The building features flexible exhibition galleries for the Art Museum's important permanent collection of 19th and early 20th century American art, contemporary art, and regional crafts; education facilities with a library, studio and study center; a multi-purpose auditorium; a café; a book and gift shop; a black-box theater; and outdoor terraces providing unique vistas of the city.

Located on a prominent corner of Roanoke's downtown, the new Art Museum, renamed the Taubman Museum of Art before opening, creates a gateway for the city. As Roanoke's most contemporary structure, it is also intended as a metaphorical gateway to the future as Roanoke evolves from an industrial and manufacturing economy to a technology-driven economy.

left main entry and atrium; boardroom terrace; temporary exhibition gallery.
right salem avenue facade facing roanoke's market district

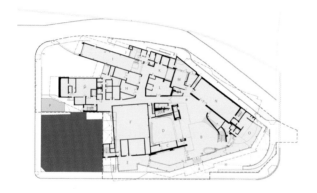

ground floor plan

second floor plan

third floor plan

far left main atrium. above, left to right grand
stair; atrium view from gallery level landing;
atrium peak and café exterior

section

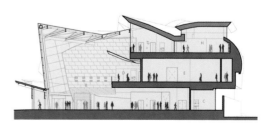

section

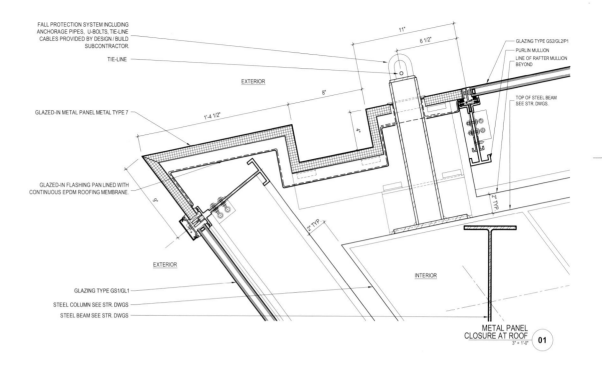

FALL PROTECTION SYSTEM INCLUDING
ANCHORAGE PIPES, U-BOLTS, TIE-LINE
CABLES PROVIDED BY DESIGN / BUILD
SUBCONTRACTOR.

TIE-LINE

GLAZED-IN METAL PANEL METAL TYPE 7

GLAZED-IN FLASHING PAN LINED WITH
CONTINUOUS EPDM ROOFING MEMBRANE.

GLAZING TYPE GS1/GL1

STEEL COLUMN SEE STR. DWGS

STEEL BEAM SEE STR. DWGS

EXTERIOR

EXTERIOR

INTERIOR

11"

6 1/2"

8"

1'-4 1/2"

4"

2" TYP

2" TYP

GLAZING TYPE GS2/GL2/P1

PURLIN MULLION

LINE OF RAFTER MULLION
BEYOND

TOP OF STEEL BEAM
SEE STR. DWGS.

**METAL PANEL
CLOSURE AT ROOF** | **01**
3" = 1'-0"

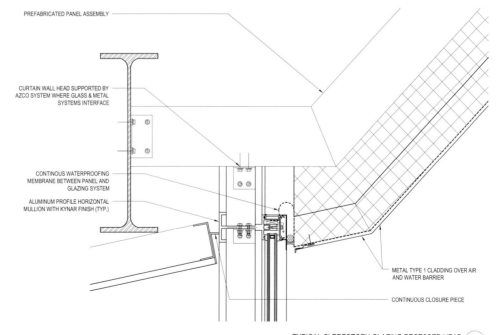

PREFABRICATED PANEL ASSEMBLY

CURTAIN WALL HEAD SUPPORTED BY
AZCO SYSTEM WHERE GLASS & METAL
SYSTEMS INTERFACE

CONTINOUS WATERPROOFING
MEMBRANE BETWEEN PANEL AND
GLAZING SYSTEM

ALUMINUM PROFILE HORIZONTAL
MULLION WITH KYNAR FINISH (TYP.)

METAL TYPE 1 CLADDING OVER AIR
AND WATER BARRIER

CONTINUOUS CLOSURE PIECE

TYPICAL CLERESTORY GLAZING RECESSED HEAD | **01**
3"=1'-0"

left, top metal panel closure at roof.
bottom typical clerestory glazing

HUNTER MUSEUM OF AMERICAN ART

YEAR OF COMPLETION 2005
LOCATION Chattanooga, Tennessee
SIZE 26,000 square feet (addition), 55,000
square feet (renovation)
PHOTOGRAPHY Timothy Griffith

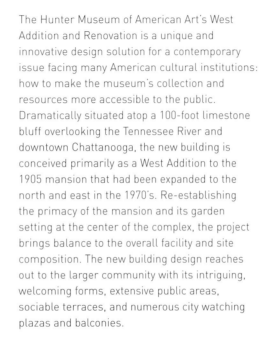

The Hunter Museum of American Art's West Addition and Renovation is a unique and innovative design solution for a contemporary issue facing many American cultural institutions: how to make the museum's collection and resources more accessible to the public. Dramatically situated atop a 100-foot limestone bluff overlooking the Tennessee River and downtown Chattanooga, the new building is conceived primarily as a West Addition to the 1905 mansion that had been expanded to the north and east in the 1970's. Re-establishing the primacy of the mansion and its garden setting at the center of the complex, the project brings balance to the overall facility and site composition. The new building design reaches out to the larger community with its intriguing, welcoming forms, extensive public areas, sociable terraces, and numerous city watching plazas and balconies.

Drawing from the natural setting of the site, the architects developed a building design that embodies a contemporary interpretation of the rock outcroppings and strata within the cliff below, while the undulating forms of the roof reflect the dynamic movements of the neighboring river. Contributing to the bold exterior is a material palette consisting of glass and aluminum curtain wall, oxidized zinc cladding and a stainless steel roof with angel hair finish. While floating above the glass atrium lobby, the fluid-like roof separates the addition from the body of the existing building. The contemporary language of the 2005 addition is a dramatic contrast to the museum's turn of the century mansion home.

The new design solves long-standing staff and art circulation problems by creating state-of-the-art receiving, storage and work areas, as well as including oversized art freight elevators. It allows the lower level to be dedicated to administrative and museum support areas. A new below-grade loading dock minimizes delivery traffic presence on the site and supports a new suite of spaces for registrar receiving exhibit preparation, security, and art storage.

The project is an integral component to Chattanooga's 21st Century Waterfront plan, an ambitious public/private redevelopment partnership. Reinforcing the museum's program for civic engagement, the city's First Street axis has been extended, with museum's complex as its focus. A new pedestrian bridge connects a public plaza at Walnut Street and First Street, allowing visitors to walk from the downtown, above the traffic, to the sculpture garden. This revitalized urban project reverses the site's previous isolation, created in the 1970's when Riverfront Drive was excavated. The museum is a notable tourist attraction for the city's newly revitalized downtown and riverfront. The design of the West Addition, its terraces, and expanded garden transformed the Hunter Museum's public image from that of a private, reserved manor to a lively, open civic forum for all the arts.

far left panoramic view from across tennessee river. left west addition main entry view from sculpture garden; lobby view looking north toward tennessee river; grand stair viewed from lobby

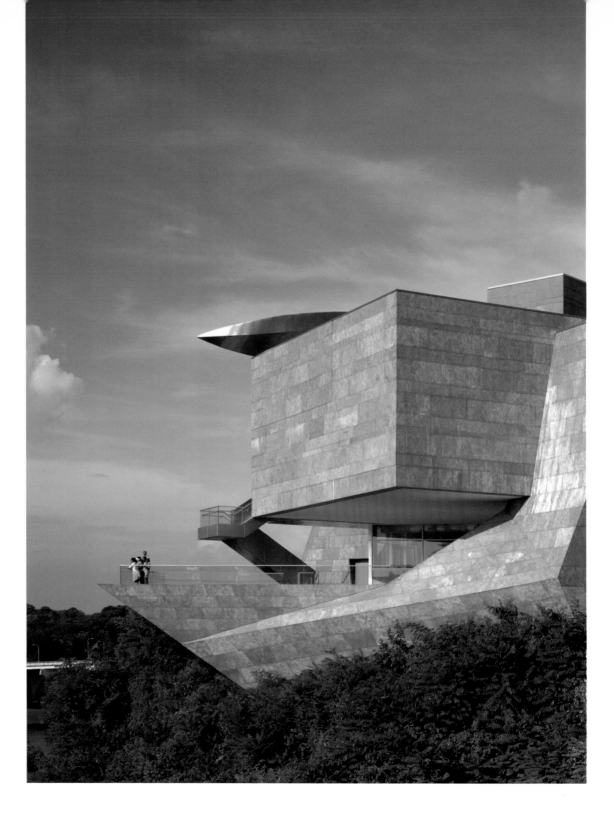

right public view deck and temporary exhibition gallery seen from first street. **opposite page** view looking east from walnut street pedestrian bridge; view of west addition at night

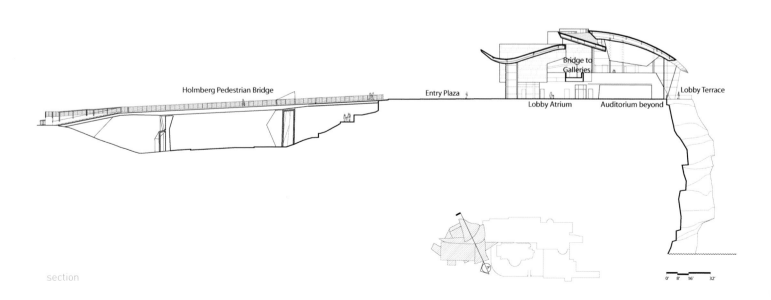

Holmberg Pedestrian Bridge

Entry Plaza

Bridge to Galleries

Lobby Atrium

Auditorium beyond

Lobby Terrace

section

0' 8' 16' 32'

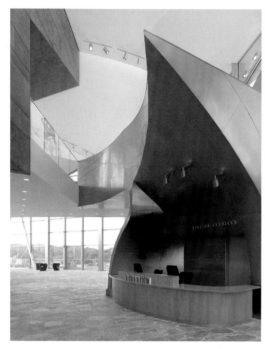

above entry area and visitor services desk;
lobby view looking south toward entry.
right interior bridge access to temporary
exhibition galleries

ART GALLERY OF ALBERTA

RANDALL STOUT ARCHITECTS, INC

YEAR OF COMPLETION 2009
LOCATION Edmonton, Alberta, Canada
SIZE 85,000 square feet
PHOTOGRAPHY Robert Lemermeyer

The new Art Gallery of Alberta is an engaging and inviting visual arts center in downtown Edmonton, Alberta. Celebrating its prominent location on Sir Winston Churchill Square, the city's arts and government core, the building's architectural design formally and philosophically extends out into the community, welcoming visitors of all ages and backgrounds to experience contemporary art firsthand. Designed by Los Angels-based Randall Stout Architects, the Gallery will open to the public in January 2010.

Crafted of patinaed zinc, high performance glazing, and stainless steel, the building has a timeless appearance and extraordinary durability in the northern climate. Transparent glazing planes and reflective metal surfaces animate the building, exposing the activities within and engaging people and art at multiple levels on both the interior and exterior. Selected to reflect Edmonton's dramatic weather patterns and the extreme contrast of the long days of summer and the short days of winter, these materials create a dynamic quality that allow the building to transform along with its natural surroundings. Not only does the building change throughout the day, it changes from season to season. More static building materials would not allow for this type of ephemeral connection between the building and the site.

The design reinvents the museum's public spaces through a continuous stainless steel surface that moves lithely through the museum's interior and exterior spaces. Wall and ceiling become one fluid surface which captures the spatial volume while guiding the public through entry points, wrapping event and gathering spaces, and leading on to the galleries. Galleries were conceived as more conventional spaces in order to maximize flexibility for curators and maintain the high level of environmental control necessary to house traveling exhibitions and the Gallery's collection. On the exterior, the galleries are expressed as simple stacked rectangular boxes, establishing a dialogue with the existing building mass as well as a heightened juxtaposition with the undulating surfaces of the public spaces. These two languages of mass and curvilinear form define an inviting rhythm of destination and path in a unique way-finding experience for visitors.

The original museum building, a 1960s Brutalist-style concrete structure, was undersized and not taking full advantage of its high-profile location on the public square. The addition/renovation project has upgraded the previously below-standard galleries and art handling facilities and includes new celebratory public event areas including the entry lobby, Gallery Great Hall, multi-purpose theatre, café, museum store, Member's Lounge, and outdoor sculpture terrace. Edmonton's underground light rail transportation system (LRT) and public pedway are accessible from the main entry lobby. The new building totals 84,000 square feet, adding 27,000 square feet of new public spaces and galleries and includes approximately 24,000 square feet of interior exhibition space.

opposite page view of the aga and edmonton city hall; exterior rendering of building at night; rendering of the member's lounge. left art gallery of alberta main entry; main atrium and grand stair; third floor landing looking out to downtown edmonton

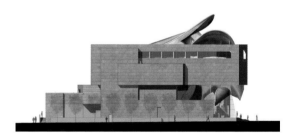

north elevation

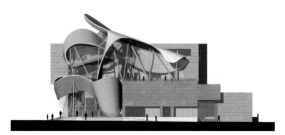

south elevation

SHUBIN + DONALDSON ARCHITECTS

www.sandarc.com

Robin Donaldson and Russell Shubin

Shubin + Donaldson Architects Inc. was founded in 1990 by principals Russell Shubin and Robin Donaldson as a design-based architectural practice which specializes in developing livable environments with a refined sensitivity toward the land, its users, and context. With offices in both Los Angeles and nearby Santa Barbara, California, the firm jointly strives for distinction through the imaginative design of sophisticated, context-driven buildings and communities standing as expressions of the users, the environment, as well as the architects. A highly rigorous and collaborative design process is employed by the principals and staff of designers and support personnel, in pursuit of a refined balance between the needs for building and housing and a respect for the preservation of natural habitats and watersheds. With extensive experience in residential multi-family master planning, community planning, hospitality, mixed use projects, commercial buildings, educational facilities, custom residential, and commercial interiors, Shubin+Donaldson Architects pride themselves on an explorative approach to design combining function with efficiency, and innovative tactile and material expression with social and environmental conscience.

Shubin + Donaldson Architects are committed to the belief that the environment and human endeavor are not mutually exclusive and through creative and thoughtful planning, can effectively cohabit and perpetually enhance one another sustainably, socially, as well as economically. We believe that the careful stewardship of the built environment can stimulate the regeneration of natural systems and processes which will in turn step towards restoring and strengthening the fabric of social interaction. In light of current trends toward global population growth and densification, Shubin+Donaldson Architects believe that the bold declaration 'The more we build, the better it is for the planet' is an ambitious yet achievable vision if approached strategically and guided by the tenets of reduction, conservation, and sustainable use of natural resources.

BISCUIT FILMWORKS

YEAR OF COMPLETION 2009
LOCATION Hollywood, California
SIZE 11,750 square feet
PHOTOGRAPHY Tom Bonner

Biscuit Filmworks is a project that stands in contrast to many of the tendencies in contemporary commercial spaces in Los Angeles. Both the client and the architects were looking to design a space that was more modest, forgiving, and broken in; a place for making comfortable creative work.

The architect began with the adaptive reuse of two warehouse buildings; thinking of them as found objects and proceeded to gut them, tie them together, and create a new structure inside this grafted condition. The relationship between the new construction and existing buildings achieves a complex and nuanced order that attempts to blend the new and old in a way that is not easily distinguishable. This sense of blending also comes from the materiality of the project; using reclaimed wood, handmade tile, ribbed glass, and board-formed concrete, the architect was able to achieve not only a range of textures and sources but an industrious spirit that speaks to the company's philosophical learnings as a factory for doing.

The architect also saw this design trajectory as an emerging philosophy about how we design for creative companies in a evolving digital world, and how these environments begin to blur the distinction betweeen the comforts of home and the stress of work.

right upon entrance, the reception area with conference room reflects the warm palette of materials used throughout this adaptive reuse project

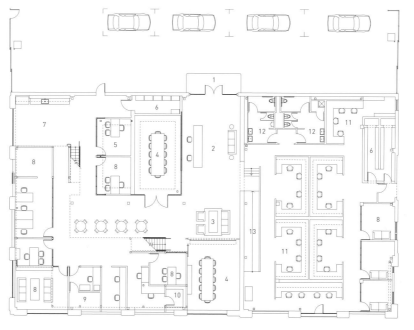

01 entry
02 reception
03 lounge
04 conference
05 library
06 storage
07 kitchen
08 office
09 server
10 vault
11 production bay
12 restroom
13 ramp

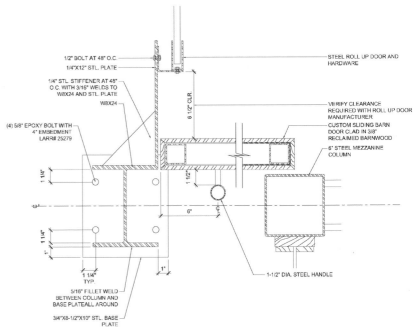

1/2" BOLT AT 48" O.C.

1/4"X12" STL. PLATE

1/4" STL. STIFFENER AT 48"
O.C. WITH 3/16" WELDS TO
W8X24 AND STL. PLATE

W8X24

(4) 5/8" EPOXY BOLT WITH
4" EMBEDMENT
LARR# 25279

6 1/2" CLR.

1 1/4"

1 1/2"

1 1/4"

1"

1 1/4"
TYP.

6"

1"

5/16" FILLET WELD
BETWEEN COLUMN AND
BASE PLATEALL AROUND

3/4"X8-1/2"X10" STL. BASE
PLATE

STEEL ROLL UP DOOR AND
HARDWARE

VERIFY CLEARANCE
REQUIRED WITH ROLL UP DOOR
MANUFACTURER

CUSTOM SLIDING BARN
DOOR CLAD IN 3/8"
RECLAIMED BARNWOOD

6" STEEL MEZZANINE
COLUMN

1-1/2" DIA. STEEL HANDLE

left, and right the architects blended new construction elements into the existing buildings, using reclaimed wood, handmade tile, ribbed glass, exposed steel profiles, and board-formed concrete

NATHAN RESIDENCE

YEAR OF COMPLETION 2008
LOCATION Bel Air, California
SIZE 7,100 square feet
PHOTOGRAPHY Ciro Coelho

This residence in Bel Air was designed on a site formerly occupied by the home in which the clients raised their family. Their intimate knowledge of the location and its sense of place guided the design of the new residence. A large tree that the clients planted when their children were small is at the heart and center of the design and shades a courtyard around which the new house is designed.

The house turns its back towards the busy street with a solid formal façade, while the other side of the house opens up to the courtyard providing light, air, and views over the city. A series of volumes are focused around the tree in the central courtyard and allow for flow between the interior and exterior of the home. A gallery for showcasing the clients art collection ties these volumes together, and is book-ended with a water feature wall and a fireplace.

This design generously accommodates formal and informal entertaining as well as the archetypal california lifestyle of indoor-outdoor living.

right the solid formality of the street-facing cubes is contrasted on the courtyard side with openness

above, from left to right entrance stair,
main interior stair, formal dining room,
kitchen with outdoor fireplace

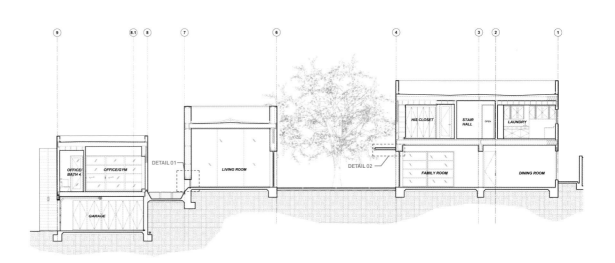

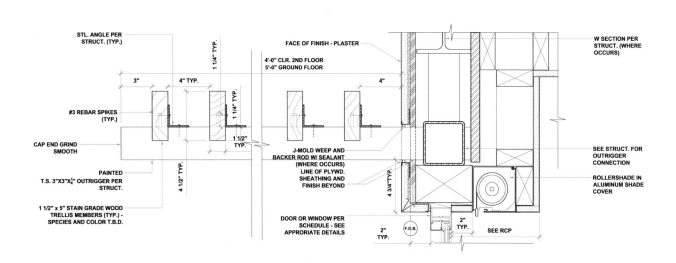

STL. ANGLE PER
STRUCT. (TYP.)

1 1/4" TYP.

FACE OF FINISH - PLASTER

W SECTION PER
STRUCT. (WHERE
OCCURS)

4'-0" CLR. 2ND FLOOR
5'-0" GROUND FLOOR

3"   4" TYP.   1 1/4" TYP.   4"

#3 REBAR SPIKES
(TYP.)

1 1/4" TYP.

CAP END GRIND
SMOOTH

1 1/2"
TYP.

SEE STRUCT. FOR
OUTRIGGER
CONNECTION

J-MOLD WEEP AND
BACKER ROD W/ SEALANT
(WHERE OCCURS)
LINE OF PLYWD.
SHEATHING AND
FINISH BEYOND

PAINTED
T.S. 3"X3"X¼" OUTRIGGER PER
STRUCT.

4 1/2" TYP.

ROLLERSHADE IN
ALUMINUM SHADE
COVER

1 1/2" x 5" STAIN GRADE WOOD
TRELLIS MEMBERS (TYP.) -
SPECIES AND COLOR T.B.D.

DOOR OR WINDOW PER
SCHEDULE - SEE
APPROIATE DETAILS

4 3/4"TYP.

F.O.S.

2"
TYP.

2"
TYP.

SEE RCP

left views to central courtyard and onto the
reflecting pool **left below**, construction
section detail of courtyard-facing sunscreen
elements **below** construction section detail
of window niche facing the reflecting pool

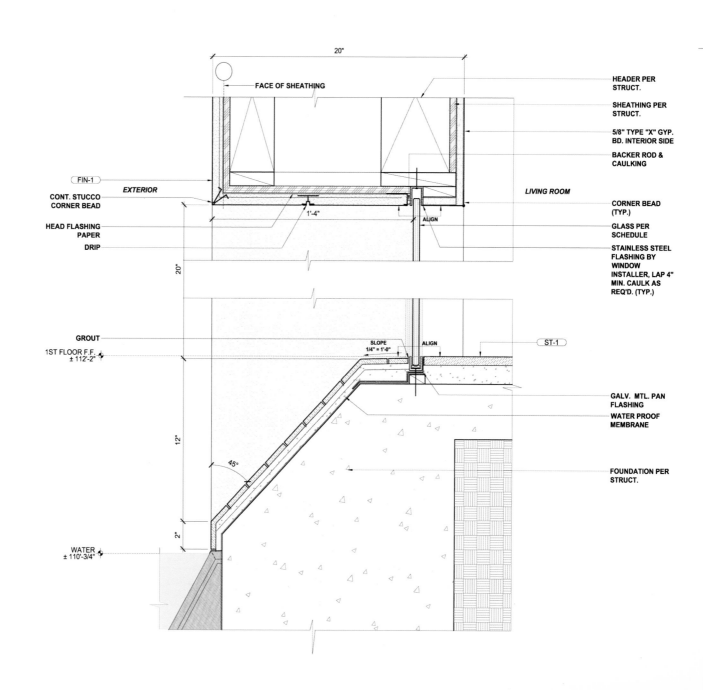

20"

FACE OF SHEATHING

HEADER PER
STRUCT.

SHEATHING PER
STRUCT.

5/8" TYPE "X" GYP.
BD. INTERIOR SIDE

BACKER ROD &
CAULKING

FIN-1

EXTERIOR

LIVING ROOM

CONT. STUCCO
CORNER BEAD

CORNER BEAD
(TYP.)

1'-4"

ALIGN

GLASS PER
SCHEDULE

HEAD FLASHING
PAPER

STAINLESS STEEL
FLASHING BY
WINDOW
INSTALLER, LAP 4"
MIN. CAULK AS
REQ'D. (TYP.)

DRIP

20"

GROUT

SLOPE
1/4" = 1'-0"

ALIGN

ST-1

1ST FLOOR F.F.
± 112'-2"

GALV. MTL. PAN
FLASHING

WATER PROOF
MEMBRANE

12"

45°

FOUNDATION PER
STRUCT.

2"

WATER
± 110'-3/4"

SAATCHI & SAATCHI

YEAR OF COMPLETION 2008
LOCATION Torrance, California
SIZE 106,000 square feet
PHOTOGRAPHY Tom Bonner

"Homing at work" instead of working at home was the concept for the renovation of saathci and saatchi's los angeles advertising office, intended to boost creative collaboration and work flows among the more than 500 employees.

The architect social engineered the plan to incorporate a "destination floor" that incorporated residential design elements such as a large kitchen and dining area, a grand staircase / meeting space, living room areas, and a "backyard" for causual gathering. The intention was to create a space that saatchi team members could comfortably meet and form creative teams in a relaxed home-like atmosphere. The advertising agency's branded orange color drove the selection of furnishings and materials.

left moving away from conventional office typologies, the architects sought to create spaces with a touch of "home." The staircase element serves the double purpose of recalling residential architecture while at the same time acting as a amphitheater-like center for community and working functions

left the advertising agency's branded orange color drove the selection of furnishings and materials. informal niches and comfortable furniture offer employees multiple opportunities to work away from the confines of a typical desk

section

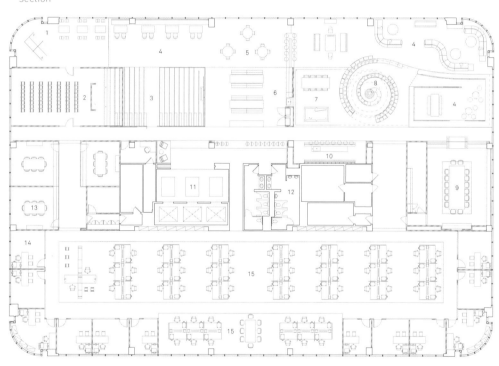

floor plan   third floor

01	"rec room"	09	library
02	sisomo room	10	conference
03	grand stair meeting	11	bar
04	area	12	elevator / lobby
05	focus area	13	restrooms
06	"dining room"	14	war room
07	break room / kitchen	15	office
08	"game room"	16	work area

STUDIO PALI FEKETE ARCHITECTS
SPF:a

Zoltan Pali and Judit Fekete

www.spfa.com

Studio Pali Fekete architects [SPF:a] was started by Zoltan Pali in 1988, joined in 1990 by partner Judit Fekete. Since that time, the studio has methodically grown and matured with the skill sets to handle most any project. Houses, apartments, condominiums, offices, schools, museums and theatres exemplify the studio's work.

SPF:a approaches each project differently depending on the situation at hand. Mostly the work is characterized by the need to balance simplicity and elegance with the desire to keep the complexity of construction minimized. However, as the quantity and quality of their commissions has increased, complexity of construction has tended to follow suit. It is against this complexity that SPF:a naturally holds the line.

Of course, that is not to say that invention is out the door; however, SPF:a does not pursue innovation for innovation's sake. They do, rather, continually re-invent, re-tool, and re-think—all the while balancing the new with the tried and true. Beautiful and responsible projects have come to fruition through this process. There is a propensity for singularity, not quantity. Mass production, prototype, prefab and tract development are words that are carefully considered before used in the studio's vocabulary.

The Studio tends towards a near obsessive level of detailing—just shy of being tiring and trite. There is a vigil against fashions fads and formalism with a penchant for honesty, integrity and morality. Their buildings are responsible, efficient and watertight.

SPF:a's view is that architecture is not a lofty profession with gods and masters to be revered and sanctified but that architecture itself comes from the basic human need to build- as if it were imprinted in the millions of years of our evolution. There is no agenda [political nor social] besides allowing the beauty of each project to emerge as its own.

Contributions of talented individuals such as Gregory Fischer, Greg Stutheit, Sandra Hutchings, Kyle Pfister, Frank Lopez, and Damon Surfas, Michael Lindell, Michael Zahn and Siddhartha Majumdar are key to the studio's success.

OBERFIELD RESIDENCE

YEAR OF COMPLETION 2009
LOCATION Los Angeles, California
SIZE 10,000 square feet
PHOTOGRAPHY Russell Abraham

From the street, the crisp, white Swisspearl panels that clad the Oberfeld Residence's exterior rise a modest 18' from the street, by code. Tucked away on the other side of the hill, a clean, modern 10,000-square foot home contains two main floors and a basement, a grand lawn, infinity pool, and spectacular view of the Los Angeles basin below.

The home's grand entry boasts an oversized wood door, pivoting into a courtyard-like foyer, flooded with natural light. The space is deceivingly sheltered and indoors, and is punctuated at the far end by a serene lily pond framed in core-ten steel.

The house is cut into a steep hillside with large concrete retaining walls to hold up the hill behind. In plan, the structure is an L-shape, embracing the view across its angled infinity pool. Staring back at the house from its generous private landscape, a transparent glass main level is topped by the master and family bedrooms – also clad in glass, but shielded from the sun's intensity by a series of custom-designed vertical louvers, cut from the same Swisspearl concrete panel material that screens the street façade of the home. The vertical louvers provide a unique architectural contrast to the building's strong horizontal elements.

The interiors feature a myriad of luxury finishes and imported stone, atop textured Mafi wood floors throughout. The 5-bedroom, 6-bathroom and 2-powder room program includes family living quarters on the upper floor, and a guest suite or maid's quarters on the first floor of the opposing wing. The master suite includes a private balcony overlooking the pool, and features a connected his and hers bathroom and walk in closet/dressing room, day lit by Solatubes – a product that channels indirect natural light into the space during the day, and contains electrical fixtures which can be illuminated at night. Tucked away in a level below the main living space are a home theater, home office, spa suite, guest quarters and wine cellar.

The living room is adorned with floor-to-ceiling, 13-foot high glass sliders, direct views of the city, and a wall-to-wall gas fireplace. A generous bar separates the living room from a more formal dining area, which spills out onto a trellised patio for indoor/outdoor dining occasions. A large kitchen area is located just on the other side of the dining room, providing a light separation that is desirable for entertaining. Outside, the overhang from the master bedroom creates a sheltered outdoor living room.

The composition of the home is fluid, blending indoor and outdoor spaces with subtle divisions and natural material integration throughout. Ample public and private areas make the home overwhelmingly livable – a private oasis, harmoniously nestled into its urban environment.

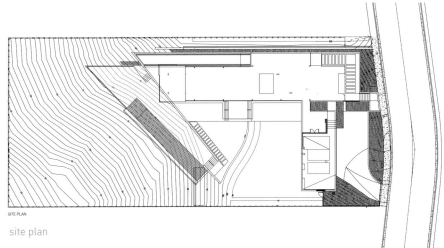

SITE PLAN

site plan

above looking from inner foyer toward front door. view across kitchen. **right** courtyard view upon entering the home

1 2-5/16" cement panels
2 stainless steel bolt with acorn head
  nuts and plastic spacer
3 slot connection allow for
  1/4"movement
4 3/8" continuous steel plate floor mount
5 1/4" steel plate
6 beam per structural where occurrs
7 9x23 wide flange weld to steel beam

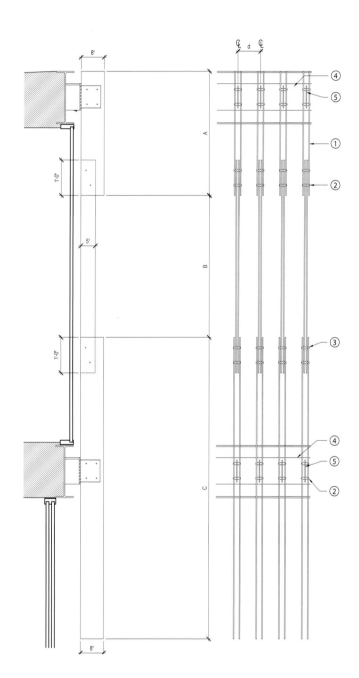

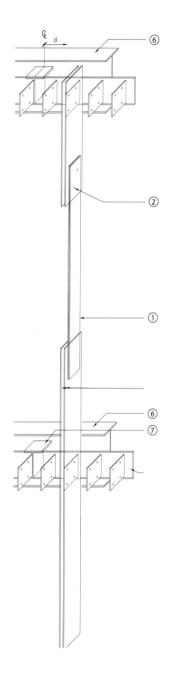

left architectural louvers, made from
concrete fiber panels, filter the sun's
direct rays and give the home its unique
character

SPF:a HEADQUARTERS

YEAR OF COMPLETION 2005
LOCATION Culver City, California
SIZE 28,000 square feet
PHOTOGRAPHY John Edward Linden

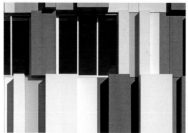

When SPF:a sought to create a new headquarters for its studio, it chose a part of Los Angeles that was on the edge of a burgeoning revival, namely Culver City. The building, with its dynamic façade, and culturally stimulating mixed-use program, amplifies the enthusiasm and motion of the city's growth and serves as a visual bridge between the city's downtown art deco theater district and the world-class art gallery district emerging directly to the east. In the heart of the ground floor, Studio Pali Fekete architects (SPF:a) opened a public gallery to explore the synergistic relationship between design, art, and architecture, animated through a series of exhibitions, lectures, and cultural events. The SPF:a Gallery is a microcosm for the convergence of creative forces that also make up the mixed use program of the building: an architecture studio, a restaurant, and gallery on the ground floor, plus seven live-work lofts on the second floor, populated by a variety of artists and creative businesses. The architecture studio is open to visitors, as is the gallery itself, with its changing exhibitions throughout the year. Ceilings are 20-feet high, with partial mezzanine space.

The physical aspects of the building explore the variation, movement, velocity and tempo of the city on all scales, using materials, textures, and variations that stimulate and delight the imagination. Concrete fiber panel boards on the exterior provide a unique rain-screen that also serves to break up street noise from busy Washington Boulevard below, and to insulate the building from the constant rays of the California sunshine. The variation of the panels in width

and depth is intended as a visual "music," playing changes in variations of 8", 16", and 32" panel widths, and three different colors that randomly alternate on the surface of the building.

Upstairs, the live/work lofts feature 16-foot high ceilings with mezzanine space, 8'-high Fleetwood sliding doors mounted on the high walls as windows, and two separate entrances per loft, serving alternate live and work functions for occupants.

Structurally, the building is based on a rigorous system, beginning with the three-car parking bay concrete column and beam layout that divides the parking bays in the basement. Standard wood-framed shear walls over the concrete beams divide the commercial bays on the ground floor and in the loft units above. The format allows the owner complete flexibility to open or close access between bays, as the building's use and tenants change over the years.

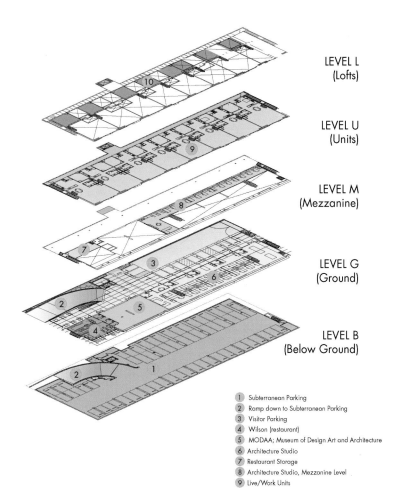

LEVEL L
(Lofts)

LEVEL U
(Units)

LEVEL M
(Mezzanine)

LEVEL G
(Ground)

LEVEL B
(Below Ground)

1 Subterranean Parking
2 Ramp down to Subterranean Parking
3 Visitor Parking
4 Wilson (restaurant)
5 MODAA; Museum of Design Art and Architecture
6 Architecture Studio
7 Restaurant Storage
8 Architecture Studio, Mezzanine Level
9 Live/Work Units
10 Live/Work Units, Loft Level

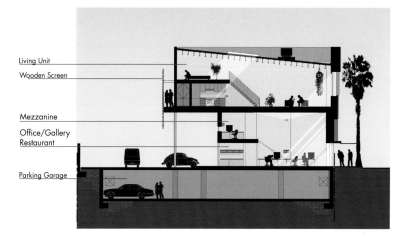

Living Unit

Wooden Screen

Mezzanine

Office/Gallery

Restaurant

Parking Garage

left view inside one of the loft units.
right view inside the ground floor SPF:a
Gallery, the architectural studio, and a
section of the building

SOMIS HAY BARN

YEAR OF COMPLETION 2004
LOCATION Somis, California
SIZE 3,000 square feet
PHOTOGRAPHY John Edward Linden

A client commissioned SPF:a to design a house on a 40-acre lemon grove in Somis, California, a small coastal farming community about 45 miles West of Los Angeles. At the same time, the client asked the architects to design a barn for his horses on the site. Reconceiving of the traditional hay barn, SPF:a explored a creative and poetic way of storing hay and providing shelter for the client's equestrian program. The architect was guided by two contrasting styles: the rhythmic rigor and permanence of Modernism, and the rough, ever-changing quality of wabi-sabi, a Japanese aesthetic that finds beauty in imperfection. Modernism's order is expressed by the barn's sleek 12-by-12-foot structural steel system, while wabi-sabi is represented by the ever-changing color and positioning of the hay as cladding on the barn. When hay is stacked along the outer storage shelves in the winter, it is green; as the season unfolds, the hay turns yellow, and the caretaker removes it from the shelves as it is used for feed. Both factors keep the facade forever in a state of evolution. The building is a metaphor for life, death and birth, common seasonal themes in an agrarian society.

The steel and cedar-wood frame is conceived as a grid system with large shelves supporting the stacked bales of hay, so forming a well-ventilated and insulated wall. A metal roof deck extends well beyond the barn's edges to protect interior spaces and the stacked bales of hay from the rain. A breezeway separates the horse stalls from the client's storage areas and office. SPF:a originally designed movable cables to hold the bales in place, which proved unnecessary—the friction created by the hay is enough to do the job.

The barn itself can house four horses, tractors, tack room, and other farm equipment needed for maintaining the forty-acre lemon grove that surrounds it. The steel structural system is constructed to the ideal dimensions for a horse stable. Natural ventilation is encouraged via open clerestories.

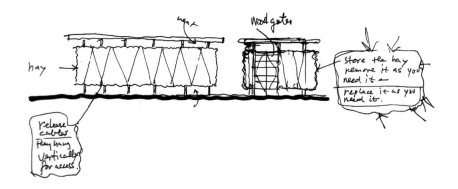

CAVERHILL RESIDENCE

YEAR OF COMPLETION 2009
LOCATION Beverly Hills, California
SIZE 4,500 square feet
PHOTOGRAPHY John Edward Linden

With a long, narrow span of angled "fins" lining its sleek façade from the street, the Caverhill house looks monumental, albeit a stealth monument. Entering beneath the canopy of the carport, one is transported into the main living space, is full of air and light. The fins provide privacy from the street, while playfully welcoming and diffusing narrow strips of light onto the home's interior surfaces. The result is a beautiful dance of sunshine that changes throughout the day.

The home replaced a smaller house on the difficult hillside lot, maximizing both the narrow footprint and the spectacular views of the Los Angeles basin. A hillside building ordinance and a desire to keep the previous structure's footprint made the project a challenge – as a result, the plan is a modified wedge, one end of the house almost twice as wide as the other.

The main entrance is on the second of three levels, where the living room flows openly into the kitchen and dining area. These communal spaces and the bedrooms on the upper level are punctuated on each end by over 1,000 square feet of generous covered terraces and balconies. Each cove is protected from the sun and wind but still open to views.

Simplicity was the goal of both the architect and the client. Steel framing allowed for a fully-open plan, free from interior walls or vertical supports obstructing the views. The result is a clean viewing angle of the exterior from almost any spot in the house. All of the house controls – heating, cooling, lighting, window shades, security and more – are contained within a control panel near the front door. Ductwork was eliminated by the use of an Airfloor System, which heats or cools

rooms through a series of dome-like structures beneath the micro-finished concrete floor surface. The upper level can be accessed either through the interior stair, or through exterior staircases located on either end of the house, incorporating the terraces into the main circulation flow of the home. Bathroom vanities float above the floor, the electrical outlets tucked below, out of sight.

"In Japanese painting you have one brush stroke that gets branch, leaves and flowers," says owner, Don Caverhill. "That's what we were hoping for -- to have less things do a whole lot more."

The lowest level of the house, set on the slope below street level, contains two guest rooms, a lawn and a patio with a long fire pit running toward an infinity pool.

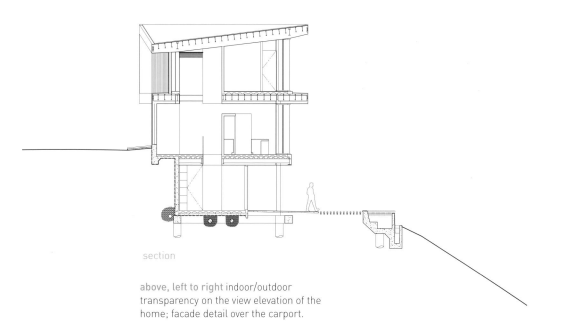

section

above, left to right indoor/outdoor transparency on the view elevation of the home; facade detail over the carport.

WALLIS ANNENBERG CENTER FOR THE PERFORMING ARTS

YEAR OF COMPLETION 2010 (design)
LOCATION Beverly Hills, California
SIZE 70,000 square feet

The project is a state-of-the-art performing arts center, built on the site of the historic, 1934 Beverly Hills Post Office. The center contains the 500-seat Goldsmith Theater, where every seat is intimately connected to the performance space. The historic post office building contains a 120-seat Lovelace Studio Theater, where ideas will be tested, workshopped, and developed into world-class material. The historic building also contains an education center with classrooms, administrative offices, and the main entry for theatre patrons, including a box office and concessions facility. A garden and courtyard connect the historic with the new building with direct visual connection to the shops and restaurants of downtown Beverly Hills.

At one point, prior to SPF:a's involvement in the project, conventional wisdom was to place the new performing arts venue within the walls of the historic post office building, and to create a small annex on the site to house the educational components of the program. SPF:a does the reverse - instead, the studio takes the smaller programmatic elements such as the rehearsal hall, classrooms, and administrative offices and locates them into the three level historic building, where they fit nicely and snugly. This preserves and celebrates the historic architecture, as well as affords the Center the opportunity to create a new, state-of-the-art, flexible performing arts facility with ample back-of-house amenities.

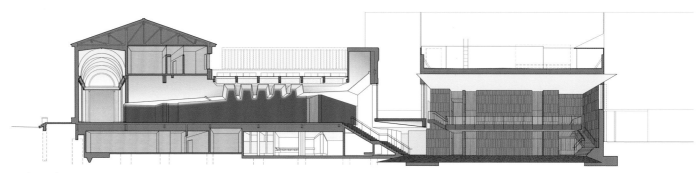

promenade section

wHY ARCHITECTURE

www.why-architecture.com

Yo-ichiro Hakomori, Richard Stoner, Kulapat Yantrasast

wHY Architecture is a collaborative workshop for creativity in architecture and design that brings a fresh and unfettered approach to each project. Each new project is considered unique and succinct, and is approached with no pre-determined style or set vocabulary. wHY Architecture brings their teamwork approach to all projects and injects new ideas and solutions in architecture so that it is executed with the highest degree of quality and intelligence in construction.

wHY Architecture's work includes many innovative architectural designs for people, the arts and the environment. The Grand Rapids Art Museum is the first new art museum in the world to receive the LEED certification Gold. wHY Architecture has been working on design for the new Tyler Museum of Art, Texas, as well as the expansion and renovation of the Speed Art Museum in Louisville, Kentucky and is in the process of redesigning and renovating multiple galleries at the Art Institute of Chicago. Community projects include the renovation of the historic Art Deco Venice Jail into the Social & Public Art Resource Center in Venice, California and the Art Bridge at the Los Angeles River. Currently awaiting groundbreaking, this bridge shall be built from trash salvaged from the LA River it spans. Recent projects also include Private residences, Art Galleries, housing projects and interesting retail spaces.

Partners at wHY Architecture include Kulapat Yantrasast, Yo-ichiro Hakomori and Richard Stoner. Kulapat, a native of Thailand, received his Master of Architecture and Ph.D. from the University of Tokyo under Japanese Government Scholarship. Yo-ichiro received his Master of Architecture from the University of California, Los Angeles, and his Doctorate from the University of Tokyo. Richard received his Bachelor of Fine Art from Rhode Island School of Design and Master of Architecture from the University of California, Los Angeles. They continue to lecture and teach at universities around the country and worldwide, Kulapat has also served on the Artist Committee for American for the Arts, the nation's oldest organization for the support of art in society. He was also awarded the prestigious Silpathorn Award in 2009 from the Government of Thailand for outstanding achievement and notable contributions to Thai contemporary arts and culture. He is the first architect to receive the award.

GRAND RAPIDS ART MUSEUM

YEAR OF COMPLETION 2007
LOCATION Grand Rapids, Michigan
SIZE 125,000 square feet
PHOTOGRAPHY Steve Hall and Scott
McDonald, Hedrich Blessing

The existing Grand Rapids Art Museum is located in Michigan and is home to one of the oldest museums in the Mid-West. The design for the building included the integration of arts and technology with a mission in obtaining a high-level certification from the Leadership in Energy and Environmental Design (LEED), thus making it the first LEED Gold certified museum in the world. The building includes 18,000 square feet of gallery space for art, a 5,000 square foot education and art learning center, 4,500 square feet of lobby/public space, a 285 seat auditorium, a conference center wing as well as museum gift shops, coffee bar and restaurant.

front elevation

left new museum spaces are characterized by understated austerity
right the covered entrance plaza creates a new public space with urban qualities.

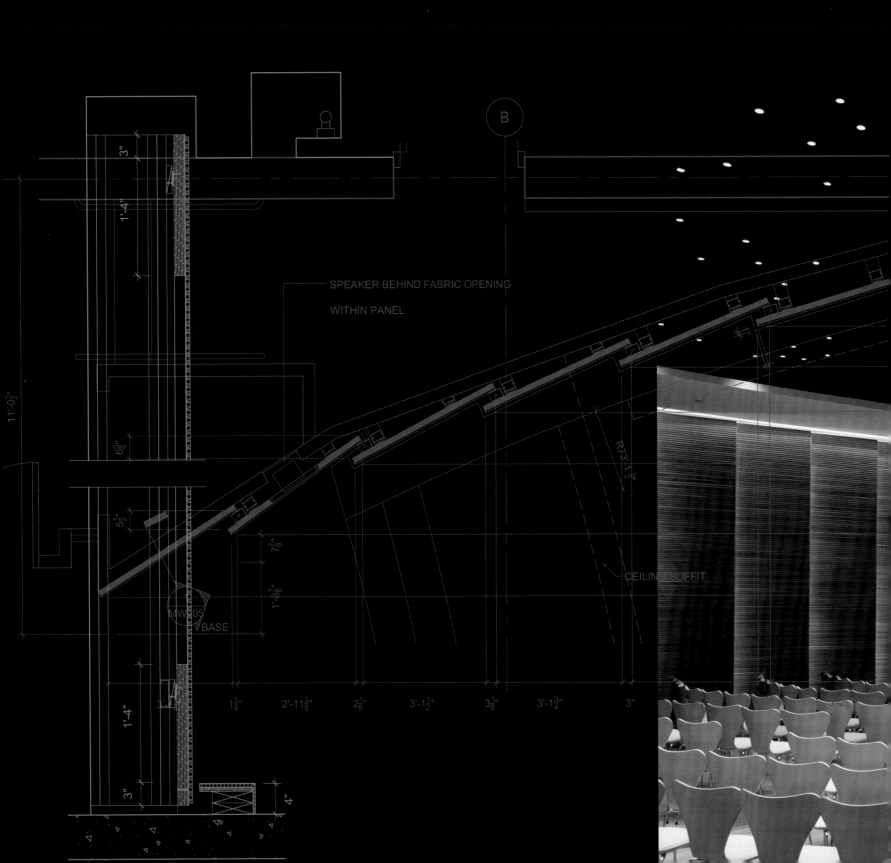

SPEAKER BEHIND FABRIC OPENING

WITHIN PANEL

CEILING SOFFIT

B.8

9¼"

R/3'-1½"

4⅝"
7¼"

7¼"

11⅞/₈"

2"

6'-9¾"

1'-1⅛"

1'-8⅜"

1'-6"

below lobby and exhibition halls **right** the exhibition spaces are interconnected by a gracious stair **far right** in addition to the entrance plaza, new urban spaces were created all around the building

a5 LOS ANGELES

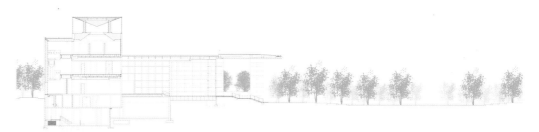

lobby lantern section

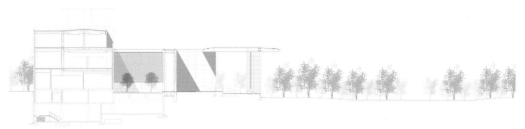

sculpt court section

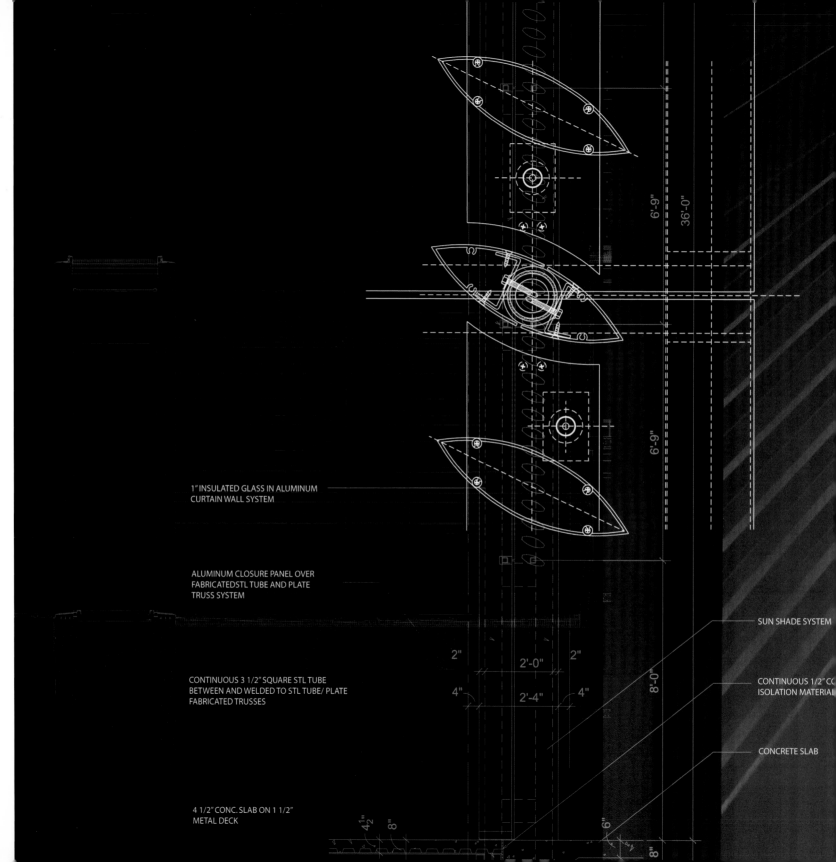

1" INSULATED GLASS IN ALUMINUM
CURTAIN WALL SYSTEM

ALUMINUM CLOSURE PANEL OVER
FABRICATEDSTL TUBE AND PLATE
TRUSS SYSTEM

CONTINUOUS 3 1/2" SQUARE STL TUBE
BETWEEN AND WELDED TO STL TUBE/ PLATE
FABRICATED TRUSSES

4 1/2" CONC. SLAB ON 1 1/2"
METAL DECK

SUN SHADE SYSTEM

CONTINUOUS 1/2" CO
ISOLATION MATERIAL

CONCRETE SLAB

6'-9"

36'-0"

6'-9"

8'-0"

2"   2"

2'-0"

4"   4"

2'-4"

6"

8"

4 1/2"

8"

8"

ROYAL/T

YEAR OF COMPLETION 2007
LOCATION Culver City, California
SIZE 10,000 square feet
PHOTOGRAPHY Basil Childers

Royal/T is a playful collision of art gallery, café and retail shop within a 10,000sf warehouse in Culver City, California. wHY Architecture designed the space unlike any other, playing upon traditional rules of gallery, retail and restaurant design. Rather than the 'white box' space, existing walls remained unpainted, and undulating ribbons of ten foot high acrylic walls contain the art and retail offerings in architectural vitrines. It is these vitrines that allow for the juxtaposition of disparate programs that yields a whole that is greater than the sum of its parts. Patrons can dine in close proximity to the multi-million dollar art collection, the only barrier being the hyper-clear, butt-glazed cast acrylic. Diners become voyeurs and participants in an architectural fusion of pop culture and high-end design. Like a private club, the Washington Boulevard entrance is covered in faux boxwood, with only the Royal/T crown logo in hot pink neon.

Inspired by the Maid Cafés in Tokyo's Akihabara district, the highly conceptualized space of Royal/T reflects the interior realm of fantasy that strongly influences the artists included in owner Sue Hancock's private collection. Recontextualizing the underground 'okaku' (geek) culture of Japan that celebrated 'cosplay' (costume play), the café servers dress in maid uniforms with a Lolita-esque touch. The look-but-don't-touch theme continues with the art and retail offerings contained within the acrylic vitrines. Even the requisite café ceiling is acrylic, allowing the existing bowstring trusses to remain visible.

below, and right scenes from the
adaptive reuse of a former industrial
building

Washington Boulevard

Lindblade Street

retail display · retail display · bar · kitchen · jan. · elec. · men · women · service corridor · office · art display

art display · art display · cafe seating · v.i.p. room · art display

floor plan

THE TYLER MUSEUM OF ART

YEAR OF COMPLETION 2010
LOCATION Tyler, Texas
SIZE 42,000 square feet

Established in 1952, the Tyler Museum of Art
moved into its present home, a 15,000 square foot
building adjacent to Tyler Junior College, in 1971.
As part of their continuing mission to enliven
the cultural landscape of East Texas, the new
TMA will be situated adjacent to the University of
Texas at Tyler on a densely wooded site bisected
by a flood plain. Meant to be both iconic and
respectful of its unique surroundings, the first
phase of construction will more than double the
existing facility's square footage and contain
6,000 square feet of gallery space to attract
traveling exhibitions and continue in its tradition
of highlighting up-and-coming Texas artists. The
new facility will also house 3,000 square feet of
educational programming, including classrooms,
a library and children's gallery. Upon completion
of future phases TMA will house over 15,000
square feet of gallery space and more than triple
the existing facility's square footage.

left, and right the gallery spaces are
stacked to create distinctly separate
galleries while at the same time defining a
unique, light-filled central atrium

section

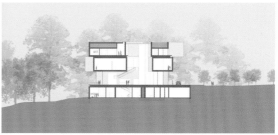

section

MULHOLLAND RESIDENCE

YEAR OF COMPLETION 2010
LOCATION Los Angeles, California
SIZE 22,000 square feet

Located on a promontory between two major arteries – Benedict Canyon and Beverly Glen – the house on Mulholland Drive is nestled between two concrete walls that cut through the contours of the land. To respond to the landform, the house is virtually formless, emphasizing instead the continuum of space that flows seamlessly from inside to outside, sheltered under a large concrete roof. The space of the house is ordered through a simple yet dynamic alternating grid. Liquid spaces – of circulation and public areas – flow around solid spaces of closed, private and contemplative rooms, made of stone and rammed earth. The seamless indoor – outdoor condition is enhanced by the connection between reflecting and swimming pools which, additionally, provides sound mitigation to traffic noise. The alternating pattern of space and form inspires the concept of "interactive borrowed scenery", where walls frame, conceal and reveal the surrounding sceneries as one moves through the house.

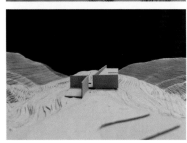

left, and right the residence nestles between two concrete walls that cut through the contours of the landscape

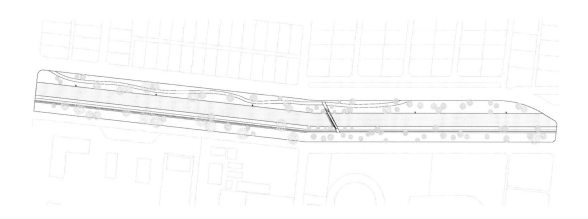

above, and right the Art Bridge is slated to be
constructed with materials salvaged from the
Los Angeles River as a symbol of regeneration
and environmentally sensitive design

GREAT WALL OF LOS ANGELES
INTERPRETIVE GREEN BRIDGE

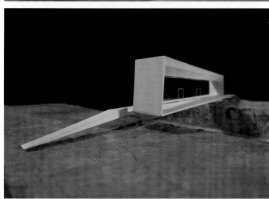

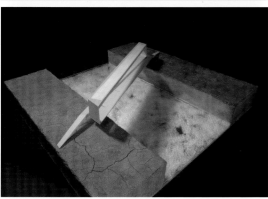

YEAR OF COMPLETION 2010
LOCATION North Hollywood, California
SIZE 1,200 square feet

The Art Bridge, designed in association with Judith Baca of SPARC, is a product and a reflection of the Los Angeles River, which in turn is the reflection of Los Angeles history. The bridge structure will be built substantially from trash salvaged from the river itself; concrete walls cast with bottle glass, cans, Styrofoam, dirt and debris; floor and pavement made from recycled tires, tennis balls and scrap metal; bridge guardrail made from recycled parts of shopping carts scattered in the riverbed as a symbol of regeneration and sustainable design. Photovoltaic panels on the canopy will generate electricity for lighting at night.

Spanning across the LA River, the Art Bridge not only serves as a pedestrian bridge for the college and school in the community, but also as an interpretative station for viewing and understanding the significance of the Great Wall of Los Angeles mural by artist/muralist Judith Baca. The slit in the bridge floor reveals the river beneath, symbolizing the scar in the landscape manifested by the concreted river, and the division it ultimately created in the community. Walking across this bridge, visitors may experience the time makers, reading about the history of the city as told by the river and by the mural. The bridge will not only serve as a physical connection from the school to the community, but it will also make a connection for the visitor between the history of the river and Los Angeles, and the void in knowledge and awareness of events depicted in the Great Wall of Los Angeles.

XTEN ARCHITECTURE

www.xtenarchitecture.com

Monika Häfelfinger and Austin Kelly

XTEN Architecture is an award winning architecture firm located in Los Angeles, California, with associate offices in Sissach, Switzerland. Founded in 2000 by partners Monika Häfelfinger and Austin Kelly AIA, XTEN Architecture is a full service architecture and design firm specializing in cultural buildings, office and commercial facilities, large-scale residential projects and custom single family residences.

XTEN has developed a distinctive method to the development of contemporary architecture, with an emphasis on open spatial configurations, material transformation and refined detailing and craftsmanship. Underlying themes in the work have focused on the conceptual use of building elements, modified with both traditional and digital techniques. In new buildings, remodels and adaptive re-use projects, the architects develop strong sculptural forms and spaces transformed by both direct and indirect connections to the building's immediate environment.

XTEN buildings and projects can be understood in two broad categories. One branch of the work starts with the structural idea: the horizontal cantilevers of the roof and floors as the defining spatial elements of the building for example, projecting beyond the enclosure line to frame views and literally extend the interior of the building into the landscape.

The other branch of the work tends toward specific volumetric objects, often in compressed conditions, defined by walls and shaped by their surroundings. In these projects the architects have been experimenting with different kinds of materials on the building itself, in an effort to again draw connections between the building and its natural (or urban) surroundings.

These two animating ideas seem to be growing together in some of the office's current work. The Sapphire Gallery Extension is both object and, due to the limited area in which the structure could be supported, also double cantilevers from a central frame. On the ground level the piers extend into the landscaping and draw the landscape/ hardscape through the building. On the upper floor the trussed structure of steel tubes is treated like a pattern itself, and the glass pushed flush to the exterior of the assembly to create a monolithic trapezoidal volume from the structural geometry. The ZPO Tower project also appears as an object from afar, but up close it is a network of structural elements, developed from a patterning idea, that flower into extreme cantilever conditions at the 160m high observation decks.

SAPPHIRE GALLERY EXTENSION

YEAR OF COMPLETION 2009
LOCATION Encino, California
SIZE 1,800 square feet
PHOTOGRAPHY Art Gray Photography

The Sapphire Gallery is a residential addition designed to display a private collection of contemporary art while also providing for a home office with views to the surrounding hills.

The owners' collection includes work by the artists Gregory Crewdson, Uta Barth, Tomoroy Dodge and the video artist Jennifer Steinkamp, and they expressed interest in a new building that would be more than just a container for their expanding art collection. The new building would have be multivalent; with suitable spaces for the artworks, but it would also have to be open to the views, provide for various domestic program spaces, and create a compelling new focal point for the approach and entry to the residence.

The new structure is grafted onto the circulation spine of the existing house and lifted off the ground to provide a minimal footprint. Freeing the ground plane creates a new multi-functional hardscape/landscape area for the family that they use as carport, children's play area, for art parties and video projections.

A structural system of lightweight braced frames was developed. They were factory built and assembled by crane in one day. These trusses rest upon moment frames that clear span the open ground plane in the perpendicular direction, and the floor and roof diaphragms are infilled with typical 2x wood framing. The system proved to be a remarkably simple, flexible and cost-effective way to achieve the program parameters of the project.

The remaining details are simple and direct: casement windows, quartz pebble flooring, steel stairs and railings with perforated panels, infill walls of gypsum board with floor to ceiling pivot doors, full height glass with a ceramic coating for UV and solar protection. An array of photovoltaic cells on the South facing sloped roof produces an average of 15kWh per day, enough to supply all the energy for the new building with a surplus directed towards the main house.

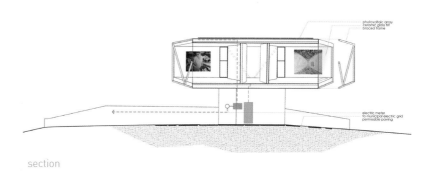

section

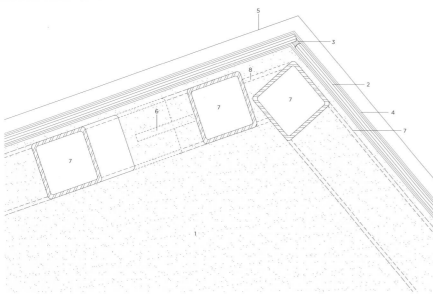

plan section

1 quartz epoxy flooring
  plywood sub floor
2 1/2" laminated glass
3 silicon joint
4 recessed aluminium glass channel
5 line of exterior stucco soffit
6 steel gusset plate
7 steel tube brace frame
8 1/2" x 5" welded steel plates at
  4"-0" o.c vertically

left gallery extension view; view
through to garden right east
gallery view

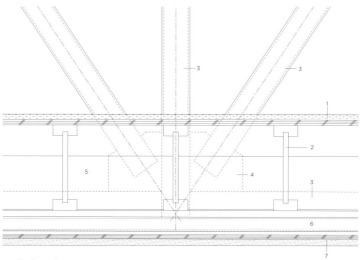

1 quartz epoxy flooring
  plywood sub floor
2 tji floor joist, 16″ o.c.
3 steel tube brace frame
4 steel gusset plate
5 batt insulation
6 cross brace
7 exterior plaster on wire
  lathe plywood sheathing

vertical section

top to bottom east gallery view; west
gallery view; west gallery view right
north-east elevation

OPENHOUSE

YEAR OF COMPLETION 2007
LOCATION Los Angeles, California
SIZE 5,500 square feet (interior floor
area), 7,500 square feet (exterior
decks/terraces)
PHOTOGRAPHY Art Gray Photography

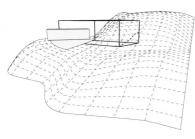

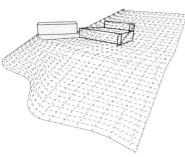

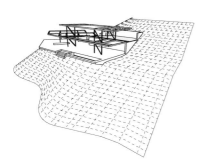

The Openhouse is embedded into a narrow and sharply sloping property in the Hollywood Hills, a challenging site that led to the creation of a house that is both integrated into the landscape and open to the city below. Retaining walls are configured to extend the first floor living level into the hillside and to create a garden terrace for the second level. Steel beams set into the retaining walls perpendicular to the hillside are cantilevered off structural shear walls at the front of the site. Lateral steel clear spans fifty feet between these beams creating a double cantilever at the leading edge of the house and allowing for uninterrupted views over Los Angeles. Front, side and rear elevations of the house slide open to erase all boundaries between indoors and out and connect the spaces to gardens on both levels.

Glass, in various renditions, is the primary wall enclosure material. There are forty-four sliding glass panels, each seven feet wide by ten feet high and configured to disappear into hidden pockets or to slide beyond the building perimeter. Deep overhangs serve as solar protection for the double pane glazing and become progressively larger as the main elevation of the building follows the hillside contours from Eastern to Southwestern exposure. This creates a microclimate which surrounds the building, creating inhabitable outdoor spaces while reducing cooling loads within. Every elevation of the house opens to capture the prevailing breezes to passively ventilate and cool the house. A vestibule at the lowest point of the house can be opened in conjunction with glass panels on the second floor to create a thermal chimney, distributing cool air throughout while extracting hot air.

Glass in the form of fixed clear plate panels, mirror plate walls and light gray mirror glass panels lend lightness to the interior spaces. These glass walls are visually counterweighted by sculptural, solid elements in the house. The fireplace is made of dry stacked granite, which continues as a vertical structural element from the living room floor through the second story. The main stair is charcoal concrete cantilevered from a structural steel tube. Service and secondary spaces are clad in floor to ceiling rift XTEN Architecture | Openhouse p.2/2 oak panels with flush concealed doors. Several interior walls are dark stucco, an exterior material that wraps inside the space. The use of cut pebble flooring throughout the house, decks and terraces continues the indoor-outdoor materiality, which is amplified when the glass walls slide away. The building finishes are few in number but applied in a multiplicity of ways throughout the project, furthering the experience of continuous open spaces from interior to exterior.

Set in a visible hillside area above Sunset Boulevard, the Openhouse appears as a simple folded line with recessed glass planes, a strong sculptural form at the scale of the site. The minimalist logic of the architecture is transformed by direct and indirect connections to the buildings' immediate environment. The perimeter landscaping is either indigenous or a drought-resistant xeriscape. An outdoor dining area implements artificial turf composed partly of recycled rubber. With the glass walls completely open the house becomes a platform defined by an abstract roof plane, a palette of natural materials, the hillside and the views.

left to right dining/terraced garden, view
towards kitchen, main stair, garden/
exterior dining area

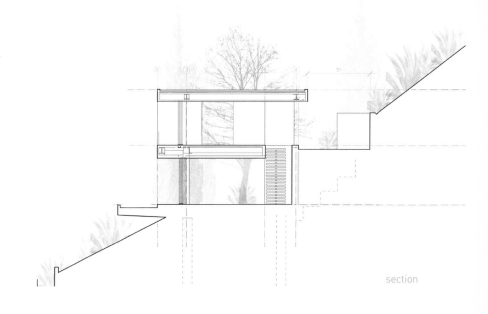

section

DUBAI ZPO TOWER

YEAR OF COMPETITION 2009
LOCATION Dubai, United Arab Emirates

The site plan for the Za'abeel Park Observation (ZPO) Tower is organized according to a traditional Islamic geometric pattern found in the regions' decorative arts. At the scale of the plaza, this pattern takes the form of the granite paving, lines of grass, flowers and trees, and a ribbon of water that draws one in and through the base of the ZPO Tower. This same pattern at a larger scale delineates four distinct landforms around the base of the tower, creating different pathways and approaches to the base as well as providing required program spaces for parking, conference center, children's library and service areas.

A flexible conference center for one hundred persons is located along a pathway to the North of the tower, with access to the lake, Za'abeel Park and a garage located within a second landform. A Children's Library is located in a smaller landform adjacent to the main tower entry, and a fourth landform shielding the site from highway traffic is provided for mechanical and service spaces.

The Islamic pattern is rendered in different grasses and plantings at a larger scale over these landforms, with the intention that they are accessible for the public to climb upon and to sit to watch the crowds or the lights of the tower above. The landforms serve to both frame and guide the activity around the entry points to the tower and also to create a gradual transition between the scale of the ZPO Tower and the larger Za'abeel Park as it extends to the North and West.

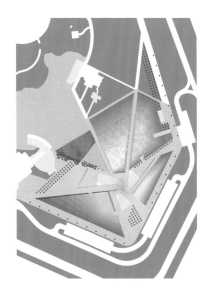

rotating tubes

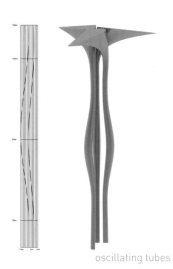

oscillating tubes

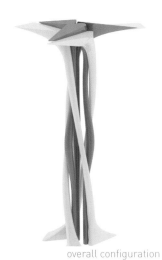

overall configuration

WHITE TUBES:
tubes 1,2 & 3 rotate 160 degrees along the full height of the tower.

BLACK TUBES:
tubes A,B & C oscillate back and forth towards the center of the tower, moving in as the rotating tubes pass and moving out to create structural diaphrams at key elevations of the tower.

DIAMONDHOUSE

YEAR OF COMPLETION 2009
LOCATION Santa Monica, California
SIZE 820 square feet (interior),
1,200 square feet (deck/terraces)
PHOTOGRAPHY Art Gray Photography

Silverspur is a 30,000 square foot renovation to a modernist office building located on the Palos Verdes peninsula in Southern California. On the interior small offices were removed to create large, open loft spaces and sustainable design elements were integrated. On the exterior a new façade was developed to modernize and increase the energy efficiency of the building.

A green roof was added to provide thermal mass and insulate the interior from solar gain while allowing for rainwater collection and percolation on site. Radiant heat was added below the new concrete topping slabs to reduce reliance on the forced-air heating system. New high-efficiency fixtures and equipment, recycled carpeting and tile were added through-out the building, and full height vision glass was used to maximize daylight and reduce the need for artificial light.

The building façade is composed of perforated, micro-laminated solar fabric stretched over steel frames that are anchored to the cantilevered concrete building slabs at various angles depending on solar orientation and building program. The solar fabric reflects 80% of the incoming solar gain while allowing for full transmission of natural daylight so that from inside one has complete views of the landscape and city beyond. The material also changes the appearance of the building throughout the day depending on the position of the sun, appearing opaque in the direct sun, translucent as the sun moves oblique to the façade, and transparent as a theater scrim at night.

site section

opposite page roof deck, north elevation
above terrace view, upper studio, roof stair

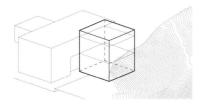
initial site condition

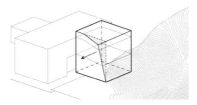
programmatic deformation

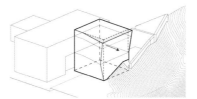
roof terrace deformation

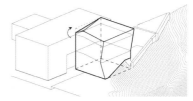
fold/delamination over from existing

YEAR OF COMPLETION 2006
LOCATION Rolling Hills Estates, California
SIZE 30,000 square feet
PHOTOGRAPHY Art Gray Photography

Silverspur is a 30,000 square foot renovation to a modernist office building located on the Palos Verdes peninsula. On the interior small offices were removed to create large, open loft spaces and sustainable design elements were integrated. On the exterior a new façade was developed to modernize and increase the energy efficiency of the building.   A green roof was added to provide thermal mass and insulate the interior from solar gain while allowing for rainwater collection and percolation on site. Radiant heat was added below the new concrete topping slabs to reduce reliance on the forced-air heating system. New high-efficiency fixtures and equipment, recycled carpeting and tile were added through-out the building, and full height vision glass was used to maximize daylight and reduce the need for artificial light.

left exteriors by day with fixed silver fabric solar screen elements right at night, the veil-like solar screen elements become transparent when backlit from the offices behind

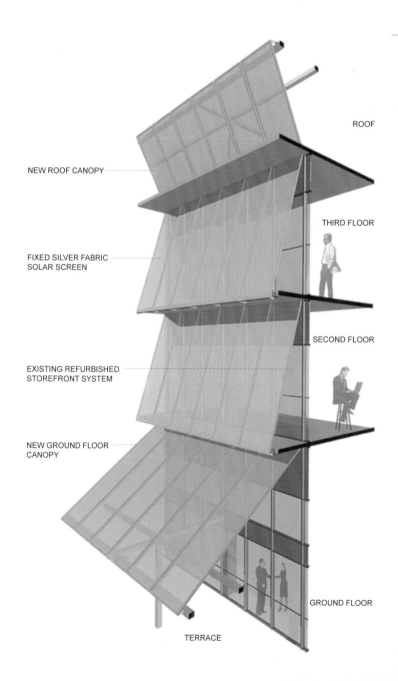

ROOF

NEW ROOF CANOPY

THIRD FLOOR

FIXED SILVER FABRIC
SOLAR SCREEN

SECOND FLOOR

EXISTING REFURBISHED
STOREFRONT SYSTEM

NEW GROUND FLOOR
CANOPY

GROUND FLOOR

TERRACE

Which Way LA? A Roundtable Survey

by Frances Anderton

It's been said that many of the projects in this book, especially the single family houses, represent a continuation of the Case Study and/or Southern California Modernist tradition, in terms of material choices and the inside-outside relationship. Is that how you see your project?

THOMAS SCHNEIDER
SENIOR ASSOCIATE, BARTON MYERS ASSOCIATES
Yes, the work and research begun by the CSH program can be seen as ongoing. The desire to translate designs into mass-produced/prefabricated housing has been a constant driver, although it has not proven to be successful in commercial terms. But certainly the experimentation spirit from the Case Study Houses continues to this day.

ZOLTAN PALI
Truth be told, much of the present architecture [residential] in Los Angeles appears to be highly derivative of the Case Study Period. Modernism [the mid-century version] became a fad and a fashion largely after its heyday interruption. However, when it came back, it did with all the neuroses of its clients and architects who truly did not understand its underlying tenets- or if they did they simply chose to push it aside and used it more as an aesthetic crutch. Although we are interested in its core tenets, we are less interested in its aesthetics.

FRED FISHER
We work in Quincy Jones' original 1954 office building and it truly affectd our thinking about the continuity of indoor/outdoor space and the psychological importance of even small garden spaces attached to living and working spaces.

AUSTIN KELLY
XTEN ARCHITECTURE
Building our work upon the example of all these exceptional and accessible works of great architecture is one of the amazing things about starting a practice in Los Angeles. From Neutra we learned how to separate a glass wall from a structural element, so that they read independently and slip past one another. From Schindler we learned about interlocking spaces and the plasticity of surfaces. From Ray and Charles Eames we learned about a collaborative and open-ended design process...it's endless, and every day you see fascinating new things going up.

Where are the differences that mark your project out as contemporary? In the generally greater house size than in midcentury ? New materials? More formal complexity? Demand for thicker insulation and structure? What else?

AUSTIN KELLY - XTEN ARCHITECTURE
Although I think you can sense the spirit of those lessons behind some XTEN projects, we do not think that the buildings really look or behave like Case Study or Cal Modern buildings. XTEN buildings are not that pure. The structures are more complex, the spaces are more irregular and the buildings are more precisely shaped by and tuned to their specific surroundings than by any a priori ideas about architecture.

JOHN FRIEDMAN
So many of the Case Study Architects were concerned with order and clear construction systems. Our generation is typically less concerned with these pursuits – partly because the current

codes make it nearly impossible to develop a pure system that is lightweight, utilizes simple connections, and is not compromised by what seems like an excessive number of shear walls – and more interested in spatial and formal complexity - typically for the dynamic lighting and sculptural qualities that come as a result, but often spurred by complex sites, more complicated living and familial relationships, and challenging city requirements (complicated setback requirements, etc.)

FRED FISHER

The ethos of Mid-Century houses stressed economy and efficiency. Today's clients tend to want bigger, more elaborate kitchens; media areas; home office areas; and more storage, none of which were part of post war middle class standard of living.

The Mid-Century houses were light constructions that took advantage of the gentle climate. Simple heating/ air-conditioning was switched on a few weeks per year. Today's energy codes and a growing consciousness of sustainability as well as a narrower range of comfort demand more attention in construction and systems to maintain the sense of openness and lightness.

THOMAS SCHNEIDER
SENIOR ASSOCIATE, BARTON MYERS ASSOCIATES

The inside-out relationship is an important feature of the "California experience" that we all relish. While for the most part idyllic it can also be quite harsh (wildfires, earthquakes, droughts, etc) architects working in LA have come up with inventive ways to deal with some of these problems. Structural engineering requirements become more rigorous after each code update, environmental technologies

have improved greatly, and interest in sustainability on the part of clients has never been higher.

ERLA DÖGG INGJALDSDÓTTIR

Our contribution on this aspect is to employ the least amount of NEW MATERIALS; the New Materials are the NO-Materials and the Renewed Materials. A "no-paint, no-carpet, no-tiles, no-a/c" philosophy keeps unnecessary chemicals away from the dwelling spaces we design.

JOHN ENRIGHT

The relationship of contemporary residential work in Los Angeles cannot avoid the reference to the early modernist traditions, particularly regarding the relationship of interior to exterior space so pervasive in this climate. Our work certainly nods to this tradition but we are interested in a more plastic relationship between interior and exterior spaces that relate to notions of fluidity and movement.

How would you characterize the drivers behind your project?

RON RADZINER

We are constantly exploring the concept and practice of modern living. Our differences arise from the study of the architectural precedents to which you refer. There are incredible benefits from the hands-on learning involved in our restoration projects. Restoration is a heavily academic exercise, involving research and reflection, where we witness how the designs and materials age and evolve. We believe the restoration process has made us better architects of contemporary projects as well.

TREVOR ABRAMSON
FAIA AND DOUGLAS TEIGER, AIA

We believe that architecture can raise your soul to a higher spiritual level. This philosophy goes hand in hand with the new direction architecture is taking called "Warm Modernism," accomplished through the use of natural earth materials, warm colors, and sculpting with light and space. As the world around us grows to be more fast paced, coming home after a busy day has taken on a deeper meaning. Warm Modernism evokes a sense of tranquility in such a way that the home becomes a sanctuary.

ERLA DÖGG INGJALDSDÓTTIR

Energy efficiency

How would you characterize the detailing? The detailing DEFINES the design? The detailing SERVES the design? Do you think LA architects are more concerned with buildability than they were reputed to be in the recent past?

THOMAS SCHNEIDER
SENIOR ASSOCIATE, BARTON MYERS ASSOCIATES

The detailing defines the design. We strive to highlight each material's inherent characteristics, which very often include approaches that are slightly unconventional. For example, exposing steel structure and building systems can be challenging in a construction industry accustomed to "hiding" everything.

TREVOR ABRAMSON   **JOHN ENRIGHT**   **FRED FISHER**   **JOHN FRIEDMAN**   **ERLA DÖGG**   **AUSTIN KELLY**   **MICHAEL LEHRER**

INGJALDSDÓTTIR

RON RADZINER

The detailing serves the design. It is still about the big picture, the overall concept of the design. I think now LA architects are more concerned with longevity of the details. LA has matured and now values a building that will last.

MICHAEL LEHRER

What is characteristic of my work, and possibly an LA attribute, and certainly an attribute of anyone who has passed through Frank Gehry's office, is the APPROPRIATENESS of detail. In all of my work, the main driver is spatial clarity, then tectonic/volumetric clarity...nailed by rigorous, appropriate detailing.

KULAPAT YANTRASAST

I think LA architects are more interested in craft and buildability, yet detailing and materials have not been a defining factor as much as in Europe.

RANDALL STOUT

I believe that the diversity of practices in LA, with many firms doing work abroad in extreme climates, has lead to more discipline and technical proficiency among architects here.

ERLA DÖGG INGJALDSDÓTTIR

Details create themselves effortlessly throughout the project.

JOHN ENRIGHT

Detailing is paramount in our work, and within architecture has a paradoxical relationship to the size of the project. That is to say, the smaller the project, the more attention to detail is required. That is why smaller installations and interior projects can sometimes be just as labor intensive as larger commissions. Detailing both serves and defines the design intent of a project, but we would say the smaller the project, the more the detail actually begins to define the design.

ZOLTAN PALI

I never realized that the 'buildabilitiness' of Los Angeles architecture was ever in question. Architecture in Los Angeles is presumably 'easier' to build than anywhere else- the weather is way more forgiving- ergo the complexity is presumably less than in other places . . . (But) the fear of earthquakes has significantly compounded things as have ADA requirements, energy requirements, a whole host of fire life safety issues and the rise of the construction defect attorney - making the building process more complex - and in my mind - NOW - no less complex than anywhere else.

JOHN FRIEDMAN

Crude detailing is typically a thing of the past in LA. Architects here care deeply about how all the pieces of a project come together - from an exterior material change to a stair guardrail. These details may not be the central feature of a project – typically, it is still the space and the form that create the larger impression – but if the details don't support the large idea, or are executed poorly, the impact of the project is not as high.

AUSTIN KELLY
XTEN ARCHITECTURE

This generation of architects does not fetishize the detail. We are interested in spatial relationships, structure, technology. Nothing is pure.

Are sustainability needs integrated into the design or the dominant features of the design?

THOMAS SCHNEIDER
SENIOR ASSOCIATE, BARTON MYERS ASSOCIATES

Both. The design of buildings and grounds themselves must inherently respond to climate, orientation, prevailing winds, etc. At the same time, they must be outfitted with the latest technologies. . . In our point of view, the greatest potential for improvement in this area lies not in new construction (all new buildings should of course be "green") but in the retrofit of the enormous existing building stock (a topic not really dealt with in this book).

CLIVE WILKINSON

Sustainability is the new black, with the strengths and shortcomings that implies. We have always thought resource efficiency is fundamental to good design, and good design always incorporates that approach. There is value, however, in exhibiting sustainable features as the visual language of buildings helps drive behavior change and persuade people that ecological consciousness is a vital part of our future.

RANDALL STOUT

I believe sustainability should be fully integrated to the point that it is so fundamental that it is generative to the form and concept of the building. Buildings where sustainable features read as "dominant", especially where features are "appliqué" are less interesting.

ZOLTAN PALI   **RON RADZINER**   **THOMAS SCHNEIDER**   **RANDALL STOUT**   **DOUG TEIGER**   **CLIVE WILKINSON**   **KULAPAT YANTRASAST**

ZOLTAN PALI

Integrated and dominant- depending on the situation at hand. The word 'sustainability' gives me pause and it always has. A well sited building, properly oriented, with appropriate levels of natural light penetration, appropriate levels of natural ventilation, sun shading, permeable surfaces, water capturing devices, water minimizing devices, state of the art mechanical systems, energy efficient lighting systems, minimized waste in construction and a 'built to last-ness' quality is simply logical and good architecture and should not require a "movement", nor should it require another layer of bureaucracy.

ERLA DÖGG INGJALDSDÓTTIR

A design without a concern for sustainability lacks any value.

To what extent do you feel influenced by movements in fine art and installation? Which artists? Or, which architects influence you?

AUSTIN KELLY
XTEN ARCHITECTURE

We see art as seamless with architecture now, and the two worlds are intertwined in LA. Many of the our greatest, most supportive and most creative clients come from the art world or are involved in some way in the arts. . . .Many of the artists we are tuned into are using similar strategies to the ones we use in developing projects: relational strategies, accumulation strategies, banding, lamination and delamination, webs, networks...
The influences are endless...Martin Puryear, Anish Kapoor, Robert Irwin, the 2nd gen space and light artists, Eliasson, Steinkamp, Serra, Zumthor, Ray and Charles Eames, Herzog deMueron, Sejima,

Richter, Lautner, Tarkovsky, Pamuk, Heizer, Ellsworth, Uta Barth, Joseph Beuys...

MICHAEL LEHRER

Art is a profound formative part of my architectural thinking. Reading *Vitruvius* in 9th grade Latin I learned that architects had to know sculpture, painting, and drawing. I still believe that profoundly.

ERLA DÖGG INGJALDSDÓTTIR

Minarc takes its inspiration from LIFE.

JOHN FRIEDMAN

Like most architects of our generation, we've followed the example of Gehry and looked closely at the work of various artists – some for their spatial, material, or phenomenological qualities, such as James Turrell, Robert Irwin, and Anish Kapoor - and some just for their attitude, political stance, and humor, such as Chris Burden, Robert Gober, Sarah Sze, and Rene Magritte. Their work contributes to the knowledge and experiential base that suffuses our thinking about everything we do (along with poets, philosophers and, of course, other architects). Qualities of their work find their way into our projects, but always indirectly. We never directly quote from their work.

RON RADZINER

James Turrell. We have had the opportunity to work with him on a number of projects over the years. I feel like what he does is a direct extension of who he is as a person. His art is a pure and sincere reflection of his being. Even after just a few moments with him it becomes apparent how much he values the concepts of light, space, and form. I think that kind of unbridled wonder and creativity is characteristic of great artists.

ZOLTAN PALI

Simply put, we are influenced by all of them and none of them. We force ourselves to not worry about what others do even though we are constantly bombarded by what others do. It is like being on a diet and your mate constantly tempts you with the most delicious, fattening, scrumptious, mouth watering delights. Hard to not get sucked in.

Do you find LA to be as receptive to experimentation as it's long been? If not, in what way and how do you get around the limitations?

AUSTIN KELLY
XTEN ARCHITECTURE

Absolutely, experimentation and creativity are built into the DNA of California... restlessness, questioning, testing, building. . . In other cities young architects write and teach and make competitions. In LA young architects have the opportunity to build, and as they build they test their ideas and the ideas develop.

JOHN FRIEDMAN

As LA matures, one might worry that it would be less receptive to experimentation – more conservative, more risk averse - but if that's the case, we haven't seen it. Additionally, the development of new, high performance materials combined with the incredible computing power that now exists through all industries has meant that experimentation is more accessible and can occur on more planes than ever. General acceptance of sustainability has also created a new avenue for experimental research – it's a cause that people, who before might have wanted to play it safe, are now willing to push the envelope for in the interest of protecting the environment.

FRED FISHER

LA continues to be a "frontier town" that has physical and mental room for new ideas. It is not a precious environment and as such, it gives artists and designers room to breathe and work. It draws people from around the world looking for that freedom.

JOHN ENRIGHT

Despite Los Angeles' reputation as being a receptive 'anything goes' hotbed of experimentation, those who have practiced here for any length of time know that this is not as it is sometimes portrayed. Yet there is obviously a strong history of critical invention within Los Angeles architecture. So each generation has to face their own resistance to that challenge within their own time and specific cultural, social, and political context.

CLIVE WILKINSON

The local receptivity to experimentation is buttressed by an overwhelming lack of a 'built culture'. Los Angeles is a place where the incongruity between public poverty and private wealth became visibly zoned into the landscape. Disparities are celebrated as diversity, and it became everyone's right to use their money in whatever way felt good. With the diaspora of 20th century immigration descending on Los Angeles, self-reinvention became the new morality, and that meant old models were bad models. We have entered the era of environmental plastic surgery.

RON RADZINER

Clients in LA are often creative people themselves and are consequently more open to the creative process in architecture, especially with a home.

THOMAS SCHNEIDER
SENIOR ASSOCIATE, BARTON MYERS ASSOCIATES

LA is still very receptive to experimentation, especially in houses, although in some ways it is getting more difficult. The difficulty comes not from clients but from the increasingly tougher requirements of building codes (such as "title-24" energy efficiency standards) that are mostly written to deal with "conventional" construction, and do not make room for experimentation. For example T-24 assumes every house will be air-conditioned even if the design calls for no such system!

ZOLTAN PALI

After the Case Study Period innovation in Los Angeles remained largely in the form-making aspects not the technical aspects of buildings. LA architects tried to make architecture sculpture and art. They succeeded - and LA wears it full of pride- with a Pritzker or two to prove it. I actually now see Los Angeles falling behind. That is not to say that Los Angeles architects themselves are falling behind and in some ways some of our big boys are still producing compelling work- in other places.

How do your overseas projects compare?

AUSTIN KELLY
XTEN ARCHITECTURE

Openness to new architectural ideas is stronger here in LA for private commissions, especially residential projects. But the opposite is true of public and larger scale buildings. In Switzerland there are architectural competitions for all public buildings, and for most medium sized buildings even if privately funded, and the public becomes very involved in the

process. If LA were to have that level of commitment to architectural competitions the city would look very different!

ERLA DÖGG INGJALDSDÓTTIR

On every architecture project, we bring our design philosophy and the location does the rest.

CLIVE WILKINSON

When we work overseas, the clients frequently bring more prior experience and notions of appropriate culture to the table. These constraints may sometimes allow more transformational thinking, but sometimes less. The pure idea is probably most free in the context of low constraints, as in LA, but purity is valuable more as a systematizing of thought than as any kind of reflection of our messy, vibrant world.

KULAPAT YANTRASAST

I think it is the same for around the world now.

If there were any common themes in the work being shown in this book, what would they be in your view?

RON RADZINER

Site-specific projects - setting and location are key.

RANDALL STOUT

The variety of firms and the quality of the work in the book proves that the "California" or "Los Angeles" architect is not limited by assumed styles or pre-assigned sensibilities but can be an influential catalyst for shaping the way we live, work and play.

JOHN FRIEDMAN

The innovation that occurred primarily in LA's private residences in the past has finally been welcomed into the city's public spaces and structures – Disney Hall, Caltrans, the Cathedral, and the Performing Arts school being the most prominent examples. There is vibrant public debate about the success of these environments, but no one suggests that the City should not expand its progressive sensibility into the public realm.

KULAPAT YANTRASAST

I think the common theme may be how architecture defines people's thought and experience.

AUSTIN KELLY
XTEN ARCHITECTURE

Rather than stylistic or formal themes, I think about how the work by this latest generation of LA architects is produced now, versus 20 years ago perhaps. Many of the offices represented in this book work in teams, husband-wife in the Eames mode, or from different cultures, bringing different experiences to bear on the work. The work is less about one person's ideas being carried out by an office staff, and more about a kind of working dialogue and process -- the architecture office as a studio.

ZOLTAN PALI

A book is like a photograph- a snapshot in time- of where we are. This one will show that Los Angeles is producing competent work but clearly really needs a jolt- somewhere on the proverbial 8.2 Richter scale [not literally- I hope] if it is to remain as one of the hotbeds of world architecture. Otherwise, we should focus on creating quiet confident, subtle, peaceful, solid, timeless work- hard to do- in a world where everything is supposed to be [so-o-o-o] "exciting."

Is there any other question you think I should have asked?

AUSTIN KELLY
XTEN ARCHITECTURE

What's the future of the city of the perpetual future...? Greater density and urbanism necessary -- more public space, more housing, more walkable and mixed use neighborhoods. More bicycle lanes, one way streets, more public transportation...

GENEROUS SUPPORT FROM THE FOLLOWING SPONSORS HAS MADE THIS BOOK POSSIBLE:

SPECTRUM OAK PRODUCTS

HINERFELD - WARD, INC
Los Angeles, CA 310-842-7929
www.hinerfeld-ward.com
Phillip Lim 3.1 L.A. - Photo by Iwan Baan

rjc builders, inc.

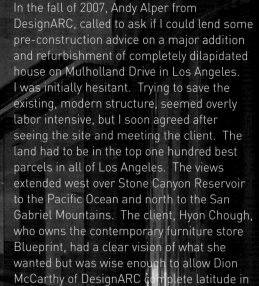

THE CHOUGH RESIDENCE
NOTES FROM A COLLABORATIVE
CONSTRUCTION PROCESS

In the fall of 2007, Andy Alper from DesignARC, called to ask if I could lend some pre-construction advice on a major addition and refurbishment of completely dilapidated house on Mulholland Drive in Los Angeles. I was initially hesitant. Trying to save the existing, modern structure, seemed overly labor intensive, but I soon agreed after seeing the site and meeting the client. The land had to be in the top one hundred best parcels in all of Los Angeles. The views extended west over Stone Canyon Reservoir to the Pacific Ocean and north to the San Gabriel Mountains. The client, Hyon Chough, who owns the contemporary furniture store Blueprint, had a clear vision of what she wanted but was wise enough to allow Dion McCarthy of DesignARC complete latitude in the design.

As builders, the first challenge to us was to save the existing walls, structure and much of the floor plan while essentially inserting a new building within the old envelope. The City's planning rules forced us to maintain the footprint of the original house, otherwise we would have lost the right to begin any project on this spectacular site. It was also critical to Hyon that we operate with a fixed

price from start to finish. We had no problem meeting her desire to stay on-budget. At the outset, I convinced Hyon that we could save money, and shave a few weeks off the schedule, by doing demolition first, during the design phase. This served us well financially over the long run too because with the walls stripped bare we could see exactly what had to be replaced and how and where we could insert the structural steel. We limited the unknowns so, for instance, when our rough carpentry went to open bidding, not only did we get a fair price, but we got a bid that incurred no additional costs during that phase of the work.

Andy Alper (he and I graduated SciArc together in 1984) gave me development drawings through the design and construction document phases. This proved vital to the successful outcome of the project. Not only was I able to develop a detailed cost outline that met Hyon's expectations, but I was also able to integrate some of my "means and methods" suggestions into the design detailing. This saved more time as we were literally ready to start construction the day the building permit was issued. Nailing down construction costs and strategies with the architect had the added benefit of letting subcontractors weigh-in on critical systems such as electrical, plumbing, and HVAC.

As construction progressed our weekly meetings with Hyon and Andy virtually eliminated the need for the formal mass of paperwork that can be generated in these litigious times. We could tackle a problem in the field, with Andy, often brought the subcontractor into the discussion and solved the issues on the spot. To Dion and Andy's credit, formal drawings and specifications followed, but usually as a matter of record, not information that left us (and the schedule) lagging behind.

As a business person I found Hyon easy to work with. In the past, she had commissioned DesignARC to build her beach house, so was no stranger to the give-and-take of the design process. Her business experience also served her well during the course of construction. She could make immediate decisions on subtle design questions and was adept at horse trading costly choices. For example, Hyon could quickly see that the electric roller shades in each guest bedroom were worth forfeiting in order to add exterior stonework – without adding a penny to the overall project.

In the end, we completed the project on time and on budget. This achievement is always the product of a team effort among designers and builders. Designers are wise to exhibit some agility in the field and to favor reasonable solutions over rigid concepts. Builders, for their part, need to show a firm commitment to their bids and to avoid viewing every conflict, or minor detail not denoted in plans and specifications, as warrants for added costs.

As a contractor with a background in architecture I like to think I have the ability to understand the design vocabulary the architect is striving to articulate. For example, a ¼" reveal in-between differing materials will establish a set of rules as it traverses the planes and edges of a building, not all of which can be drawn. By understanding the intent of the detail, good builders can keep building. There's no reason to halt construction and instead hammer out a week's worth of memos. The old adage, "time is money," is as true on a job site as anywhere else, and if we have to stop and send memos for every little question it will surely be reflected in the final cost.

It's a great feeling for a builder to have completed a well-crafted, beautiful project and of course even better to have the project completed on time and on budget – and that is always a team effort.

John Cordic, president
RJC Builders, Inc.

TRESPA®

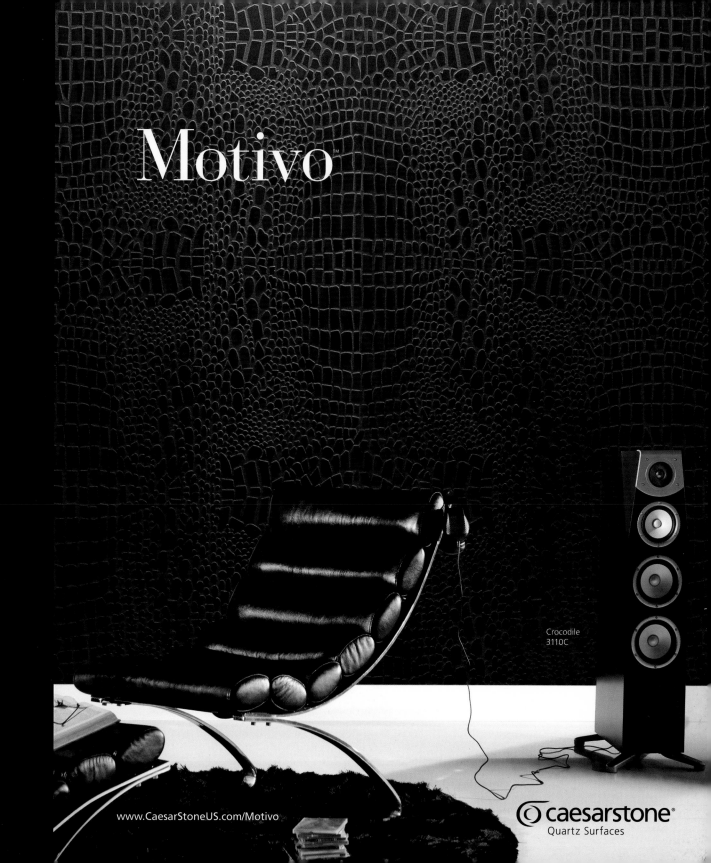

Motivo™

Crocodile
3110C

www.CaesarStoneUS.com/Motivo

caesarstone®
Quartz Surfaces

Fleetwood Innovation Makes Your Home Designs Shine

By simple definition, Fleetwood Windows & Doors offers a complete package for the modern luxury home.

In particular, Fleetwood offers a unique approach to LARGE openings. Because of its extensive family of multi-slide/pocketing door systems, customers can create affordable, custom configurations. Imagine a thirty-foot (30') wide door opening: In this opening are five door panels with narrow sight lines. These panels will slide into a hidden pocket, leaving the entire opening to blend into the home. Each door weighs about 300 lbs. but can be moved by a child,

or this same door can be automated. This is one of many 'home dreams' that can come true with Fleetwood.

No Detail Is Overlooked

Fleetwood specializes in the often-overlooked 'little things' that make or break a product.

For example, the company's patent pending Archetype Hardware is constructed of stainless steel and recesses into the aluminum stile. This proprietary hardware even offers an ADA lever and keyed lock option and is available in a natural brushed finish or black paint.

Other 'little things' are the authentic Swiss precision bearing rollers, which—like the Archetype—are constructed of stainless steel and made in the USA to insure the highest quality standards are met.

A Company You Can Trust

Fleetwood Windows & Doors has been manufacturing aluminum products for almost 50 years. They are proud of their roots and believe in helping support the American dream of success by relying upon God and this country's ingenuity and work ethic. The company continues to blaze a trail of top quality and innovative designs, while taking the industry lead in providing responsible products that exceed global needs and desires.

For more information, visit
www.FleetwoodUSA.com.

FLEETWOOD
WINDOWS & DOORS
WWW.FLEETWOODUSA.COM

A full-service builder for those with an extraordinary outlook.

CAPUTO
CONSTRUCTION

CASEY C.M. MATHEWSON, EDITOR

Native Californian Casey C.M. Mathewson studied architecture in Oregon und Stuttgart. After settling in Berlin, Germany in 1988, he founded mab – mathewson architektur berlin (www.ma-b.net), his institute devoted to building, and research in architecture. The themes of his publications include human focus in architectural design, urban design in Germany, and the history of residential architecture. In 2009, Casey partnered with ORO editions to create the a5 Architecture Series – a series of books focusing on the most innovative architectural developments of key world metropolises. He continues to develop new book projects from the newly founded ORO editions office in Berlin, while at the same time leading his own architectural practice.

ANN VIDERIKSEN, LOS ANGELES EDITOR

Ann Videriksen established her own PR and Marketing firm in 1993 after filling that role in-house with architectural firms in Los Angeles and Copenhagen.   She represents architecture firms in Los Angeles as a media and marketing consultant for her own firm Design Communication. She is a contributor to numerous magazines and books on architecture and design, an advisor to the *Masters of Architecture* lecture series at LACMA, and serves on the board of directors of the *A+D Architecture and Design Museum>LA*.

FRANCES ANDERTON, INTRODUCTION

Frances Anderton is the host of DnA: Design and Architecture, aired monthly on 89.9 KCRW and KCRW.com. She is also producer of KCRW's national and local current affairs shows, To The Point, and Which Way, LA?, both hosted by Warren Olney. She studied architecture at University College London (Bartlett School), and then traveled to Jaipur, India, to study the haveli courtyard house for a Royal Society of Town Planning paper. She then became associate editor of The Architectural Review magazine, one of the oldest architecture publications; her first assignment was to produce a special issue on Los Angeles. In addition, Ms. Anderton is the L.A. Editor for Dwell Magazine, a contributor to Huffingtonpost.com and a frequent public speaker on architecture and design on the West Coast. In 2009 she was made an honorary member of the AIA/LA for her work in highlighting the LA design and architecture sceneShe has also been featured on TV and documentary programs about architecture; the latest are the documentary films, Visual Acoustics: The Modernism of Julius Shulman and A Necessary Ruin: The Story of Buckminster Fuller and the Union Tank Car Dome.

ORO *editions*
Publishers of Architecture, Art, and Design
Gordon Goff – Publisher
USA, ASIA ,EUROPE, MIDDLE EAST
www.oroeditions.com
info@oroeditions.com

Copyright © 2010 by ORO *editions*

ISBN: 978-0-9819857-1-8

Designed and Produced by ORO *editions*
Art Direction: Gordon Goff
a5 Series Concept: Casey C.M. Mathewson, Gordon Goff
Graphic Design: Davina Tjandra
Cover Design: Usana Shadday
Copyediting: Jana Balik FitzGerald
Project and Production Manager: Joanne Tan, Christyanna M. LaFaver and Usana Shadday
Color Separation and Printing: ORO Group LTD

Text printed using offset sheetfed printing process in 4 color on 157gsm premium matt art paper with an off-line gloss spot varnish applied to all photographs

ORO *editions* has made every effort to minimize the overall carbon footprint of this project. As part of this goal, ORO *editions*, in association with Global ReLeaf, have arranged to plant two trees for each and every tree used in the manufacturing of the paper produced for this book. Global ReLeaf is an international campaign run by American Forests, the nation's oldest nonprofit conservation organization. Global ReLeaf is American Forests' education and action program that helps individuals, organizations, agencies, and corporations improve the local and global environment by planting and caring for trees.

North American Distribution:

Publishers Group West
1700 Fourth Street
Berkeley, CA 94710
USA
www.pgw.com

International Distribution:
www.oroeditions.com

Printed in China by ORO Group LTD.